DECONSTRUCTION
AS ANALYTIC PHILOSOPHY

Cultural Memory
in
the
Present

Mieke Bal and Hent de Vries, Editors

DECONSTRUCTION
AS ANALYTIC PHILOSOPHY

Samuel C. Wheeler III

STANFORD UNIVERSITY PRESS

STANFORD, CALIFORNIA

2000

Stanford University Press
Stanford, California
© 2000 by the Board of Trustees of the
Leland Stanford Junior University

Printed in the United States of America

CIP data appear at the end of the book

Contents

DECONSTRUCTION
AS ANALYTIC PHILOSOPHY

Introduction

Deconstruction as Analytic Philosophy primarily addresses analytic philosophers, especially those who do not think that other traditions in philosophy might be capable of contributing something of interest to philosophy. I start from a conviction that Jacques Derrida and Donald Davidson are both right about a number of central philosophical topics. The chapters try to work out this common core, sometimes by discussing analytic philosophers and deconstructors who are importantly similar to Davidson or Derrida, such as Ludwig Wittgenstein, W. V. O. Quine, and Paul de Man. For the most part, this book seeks connections and affinities, since the contrasts are so obvious. Having achieved some grasp of commonalities, however, I have begun to see what issues separate Davidson and Derrida beneath the obvious surface differences.

"Analytic philosophers" is a family-resemblance term, a diffuse category defined partly by the texts one assumes will be familiar to one's readers and partly by a family of styles of argument. The texts to which analytic philosophers commonly refer include works by J. L. Austin, Rudolf Carnap, Alonzo Church, Gottlob Frege, Nelson Goodman, Quine, Gilbert Ryle, P. F. Strawson, and the early Wittgenstein. Some familiarity with mathematical logic is also presumed. The style of argument tends toward linear exposition with explicit premises and conclusions.

However, philosophers such as O. K. Bouwsma and the later Wittgenstein, whose expositions are not exactly linear and explicit, also belong to the analytic camp, as do figures such as Hubert Dreyfus, Dagfinn Føllesdal, and Richard Rorty, who read and write about Husserl or Heidegger. Analytic philosophers often seem to define themselves in opposition to "continental philosophers," a similarly diffuse group that excludes such geographically continental people as Carnap, Hempel, and Jaakko Hintikka.

One might suggest the following criterion for defining analytic philosophy: clear writing. This criterion, however, is relative to one's training. In the interest of "communication across a schism," I once gave Derrida a copy of Saul Kripke's *Naming and Necessity,* which I regard as a nearly transparent text, absolutely clear and brilliant. Derrida said he had tried to read this before but had not been able to understand what was going on. In contrast, he said, Heidegger was very clear. So: You are an analytic philosopher if you think Kripke writes clearly; you are a continental philosopher if you think Heidegger writes clearly.

These chapters discuss Derrida and other "deconstructive" thinkers from the perspective of an analytic philosopher willing to treat deconstruction as philosophy, taking it seriously and looking for arguments. This attitude has often proved not to the liking of other analytic philosophers, who tend to view deconstruction and Derrida as enemies of rational thought rather than as interesting sources of new ideas. My argument against such an attitude appears in this book.

These pages arose not primarily from an interest in the contemporary history of philosophy but from the hope that thinking through the metaphysical issues addressed by Derrida and Davidson would give me answers. My guiding thought has been that philosophers ought to be able to understand one another, even those from very different backgrounds of reading and philosophical practice. Reading first Husserl's logical works, and then some Heidegger, convinced me that continental and analytic philosophy have to some extent developed in parallel. Frege and Husserl dealt with some of the same issues and had similar views about the nature of logic. Wittgenstein, Quine, and Heidegger started to overturn some of the presuppositions about meaning and experience that the traditions stemming from Husserl and Frege accepted.

Davidson and Derrida seem to have arrived at analogous positions, having rejected, respectively, even more dogmas of empiricism and phenomenology. Derrida and Davidson are quite different, of course. Certain problems that occupy them, their styles, and their textual backgrounds all differ. Further, as I will explain below, a fundamental philosophical difference separates them as well, a difference I have only recently begun to understand. Nonetheless, I continue to find their disparities mutually illuminating. Much the same is true of Quine and Wittgenstein, the two other modern analytical philosophers I have thought about in relation to Derrida. (Perhaps no similarity I allege is more startling than that between Quine and Derrida.) Interesting papers could also be written about Sellars and Derrida.

Similarities Between Derrida and Davidson

I believe that Derrida and Davidson are both right about a number of the same central topics. The fundamental point of agreement between Derrida and Davidson, as well as other thinkers in the analytic tradition, such as Quine and Wittgenstein, is their denial of what I call the "magic language." This is the language of *nous*, a language that is, in Wittgenstein's terms, self-interpreting. The magic language is the language in which we know what we mean, think our thoughts, and form intentions. There is no question of interpreting sentences in the magic language, since the magic language is what interpretation is interpretation into. Furthermore, there is no question of discovering what the terms of the magic language mean, since the terms of the magic language are nothing but the meanings expressed by words of natural languages.

Derrida argues that the presupposition of some form of the magic language has determined the very project of philosophy from the beginning. Direct access to the Platonic Forms, Aristotle's deliverances of *nous*, the ideas of the empiricist philosophers, and the sense data of the Vienna Circle are all versions of the magic language. We have a magic-language theory whenever a kind of item is alleged to be by its very nature "present" to the mind. Accordingly, Derrida characterizes such positions as "presence" theories, "presence" being what Wilfrid Sellars has termed "the myth of the given." Derrida's arguments work out the consequences of rejecting such self-interpreting mental contents. He conceives his project as more complex than that of the analytic philosophers, however, because he holds that the very philosophical concepts he is deconstructing have thoroughly structured the entire language. In other words, the language we use to discuss founding philosophical concepts presupposes the validity of those concepts. Thus "normal" philosophical critique takes place in a language that, to use his metaphor, "reinscribes" the very distinctions one is attempting to eliminate. Derrida's attempt to avoid this reinscription by circumventing "straight" critique is what makes his work so difficult for analytic philosophers to follow.

Derrida and Davidson also agree in denying a "given." Without a given, questions about realism and idealism cease to have a point. Without a given, there is nothing to say about the match between language and reality except "'Fred is a frog' is true if and only if Fred is a frog."

The Major Difference Between Davidson and Derrida

It has taken me a long time to figure out the central difference between Davidson and Derrida, and none of the chapters in this book make this difference clear. The exposition of this difference from Davidson's side is the burden of a long work in progress in which I show how Davidson can do metaphysics without funny stuff, such as properties, possible worlds, and the like. Let me try here to sketch the central issue that now seems to me to divide Davidson and Derrida.

Both Davidson and Derrida are committed to the textuality of all significant marks, whether in neurons or on paper. Further, they are committed to the idea that how an expression is to be interpreted is in principle epistemologically indeterminate. For Davidson and Derrida, the context of a speech act does not suffice to choose one interpretation over another. That is, epistemologically—and for Derrida, metaphysically as well—neither the intrinsic character of the representations nor the context in which they take place can determine which of several interpretations is correct.

Metaphorical extensions of terms, which are a central focus of the following essays, bring the issue of indeterminacy into sharp focus. Metaphor and the history of metaphor abound in indeterminacy, both synchronic and diachronic. To illustrate the indeterminacy that arises with metaphor, consider the possibly metaphorical use of the verb "crush" in "The Broncos crushed the Packers." Davidson's theory of metaphor would have two interpretive choices: On one hypothesis, the utterance is metaphorical: "crush" is literally false, but used for some purpose other than stating what is literally the case. Something about the vigor with which the Broncos dealt with the Packers makes the use of "crush" appropriate. On the other hypothesis, the utterance is not metaphorical: "crush" is being used literally, and we have two "senses" of "crush." The two hypotheses are equally supported by all evidence. The difference between them involves the assignment of different truth-values to an utterance, but the two hypotheses can be exactly the same in every other way. If nothing can decide between the hypotheses, then nothing can decide the truth-values of certain utterances.

Note that, practically speaking, nothing hangs on the decision. The constraint to maximize agreement in beliefs is equally served by the metaphorical and the literal understanding of "crush." Nothing short of a "magic language" term, whose very nature determined its referent, could decide this issue. This lack of practical difference supports Quine's idea that there is a "given," some basis for conceptual schemes that remains the same when different schemes are applied.

Now, one can have three responses to such indeterminacy. First, one can appeal to ontological relativity: If one accepts some kind of given relative to which schemes can differ, then one can say that the indeterminacy is not merely epistemological and that there "is no fact of the matter." So, which of the alternatives is "actually" correct is not a real question, and science can progress in the knowledge that "ontological schemes" in a way do not matter. Such schemes are required to state truths, just as metrics are required to state sizes; but just as different metrics will yield different numbers for the same sizes without missing anything, so different ontological schemes render different true statements for the same contexts without missing anything. This seems to be Quine's position in *Word and Object* and *Ontological Relativity*. The difficulty with this position, as Davidson has argued in "The Very Idea of a Conceptual Scheme," is the notion of the "given," which in effect supposes a basic conceptual scheme underlying all the others.

Second, one can appeal to the causal theory of reference, which removes indeterminacy. We can hold that, since there is no given, and since we cannot do better than use language to say what is the case, the difference between an "ontological" given and a magic-language-type given evaporates. This is why a position I once held, that Kripke's causal theory of direct reference undermined Davidson's arguments for the indeterminacy of interpretation,[1] is mistaken. Davidson's arguments, I believed, showed that reference was indeterminate only if reference was a function of sense (meaning), and if sense was in turn a function of the position of a sentence, and so of a term, in a Quinean web of belief. And given that reference was a function of sense, I argued, realism could not be true. One could be a realist only by abandoning the Quinean/Davidsonian account of meaning.

Third, one can appeal to the truth as irreducible. The above interpretation of Davidson overlooks his real view, that meaning is truth conditions. Considerations involving the Quinean web of belief give evidence for truth conditions, but there is nothing to meaning beyond truth conditions. Truth conditions, though, are expressed in a language. If one denies presence, or a given, then one has two options. (A) One can say that indeterminacy means that the notions of truth and truth conditions do not always apply, and that our understanding of life and language must abandon the idea that such notions are generally applicable. (B) Or one can say that an utterance has truth conditions and truth-value, even though all the phenomena in principle do not show what that truth-value is. Response (A) is Derrida's position; response (B) is Davidson's.

According to Derrida, the determinacy of meaning required to make utterances true is lacking, for reasons discussed in the essays in this collection. If nothing about the world or words makes utterances true, then "true" cannot be a fundamental, real feature of the world. This is not to say that we cannot continue to characterize utterances as "true" and "false" but to say that these terms cannot be theoretical tools for grasping what goes on in understanding and communication. "Truth," because of its dependence on meaning and reference, which in turn depend on either "givens" or a magic language, is a metaphysical notion that cannot be supported, after the deconstruction of the given and of the magic language.

Davidson agrees that truth cannot be reduced to anything else, that no conditions of speakers and contexts can yield an analysis of truth. That is to say, the phenomena of "indeterminacy of interpretation" show the failure of attempts to come up with criteria for truth. Without a given, and without a magic language whose tokens require no interpretation by their very nature, truth cannot be explained by anything else.

Derrida can be interpreted as requiring that any coherent account of truth must make truth dependent on a match between what is and what is said. Something about what is and its relation to the things we say must make truth sentences true. Thus Derrida would be a "truth-maker" theorist about truth, but a skeptical one, since he thinks nothing can meet the conditions for the truth-maker theory.

Davidson holds that the notion of truth is absolutely indispensable and primitive. Without this notion, nothing else we think, or even that we think, can be made sense of. For Davidson, if, as it turns out, truth cannot be reduced to reference or other notions, that is a reason to take truth as primitive. Derrida, on the other hand, holds that, while the notion of truth is indeed central to our thought, we must abandon the hope of making strict sense of that notion. For Derrida, this shows that something is wrong with our whole notion of "making sense of." Deconstruction is the exposition of the failure of "making sense" in the philosophical sense.

Davidson's position incurs some costs. Most strikingly, a vast number of truths are not only unknown but unknowable—for instance, all genuine borderline cases of vague predicates must be treated as having truth-values that cannot be known. If nothing makes such sentences true, but such sentences just are true or false, then the existence of unknowable truth-values follows from the nonreducibility of truth, together with the thesis that truth is absolutely central, that we cannot make sense of there not being truths and falsehoods. Analogs of this treatment of vagueness occur mainly in the discussions of Davidson below, in accounts of metaphor and indeterminacy of interpretation.

Derrida's and Davidson's views of necessity likewise contrast. Both thinkers deny a given and thereby deny anything from which necessity can be derived. Without a given, that is, a domain of possible worlds or entities with natures, modalities cannot be reduced to nonmodal truths. For Davidson, the truth conditions of an utterance on an occasion presuppose the truth-values of counterfactuals about the truth conditions of other utterances a speaker might have made. So, for Davidson, truth-values of modal sentences do not reduce to truth-values of any nonmodal sentences.

But the philosophical tradition has always found explanations of what must be the case in terms of what is the case. Otherwise, "necessity" has been regarded as mysterious and unfathomable. Davidson, just as he takes truth to be irreducible, must take necessity to be irreducible. Fully establishing that Davidson is committed to this position requires the above-mentioned work. But the thesis is immediately plausible in view of his commitment to the primacy of truth and the denial of a given.

Derrida's response to the same facts about irreducibility is analogous to his response to the failure to find anything adequate to "make" sentences true: he concludes that necessity, while it is a requirement for "making sense" of anything, is a notion that cannot correspond to anything real. Thus necessity, like truth, becomes a notion that is both indispensable and senseless.

Part of Derrida's thinking is that the philosophical history of the concepts of truth and necessity renders it almost analytic that truth is correspondence and necessity is grounded on permanent being. Once those analytic components are shown to be incoherent, the concepts that rest on them are deconstructed as well. Thus the issue between Derrida and Davidson becomes, once again, whether philosophical theories are central or marginal to the concepts we use to "make sense of" the world. Derrida thinks that philosophy invented a concept of "making sense," and that to deconstruct that concept is to deconstruct, for instance, truth and necessity. Davidson has a different conception of concepts, and reaches a different conclusion.

To summarize: Derrida and Davidson agree in denying a "given." Without a given, questions about realism and idealism cease to have point. Without a given, there is nothing to say about the match between language and reality except "'Fred is a frog' is true if and only if Fred is a frog."

A lot, then, depends on what one thinks about the objectivity of judgments such as that Fred is a frog.

Derrida reasons as follows: since there is no given, and since what is said is contingent on human decisions, and since many such judgments are indeterminate even within a theory, one may conclude that judgments cannot be objective in the sense of corresponding to being. So truth becomes another fiction, resting on metaphysical misconceptions.

Davidson, accepting the same premises, rejects the thesis that truth supervenes on being. If truth is absolutely central and basic to the possibility of thought, then the indeterminacy of truth relative to all other phenomena just means that truth is irreducible and that there are unknowable truths.

The Chapters

"Indeterminacy of French Interpretation: Derrida and Davidson" appeared in *Truth and Interpretation: Perspectives on the Philosophy of Donald Davidson*, edited by Ernest Lepore (Oxford: Basil Blackwell, 1986). I also presented a version of this essay at a conference on the Philosophy of Donald Davidson, held at Rutgers in 1984. This piece is the first of a series of essays on analytic philosophy and deconstruction collected in the present volume, and sets out many of the themes of resemblance developed in them. In it I argue that Derrida and Davidson substantially agree on fundamental issues in the philosophy of language, and that both philosophers are committed to some degree of indeterminacy of interpretation for the same reasons.

"The Extension of Deconstruction" appeared in *The Monist*, 69, no. 1 (January 1986): 3–21. This essay addresses the question how, if deconstruction is primarily a philosophical notion, it could possibly be relevant to literary texts. The argument that it might be relevant begins with Quine's deconstruction of the division between analytic and synthetic, which is paralleled by Derrida's rejection of "present" meanings. The especially semantic sense of "conceptual connection," which has been taken to be philosophy's bailiwick since the sciences became independent, is then argued to be so loosened that many connections can be treated in the same way that "conceptual" ones can. That is, a poem can be regarded as something like a theory. Thus, just as Quine regards logic and philosophy as continuous with science, so Derrida regards literature as continuous with philosophy. The prima facie odd phenomenon of doing a kind of philosophical critique of a work of literature therefore turns out to be not necessarily quite so odd.

"Truth Conditions, Rhetoric and Logical Form: Davidson and Deconstruction," appeared in *Literary Theory After Davidson*, edited by Reed Way Dasenbrock (University Park: Pennsylvania State University Press, 1993). This essay demonstrates relatively formally that a deconstructive thesis—that no principled difference obtains between "logic" and "rhetoric"—can be translated into a thesis about radical interpretation. Moreover, the latter thesis not only is plausible on Davidsonian and Quinean grounds but fits naturally into Davidson's actual accounts of radical interpretation. To effect the translation, I apply a version of the Gricean analysis of conversational implicature to the interpretation of truth-functional conditionals. Specifically, the version is the analysis of the logical form of "only" sentences, which would fit naturally into the truth-functional analysis of "if . . . then . . ." except that "Fred loves Susan" turns out not to be a logical consequence of "Only Fred loves Susan." Because this strikes so many people as an obvious consequence, the possibility of explaining it rhetorically, that is, via Gricean implicature, is especially noteworthy. This essay, then, proposes another variety of indeterminacy of radical interpretation, that between alternative assignments of logical form and alternative assignments of felt consequence to rhetoric or to logic.

"Davidson, Derrida, and Knapp and Michaels on Intentions in Interpretation" was started some years ago but not finished until recently. Steven Knapp and Walter Michaels had written an essay, published in *Critical Inquiry*, entitled "Against Theory." Numerous rebuttals followed, as did their reply, "Against Theory II." They believed that texts are determinate in meaning and that the intention of the author fixes the meaning of the text. Among the interesting features of Knapp and Michaels's work is its apparent allegiance with Davidson's view that convention, "rules," norms, and a public language are inessential to meaning and interpretation. Their essays challenge Derrida's view that iterability is essential to meaning. My chapter investigates the credibility of this challenge and asks whether Davidson could indeed be committed to a view that intention is the foundation for assigning meanings to texts.

"Metaphor According to Davidson and de Man" appeared as a chapter in *Redrawing the Lines*, edited by Reed Way Dasenbrock (Minneapolis: University of Minnesota Press, 1989). By interpreting Paul de Man as holding a general theory of meaning, truth, and reference analogous to Davidson's, this essay treats de Man's writings in literary theory as philosophy of language. De Man is also a literary theorist with substantial affinities to Derrida's work. For example, de Man's criticism of the romantic contrast between "signs," which are arbitrary in their relation to their referents, and "symbols," which were alleged to have a "natural" affinity with what they were symbols of, connects very clearly with Derrida's argument that everything is a sign. Of the figures in the "Yale School of Deconstruction," de Man seems to me the most original philosophical deconstructor.

De Man's account of metaphor is particularly interesting in that he treats predication in general as metaphorical. Like Davidson, his account of metaphor is based on differences in rhetorical force. To grasp predication as metaphor, one must realize that every application of a term in a new case is an extension that is not forced on the user by the new case. Thus the application of a predicate in any new case, no matter how routine, is an application that "extends" a predicate beyond its previous sense.

The primary difficulty in interpreting de Man is that his conception of the alternatives to his position is somewhat primitive. He tends to confuse the reader by talking about "verification" as what could establish that a predicate "genuinely" applied in a given case, for instance. Davidson's account of metaphor abstains from supplying a theory of the common phenomenon of a metaphor's "dying" and becoming literal. De Man's theory can thus supplement Davidson's by showing this process to be continuous with "normal" metaphors. That is, if predication itself is always unforced by previous applications of terms, then the difference between a routine predication and a daring metaphor is one only of degree.

"True Figures: Metaphor and the Sorites" was a contribution to *The Interpretive Turn*, edited by David Hiley, James Bohman, and Richard Shusterman (Ithaca, N.Y.: Cornell University Press, 1991). As the newly added preface to the version here indicates, this essay is a discussion of metaphor and predication in which I deny that any sense can be made of the notion of unknowable truths. The essay works out some of the consequences for a naturalism about language that rejects a given and treats indeterminacy as lack of truth-value. This seems to me the only alternative to accepting in-principle unknowable truths.

"A Rabbinic Philosophy of Language" serves as an appendix to the above essay, "True Figures." The initially puzzling view of language and reality implicit in a famous Talmudic anecdote turns out to be the view arrived at in "True Figures." Briefly, the Rabbinic view implicit in the anecdote is that God's commands do not cover all cases yet. In effect, God's words are construed as being like human words in that the predicates do not determine sets, at least not on the basis of anything already in their meanings. The Rabbis' applying of commands to novel cases turns out to be a model for the "True Figures" view of how social decisions create truth where none existed before.

"Deconstruction, Cleanth Brooks, and Self-Reference," a previously unpublished essay I worked on for several years, discusses several interconnected topics. I argue that Brooks, a New Critic, shares with deconstructionists an essentially Davidsonian notion of language. Much of the essay tries to explicate the role of self-reference, a concept central to Brooks and the deconstructionists, and to justify a kind of negative application of results in metamathematics to literature. Paul de Man's uses of self-reference and his appeals to "undecidability," which I regard as a metaphorical extension of metamathematical notions, are contrasted with Brooks's idea that self-reference contributes to the unity of a literary work of art.

"A Deconstructive Wittgenstein: On Henry Staten's *Wittgenstein and*

Derrida" is a much-revised version of a long review of Staten's book that appeared in *Annals of Scholarship*, 4, no. 2 (Winter 1987): 65–79. The essay begins with the relationship between philosophy and deconstruction. Staten holds them to be competitors; I argue that deconstruction is a part of philosophy well entrenched in the tradition. I describe deconstructive arguments in relation to the parts of the history of philosophy Staten discusses, and place deconstruction in a tradition of questioning that includes Quine and Aristotle as well as Wittgenstein. While Staten's book is referenced, the essay does not presuppose familiarity with it.

"Wittgenstein as Conservative Deconstructor" appeared in *New Literary History*, 19, no. 2 (Winter 1988): 239–58; this was a special issue on Wittgenstein and literary theory. I argue that Wittgenstein's approach to philosophy is akin to deconstruction, with the difference that, since Wittgenstein took philosophical concerns to be only marginally connected to "ordinary language," his deconstruction left everything as it was. This essay primarily targets a certain overreaction to deconstruction that was current in the late 1980s. The supposition common among many philosophically naive practitioners of "deconstruction" was that, if a distinction has been shown not to be strictly definable and not to rest on some deep real structure of things, it is therefore not an applicable distinction. In judgments of taste, for instance, if one cannot separate a culture's contribution from "aesthetic" values, there is no such thing as aesthetic value. Such a position, though, assumes that any genuine distinction requires that the terms in the distinction instantiate Platonic forms, or some equivalent. If the point of Derrida's and Wittgenstein's analyses is that no such Platonic forms are available, then the appropriate conclusion to reach is that some other account of how distinctions can work within a natural language is called for.

"Deconstructed Distinctions Are OK" was presented in various venues in the early 1990s. It is my most careful account of what deconstruction is in analytical terms. The explication connects Derrida's practice with a number of analytic philosophers, and addresses the general question of what results from having shown that a distinction is not founded on the nature of things.

"Derrida's Differance and Plato's Different," which appeared in *Philosophy and Phenomenological Research*, 59 (December 1999): 999–1013, argues that Derrida works firmly within the philosophical tradition. I show that his central concept, "differance," is clearly a response to Plato's "Difference Itself." Besides being verbally similar, the concepts address the same difficulty and have many of the same obscurities. Roughly, the difficulty is that in order to be sorted into categories, things have to be differentiated to start with. Thus Derrida and Plato seem to appeal to a kind of preconceptual differentiation to produce a multiplicity from which constructions can be built.

Davidson has argued that such a metaphysical requirement rests on a mistake. The idea, common to Derrida and Plato, that there must be some kind of basis from which "conceptual schemes" are generated constitutes an appeal to a "given," which is provably incoherent. Thus Davidson shows a way to avoid the mysteries of the Difference and Differance.

Why Me?

I became interested in Derrida by accident. In 1983, at a convention of the American Philosophical Association, Richard Rorty read a paper on Derrida, a name completely unfamiliar to me. I asked Rorty whether Derrida was someone I should read. Rorty said yes, he thought so. Since I have made it a habit to take seriously what Rorty says, I bought Derrida's *Grammatology* and joined a group of literature professors and philosophers at Connecticut College who were reading the book together. Thereupon I plunged into what at first seemed a very strange text. It turned out that reading the book as presupposing something like a Quinean-Davidsonian account of meaning made *Grammatology* not only make sense but show itself to consist of arguments, albeit arguments that were occasionally obscure for a person of my training. I continued reading the standard works by Derrida in print at that time, read the writers Derrida discussed, and started writing the sequence of papers collected here. Meanwhile, I took several literature courses at my own university, worked as a postdoctoral fellow in English at Yale, and became less illiterate in matters continental.

I would like to thank Richard Rorty for getting me into this sequence of projects in the first place, and the departments of English at Yale University and the University of Connecticut for their patience with a philosopher. Nancy Young, my copy editor, is largely responsible for producing the illusion that I can write clearly.

1

Indeterminacy of French Interpretation

DERRIDA AND DAVIDSON

In this chapter, I hope to persuade readers who may already be familiar with Donald Davidson's writings that Jacques Derrida supplies important, if dangerous, supplementary arguments and considerations on a topic on which Davidson has done exciting work: the thesis of the indeterminacy of radical interpretation. I show how a line of thought of the French philosopher is a version of this thesis as purified by Davidson. The two thinkers' basic conceptions of language and its relation to thought and reality are much the same. More importantly, I maintain that certain basic ideas and insights that move their respective arguments are the same for the two philosophers.

The similarity of their conclusions is partly obscured by the fact that these thinkers come from different traditions. By a "tradition" I mean a family of theories and a complex of shared metaphors, shared formulations of problems, shared texts, shared shorthands, and shared styles that shape the way philosophy is done. Just as our mention of "canonical notation" alludes to a familiar if complex part of our canon, so a continental's use of "primordial" animates a reader's prior absorption of texts from that tradition.

Frege and Husserl and the Presence of Meaning

I begin with some reminders and questions about Frege's remarks on sense. For Frege, a given term on a given occasion of use designates its referent and expresses a sense. How, according to Frege, does one know what sense one's utterance is expressing? Two phenomena are involved here: first, the connection of expression to sense, and second, the identification and reidentification of the sense. So, first, when an utterance expresses a sense, the speaker seems to bring about a connection between the word and the sense, or to endorse a connection that is already there. Second, the speaker is able to know which sense his utterance is expressing and to know a number of things about that sense. When I say "elephant," expressing its ordinary sense, for example, I know that the sense my term expresses determines no plants.

On Frege's picture, some senses must be present in themselves, directly apprehended in their own nature.[1] Senses, though signlike insofar as they determine objects, differ from ordinary signs in that somehow there is no possibility of misinterpreting them. A sense is, as it were, a sign that forces us to take it in exactly one way, and which means itself. Frege's theory seems to require, then, a kind of direct and unmediated presence of sense. At least, this object is directly present to a thinker and speaker and can be connected (presumably by *intending* that this sense be connected) with this utterance of this word.

While Husserl's examples, concerns, and even terminology are very similar to those of Frege, Husserl deals especially with the nature of propositional contents, our access to them, and their connection to human acts of language production.[2] Husserl expends much effort in describing how a person attaches a sense to a sign and exactly what senses are.[3] Both Frege and Husserl are antireductionists. Both take the defense of mathematical and logical consequence against psychologism to be of central concern. Part of this effort for both thinkers is the requirement that thought and language ultimately be grounded on a kind of nonlinguistic or prelinguistic meaning that is present to us without the mediation of a sign. "Presence," for the moment, is the unmediated, transparent access we are alleged to have to entities such as senses and to the prelinguistic "directedness" by which we can allegedly associate our acts with such entities.

A connection between a sense and a use of a term on a given occasion could be already there insofar as others have used tokens of this kind in the way appropriately connected with that sense. It is then still up to the current speaker to endorse that connection or not. This decision about endorsement, at bottom, is the decision whether to speak German, for instance.

The "presence" model common to Husserl and Frege is shared by many theories that are, on the surface, hardheaded and antimetaphysical. Any theory that claims a domain of objects or acts to which we are alleged to have direct epistemological access is a "presence" theory.[4]

Derrida, Davidson, and the Absence of Meaning

Frege and Husserl can thus be taken as very similar starting points for Davidson and Derrida, respectively, even given that Davidson's tradition and interests are otherwise very different from Derrida's. We must admit that Quine and Davidson only rarely discuss Freudian analyses of "The Purloined Letter" and that Derrida does not concern himself with first-order languages or physics. However, both Davidson and Derrida question the fundamental commitment to "presence" and nonlinguistic foundations in analyses of language, meaning, and necessity. I will show this by presenting some of Derrida's thinking as a supplement to such Davidson articles as "Radical Interpretation" and "On the Very Idea of a Conceptual Scheme."

The indeterminacy of radical interpretation proposed by Derrida can be presented as a consequence of the rejection of "present" unmediated semantic items. The rejection of presence itself turns on some fundamental reflections on the way signs must function in order to be signs.

Derrida's analysis starts with a framework taken from Saussure. He notes Saussure's point that signs are arbitrary.[5] This truism means that linguistic signs have no intrinsic characteristics that determine what they mean. A linguistic sign, then, cannot by itself force an interpretation or be self-interpreting. More importantly, Derrida accepts part of Saussure's view that both phonetic and conceptual systems are systems of differences. That is, what defines an *a* as an *a*, for instance, is its difference from other phonemes within the system, rather than any intrinsic characteristics of its sound. Analogous remarks apply to conceptual schemes (the very idea of which is not questioned by Saussure). A concept is defined by its differences from other concepts. A conceptual scheme is a system of differences.

This Saussurean idea that conceptual schemes are systems of differences is like Quine's web of belief.[6] While the Saussurean model deals with terms rather than with sentences, and its exclusive concentration on difference logically impoverishes its account of the structure of a theory, the central idea is very like that of the interanimation of sentences.[7] Just as the meaning of a sentence for Quine is (more or less) a function of its connections with other sentences, so the meaning of a term for Saussure is a function of the differences of its associated concept from other concepts. Both models for the most part make the meanings depend on relations rather than on intrinsic features of concepts or sentences. Quine's departure from the single-experience-packet theory of sentence meaning is in many ways parallel with Saussure's departure from the preexisting-concept theory of term meaning.

Now, Saussure seems to imagine a kind of conceptual field that various languages divide up in various ways. The concepts signified in a language, then, are various partitions of this conceptual field. The field itself seems to be present to thought; hence there is a fact of the matter about whether two cultures have conceptual overlaps and what those overlaps are.

For reasons dealt with below, Derrida rejects the comprehensibility of this kind of "conceptual field" and the possibilities it allows. He is left with differences that lack anchors to any intrinsic contents. The same difference divides Quine from Saussure. While the notion of stimulus meaning does retain the idea of a given field divided up among sentences, it is not a *conceptual* field. Thus Quine's theory is substantially purified of the notion that there is something isolable and *semantic* behind language for interpretation to link up to.

Let us now see how Derrida transforms Saussurean theory. He starts with Saussurean properties of words, and combines these with the more or less Husserlian idea that semantical properties must somehow be understood in terms of a relation to utterances. That is, what words mean is derived from how people have meant them. In some sense, meaning is use. This is the same starting point, albeit less behavioristically conceived, that we find in Quine's *Word and Object*. Meaning, to the extent that it is a real phenomenon, is a function of what people say and when they say it. We begin Derrida's argument with his characterizations of linguistic signs and other significant items.

1. Linguistic signs are arbitrary, so they have no intrinsic properties to tie them to any particular referent or use. Senses, contents, and meanings, on the other hand, have intrinsic features that identify them in isolation.

The sense of a term, for instance, must have enough content so that the reference can be a function of it. Even in Saussure's conceptual field, the various areas of the field seem to have properties intrinsically, even though this conflicts with the claim that a system of concepts is a system of differences only.[8] Any significant items that are like linguistic signs in being arbitrary require interpretation or supplementation to provide their meaning, since they are not self-interpreting. Arbitrary signs differ from and defer their significance.

2. Signs are essentially iterable. This is the fundamental principle on which the whole of Derrida's argument depends. Striking consequences are alleged to follow from this feature of significant items.[9]

"Iterable" sounds as though it requires that the person speaking use the expression again. The modality Derrida is driving at should be distinguished from the normal situation of language users, since the modal properties of the significant are supposed to be essential to anything that could be meaningful. The core modal formulation is the following: For something to be "iterable" is for it to be essentially something that could have had another application. "Iterable" is a thoroughly counterfactual notion that has nothing to do with conventions, lasting systems of signs, or other aspects of the philosophical notion of a language. Even if there were a person whose language varied unpredictably over time, and varied so quickly that no two utterances would be in the same language, the expressions would be meaningful only if the person could have uttered the same expression with a different meaning. The "could have" is governed by the ascriptions of law implicit in a truth-definition. In Davidson's terms, to ascribe meaning to an utterance is to ascribe a (perhaps momentary) theory to the speaker. Our theory of the speaker's theory is in part a truth-definition of all possible utterances of the speaker at the moment. That truth-definition will have consequences that include other possible occurrences of the expression in question, and those other occurrences would be parts of sentences with different truth conditions. If to be meaningful is to have truth conditions, and to have truth conditions depends on there being a truth-definition, and there being a truth-definition is for the agent being interpreted to fall under laws that support counterfactuals, then a meaningful expression necessarily has other possible occurrences in other situations. Those possibilities of other occurrences are what it is to correctly fall under a truth-definition. Hence,

Derrida's thesis about iterability is the thesis that to be meaningful is to have truth conditions.

This feature of meaningful items means that a meaningful item cannot be essentially tied to a particular situation. Its meaningfulness consists in its falling under a system of laws, the truth-definition, which requires that there are counterfactual situations in which the item would have meant otherwise. My scream in response to the car about to hit me is not meaningful, whereas "That damned jerk!" is. "That damned jerk," "that," "damned," and "jerk," even if they were items in a momentary idiolect, could have been uttered with different meanings, tied to different circumstances. The scream, on the other hand, is an individual phonic but nonlinguistic event.

A singular nonlinguistic event can be attached to a particular circumstance, but as a causal or accidental accompaniment. Insofar as an event or item is significant in any way, as a linguistic sign or not, it must be a repeatable whose import is not tied to a particular event. "The possibility of repeating, and therefore identifying, marks is implied in every code, making of it a communicable, transmittable, decipherable grid that is iterable . . . for any possible user."[10] Some iterable aspect of the semantic item is what carries the meaning. Whatever is semantic is so via and in virtue of what is taken as iterable in it.

This central concept of the argument deserves close attention, especially those aspects that undermine the possibility of fully present representations. Let us start with the apparently harmless type-token distinction.[11] Surely the simplest kind of "interpretation" of an utterance is saying what words were said, "what the person said" in the most transparent sense.

Now, a token qua token is essentially an instance of a repeatable. What makes the entity meaningful is that it is a token of a given type. Of course, as far as its intrinsic features go, a linguistic item or event could be a token of any number of types. An utterance that sounds like "bloo" could be a token of several words, even in English. Correct interpretation could be taken to specify what type a token is a token of.

How is this specification to be understood? Tokens either have absolute significance in given situations or they have significance only relative to a given language-scheme (leading to familiar "regresses to a background language"). Connecting linguistic tokens to thought tokens does not help, for it does not avert the question of which universal a token is a token of.

Thought tokens, which occur when someone is thinking of something, might be construed as a language built into the thinker. Ideas are tokens in the language of thought. In a mental tokening, it might seem the token can be correctly taken in only one way—since it "really" is a token of a given type, that is, a token of this type rather than that type—either because of some kind of intention attached by the thinker or by its very nature, or because of some privileged relational properties. That is, the question of what thought is being thought is the question of what the right interpretation of a token is.

If an item is a token of a given type, then it is necessarily repeatable. Its being of that type entails that other tokens of its type would function in other contexts in ways defined by the type. These other possibilities are built into its nature as a token of that type. Whether this necessity is conceived as intrinsic to the nature of the token or as stemming from relational properties of the token, an appeal to an apparent objective necessity is part of the notion that a token is "really" a token of precisely this one among the several types of which it could be construed to be a token.

In developing an account of meaning that allows determinacy of meaning, the difficulty is to give an account of this necessity. How are we to understand the "necessarily" in the above sentence—"If an item is a token of a given type, then it is necessarily repeatable"—so that an entity can be "really" a token of one type rather than another? The treatment of "necessarily" in both Davidson and Derrida is the point on which all the radical claims turn. Their radical claims are in fact consequences of rejecting realist conceptions of necessity and so objecthood.

There seem to be three kinds of account of the "necessarily" that makes a token a repeatable of a given type.

First, one could be the sort of essentialist that the case seems to require. Aristotle's idea would be that the token itself, at least in the case of thought, has privileged, natural sameness of kind with other tokens. A universal exists that explains the sameness of thoughts of Animals, since each of these thoughts is of the same species, without the matter. This is perhaps the model of the "idea" idea, the notion that items of thought have an intrinsic nature that identifies ideas of the same kind and ideas with the same meaning. This way of explaining the necessity (or identifying objects as tokens of given universal) amounts to essentialism about thought contents. As Nelson Goodman has pointed out,[12] objective sameness is a notion that goes together with objective necessity and non–system-relative objecthood. An explanation of the grouping of entities of a given kind by appeal to their natures requires a realist ontology of natures. Since the token's nature is the universal that is its type, the relation between a token and its type has the same problems as that between an Aristotelian substance and its essence. (Analogous problems arise if it is relations rather than intrinsic natures that constitute a token as a token of a given type.)

The second way to explain necessity and thus objecthood and objective sameness is by some version of linguistic convention or practice. I do not see how this strategy can work as an account of the objective sameness of tokens needed to account for the existence of language itself. At some level, these theories imply real *natures* and thus objective necessities about the linguistic and semantical items that constitute linguistic conventions and practices. Quine's savaging of the analytic/synthetic distinction can be taken as pointing out that "conventionalist" accounts of necessity would have to be essentialist about linguistic items.

The third way to account for necessity and natures is the Kantian strategy of treating the objects as constructed and so as having the features by which they are constructed necessarily. This seems to be the favored strategy for Husserl, and the one to which Derrida's remarks are addressed. On this account, objects are constituted by structuring some kind of raw material with concepts. The object then necessarily has properties by which it was constituted.

In the case at hand, the universal that is the type is constructed of the potentially infinite repetitions of the token, past and future. The universal is constructed out of the repeatability of the token. A token's being a token of a given type, then, is defined in terms of future and past repetitions. Now, it is only on the Aristotelian picture that repetitions of "the same thing" depend on an intrinsic sameness in the very nature of the items. On the Kantian view that Derrida supposes, the sameness of tokens derives from their being posited as the same, from being constituted as the same. The sameness is constructed, not given. The *a priori* is synthetic, owing to the constituting power of the subject. In Roderick Chisholm's terminology, then, the property of being a token of a given type is "rooted outside times at which it is had."[13]

From this point of view, the iterability of representations, their status as tokens of given types, is a feature that cannot be completely present.

What a token really is, its status as a token, extends past what can be completely there at a moment. Thus a token, qua token, is essentially nonpresent. (This dependency on the nonpresent is rather like what occurs according to one reading of Goodman's account of "grue" versus "green." That is, since whether grue or green is meant is a matter of what is said in future circumstances rather than of intrinsic properties of words, whether a token of "green" is a token of the concept "green" or the concept "grue" is nonpresent.)

If universals must be construed as constructions out of past and future instances, then iterability might arguably have the exotic consequences Derrida ascribes to it. If being a token of a given type is problematic because it essentially involves what is not present, then even determining that a token is of a type is an interpretation rather than a basis for interpretation.

The identification of items as instances of universals, even in the simplest case where the universals are word types, already involves reference to rules of language, social practices, and so forth. All these rules and practices are themselves built on repeatable, iterable significant items that are themselves tokens of types. Thoughts, intentions, and so forth are significant only qua tokens of some kind of semantic universals. So all significant items are nonpresent in the way I have argued that tokens are.

So nothing significant can be totally present. Significant items are thus always signlike in referring to something else and deferring their meaning. Displacements and nonstandard uses of a token of a type are not accidental deviations but essential to what the thing is. Its nature as a significant item *is* this displacement from full presence. Thus, in any mark, "no matter how fine this point may be, it is like the *stigma* of every mark, already split."[14] All significant items, then, are signlike in being thus incomplete. This is one reason why Derrida insists that "marginal" speech acts cannot be set aside to be dealt with as special cases of the more general theory.[15]

The core problem driving the analyses of both Derrida and Davidson, it seems to me, is that allegedly non-Aristotelian and nonessentialist accounts of the world (e.g., Kantian and "linguistic" ones) still seem to rest on essentialism about conceptual or linguistic items. That is, when we ascribe all necessity (and so objecthood, objective sameness, etc.) to the nature of linguistic or conceptual phenomena, some natures and essences still remain, namely those of linguistic and conceptual phenomena. The radical break that both Davidson and Derrida make is to work out the consequences of denying essentialism and objective necessities across the board.

Iterability, according to Derrida, most clearly undermines the meaning of speech acts, the force with which they are to be taken. The undermining of reference and sense follows, given that reference and sense are constructed out of expressive speech acts. If, following Derrida, Davidson, and Quine, we start with sentences as meant on occasions, in order to construct meanings of sentences and words, the force with which an utterance is made as well as the "contents" attached to particular words must be gotten out of iterable utterances.

Why does iterability create a problem about understanding utterances? In outline, the argument is as follows: Because of iterability, that is, the possibility of other occurrences of the linguistic item with different meanings, something beyond the linguistic item must be brought in if meaning is to be completed. The completion can only be a context that itself includes languagelike items that themselves require interpretation in context. And so on. At every point where clarification by context would be required, some languagelike phenomena require interpretation, again by context, a further context.

The possibility of occurrence with other meaning is part of the essence of what it is to be a linguistic item. That is, unless it were possible for this very sentence to be taken as, for instance, nonserious, this sentence would not have significance. The meaning of the sentence itself, in virtue of the iterability described above, is not tied to the particular personal intention that produced it. On an occasion of utterance, of course, the intention would clarify the meaning of the utterance. The only difficulty is that the intention is itself something languagelike, and so subject to interpretation in diverse ways. Only a kind of meaningful entity or state that could not be misinterpreted would finally and unambiguously fix meaning. The denial of the possibility of such a magic language of thought is the conclusion of Derrida's critique of Husserl in *Speech and Phenomena*.

Davidson has made similar remarks in discussing Austin's theories of illocutions, Frege's use of the assertion sign, and the general distinction between force and content.[16] For Davidson, one cannot put force into words or guarantee by a linguistic form that an expression is to be taken in a certain way. Any such attempt at a performative form creates an item which itself can be used in some other way—as an example, for instance. Anything that could not be misused would not be a linguistic item at all. It is necessarily possible for linguistic items to occur with different forces and so to be interpreted in deviant ways. So what?

Now we can state Derrida's argument, starting from this Davidsonian observation and the principle that iterability is a mark of any sign. The discussion of iterability makes it clear that words alone will not specify how a sentence is meant in any full way. Given that how a sentence is meant is the basis from which an account of linguistic meaning must start, any indeterminacy or lack of fullness in the meaning that comes in utterances will corrupt the whole theory. Derrida argues that this lack of fullness of meaning in words themselves used on occasions is in principle unfillable. So, to start with, what must be added to words to yield a determinate speech act?

Derrida considers two alternatives. First, there could be *present* meanings, thoughts, or intentions consisting of some kind of representation that needed no interpretation. I avoid the Husserlian complications of analyzing the intention with its object into the intending (which is present in its nature) and the object (likewise present in its nature). Second, if presence proves inadequate, then perhaps the context in which an utterance is made could suffice to fill in the gaps, that is, complete the meaning.

The problem with the first alternative considered by Derrida—presence—has been covered in the discussion of iterability: no significant item can be fully present in a way that makes it nonarbitrary or that precludes the necessity of its being interpreted. If iterability and detachability from context are required in order for an item to be significant, and iterability destroys full presence, then significant items of any kind cannot by themselves fill in what is missing to complete the specification of the meaning of a speech act.

This result holds even if the notion of presence is not tied to oddities about the notion of a sign. Suppose an organism has significant *states* that are present to it in their totality but that are not, strictly speaking, signs. In order to be meaningful, such states would have to be iterable, at least, in the sense that they are tokens of universals with semantic import.

If such a state were iterable as signs are, then interpretation would be required to say what the state meant on this occasion in this mind. If it is a sign at all, and thus functioning semantically, then it is iterable and so usable on more than one occasion. If it is iterable, though, it can be taken and used in more than one way. Iterability thus destroys the possibility of a nonarbitrary significant item, and makes all significant items like linguistic signs.

Such significant items, whether linguistic signs or thought events, cannot be fully present. In fact, no significant item, by the very nature of what significance requires, can be fully present, according to Derrida's iterability argument.

"Representations," as thought tokens of some kind that are fully present in their own nature and hence in need of no interpretation, are an illusion unless "their own nature" is understood as Aristotle understands forms without matter—that is, unless one is an essentialist about referential properties of an organism's states. Representations thus will not provide the kind of filling needed to complete meaning, but will rather be just spiritual words in need of interpretation. States that are not iterable, that is, states that are not essentially tokens of types, do not "stand for" anything but instead causally accompany events happening in and to the organism.

If all significant items are essentially iterable, then they can be no better than signs. But signs, besides being incomplete in specifying the whole speech act on a given occasion, essentially differ from and defer meanings and referents. Thus there can be no significant items that cannot be otherwise used or understood. For these among other reasons, Derrida rejects the idea that meanings or any other entities are present to us in a way that would fulfill meaning.[17] He agrees with Sellars[18] that even experience itself is not given without mediation.[19] Any awareness is mediated by language or languagelike phenomena. I will sketch some of the consequences Derrida draws below.

If totally present significant items cannot exist and so cannot complete the meanings of words, then perhaps context—the second alternative considered by Derrida—will suffice. It might be claimed that context, for instance, fixes such features as the references of words and whether an utterance is to be taken seriously, and thus freezes the repeatable expression in precisely one of its possible ways of being taken. If this were the case, then the total theory of meaning would be a theory that would pair contexts, specified nonlinguistically, and sentences to yield meanings. The difficulty is that contexts are not exhaustively specifiable without reference to intentions, beliefs, and so forth, which are themselves subject to interpretation.

With an argument very like the Brentano-Chisholm-Quine argument that either intentional entities are irreducible or translation is inde-terminate,[20] Derrida points out that the specification of a context that would fix the meaning of an utterance always falls short of a reduction of meaning. "For a context to be exhaustively determinable, in the sense demanded by Austin, it at least would be necessary for the conscious intention to be totally present and actually transparent for itself and others."[21] Without intentions that need no interpretation but carry meaning on their own, and without significant items that are purely present in themselves (as are Putnam's intuitions of the Forms),[22] there is no locking an utterance event into one fully stable and determinate meaning. Without some level of unmediated, directly present thought, the wandering possibilities of individual utterances cannot be pinned down.

To see the consequences of denying presence and holding that nothing isolable and semantic lies behind language, let us first consider Quine and Davidson's thesis of the indeterminacy of radical translation. It would be a misunderstanding of this thesis to suppose that indeterminacy is a problem of figuring out which meaning a given sentence has when the evidence gives equal support to several. This model of indeterminacy supposes that there are nonlinguistic or prelinguistic meanings, and that indeterminacy is a problem of linking a sentence to one of those meanings.

The denial of presence requires a very different understanding of indeterminacy. It requires that there are only the interpretee's dispositions as to what to say and when to say it (his theory of the world) and our dispositions as to what to say and when to say it (our theory of the world). A translation or interpretation is just a mapping of the interpretee's dispositions onto our dispositions, yielding our theory of what the interpretee means. The question of what an utterance in one language means in another language is like the question "Which football position is the short-stop?" There are no unmediated meanings and no magical links between acts of utterance and these meanings.

The same kind of theory of meaning that is rejected by Quine and Davidson is implicit in the traditional notion of polysemy as an account of what is the case when a text can be taken in several ways. That is, poly-semy—multiple ambiguity or "levels" of meaning—presupposes that there are meanings that words ambiguously express. Thus Derrida's rejection of polysemy agrees with Quine's and Davidson's accounts of the translation or interpretation situation.

On a theory that denies presence (i.e., a theory without the myth of the given), no level of meaning escapes indeterminacy problems. All the way down there is just more language. All significant items are signlike, non–self-interpreting, and thus defer something.

3. Deferral is the third feature of signs to which Derrida draws attention. Signs as signs defer or put off access to what they are signs of. The central idea is that, without presence, this deferral is never consummated; it can only regress in an unending sequence of background languages, to use Quine's term.[23] Signlike representation is never fully present but rather always leaves something out. Sentences and terms are tracks of an absent beast that is in principle inaccessible.

This structure of deferral, combined with the consequences of iterability, makes the very terminology in which we describe semantic phenomena inappropriate, much as the denial of the analytic/synthetic distinction does for talk of "meaning." If we think of the concept of "sign" as a token of a meaning or of an item separate from language, then that concept supposes distinctions that "cannot be made comprehensible." In the same way, the notion of "deferral," of putting off contact with what language "communicates," namely a meaning, is inappropriate in a theory according to which there is no interpretation into anything that is not another language.

The "distance" alleged to obtain between language and what language expresses is not exactly a deferral or delay of some presence, since the presence is in principle always deferred. On the other hand, even though language is inseparable from what it is about (that is, even though the theory/content contrast cannot be made), the world is not just words. Language differs from what it is about and defers what it is about, but without the structure of two domains, which both of these concepts ("deferral" and "differing") presuppose. Derrida's terms "deferral" and "differing" do not express the concepts, partly because of this misfit and partly because, if he is right, there are no concepts but only terms.

The inappropriateness of these dualisms removes essential conditions for the application of "sign," "reference," and so forth. This is at least part of the thinking behind Derrida's neologism "differance."[24] We are likewise cast adrift from familiar contrasts in thinking about language and the world by the abandonment of dualisms in Davidson's "On the Very Idea of a Conceptual Scheme." Davidson encourages us to be more relaxed about the destruction of the divide between our language and the world (what else could we reasonably expect?), but the abyss is still there.

If all interpretation takes place via regress to a background language (or if, in the best of circumstances, truth-definitions relate language to language), then the problem that iterability produces is in part a kind of disposition of terms to drift.[25] Without the absolute anchors of completed meaning supplied by either context or totally present representations, no one interpretation of a term or text can be privileged over others. There can be no privileged complete assignments of translations from one language to another. Drift is built into interpretation; there is always a "slack" between an interpretation and the evidence for it. Derrida assigns this slack to iterability, but that is in effect to assign the slack to the essence of language itself. That is, just as for Quine and Davidson the real reason for indeterminacy of translation is that there is nothing to language but items with languagelike properties, so for Derrida drift is a feature built into the functioning of any mark as a sign.

Derrida's rejection of polysemy as a model for problems with interpretation has a similar basis. The term Derrida uses rather than the inappropriate "polysemy" is "dissemination," which describes the kind of fluidity that "correct" interpretations will have, given that there is nothing semantic beyond language and thus nothing capable of freezing interpretation between languages or among discourses within one language.

The phenomenon of dissemination is akin to the Davidsonian variety of indeterminacy[26] rather than to the kind of global, total sets of alternatives that Quine envisions in *Word and Object*.[27] Quinean indeterminacy of translation still depends on a (perhaps correct but non-Davidsonian) dualism between observation and theory. Quine must somehow hold that there is a level of semantic content, the observation sentence, which is invulnerable to theoretical change, that is, to change of scheme. Part of what transpires can be purified and separated from language. Only if the theoretical views of a theory are separable from observation or some directly present content can sense be made of the notion that alternatives are available to our present system of organizing experience. Without some *present* experience that is separable from linguistic phenomena, the notion that there is the organized as opposed to what organizes cannot be made sense of. This paraphrases Davidson's remark, "This second dualism of scheme and content, of organizing system and something waiting to be organized, cannot be made intelligible and defensible."[28]

Davidson's apparently milder kind of indeterminacy is thus in fact more radical and pure than Quine's, since Davidson denies any subbasement of content that can be separated from the linguistic framework. Davidson absolutely abandons the dualism between "scheme and content" so that even the notion that experience is something organized by theory or that there are alternative schemes does not make sense.[29] Thus N. L. Wilson's concept of "charity"[30] applies for Davidson to ontology as well. Ontology is relative only if something stable exists for ontology to be relative to. Alternative fits between a scheme and content occur only if scheme and content are separable phenomena. For Davidson, language and what language is about are inextricably bound. Furthermore, there is no "presence" behind language; rather, what is behind language is inseparable from further language.[31] Without the crutches of dualisms, this is the view to which he and Derrida are forced.

Davidsonian indeterminacy then, shows up at specific locations where our speech and that of the other are not wholly homogeneous. In interpretation, equally good alternatives arise as to whether and where to impute falsehood (by our lights), reinterpret a predicate, or assign some unusual attitude or valuation in an area of another's discourse.

One difference between Derridean and Davidsonian indeterminacy is crucial, although it has no practical effect. Derrida assumes that truth, if anything, must be a match between an utterance and a given. Since he has shown that no such matching can be made sense of, his disparaging remarks about truth are incompatible with Davidson's theories. Davidson takes the other tack, denying not only that utterances match up with a given but that such matching is required for truth. In fact, Davidson takes the point he and Derrida agree on to be the basis for denying that truth is reducible and for making truth the central theoretical concept.

Although Davidson sometimes gives the impression that his theory is concerned primarily with assertions, he is well aware that the claim that a native sentence is a serious and sincere attempt to inform us cannot be the opening of a theory but is rather already the result of a somewhat developed theory. Some readers have taken the fact that Davidson deals with truth-definitions to mean that his theory takes "fact-reporting" discourse to be primary. But this confuses truth with assertion. For Davidson, interpretation starts with what people do and what situations they do it in, and parcels out the verbal part of this behavior into speech acts. Interpreters hypothesize holistically and simultaneously about what speech act is being undertaken and what its content is.

Davidsonian indeterminacy seems to occur only at margins, since interpretation itself depends on overall agreement. Thus global breakdown is impossible so long as interpretation is possible. It seems that, in the best of circumstances, Davidson's theory implies stability. According to Derrida, on the other hand, since iterability itself brings about displacement of interpretation, indeterminacy obtains even in the best of circumstances. Even though not everything is overturned at once, no part of our theory is safe from drift.

Even Davidson's principles, however, would seem to allow the germ of insidious Derridean piece-by-piece global indeterminacy, a germ that Davidson tries to conceal from us by his calm reassurances. First, given the interanimation of sentences, indeterminacy may well seep into other areas from the original problem areas. Second, if we extend Davidson's ideas to the interpretation of discourse from our own past and from our culture's past, indeterminacy of translation, especially about the cultural, social, and moral topics on which much of our literature dwells, becomes much more creeping and pervasive. Third and most importantly, if we do not make the simplifying assumption that a person's language or theory *at a time* is a unified whole, then areas of our own language are indeterminate relative to other areas of our own language. This kind of indeterminacy threatens to supplant Davidson's calm and comforting picture of indeterminacy as largely concerned with minor aspects of the psychology of the other.

Derrida's indeterminacy of interpretation starts out being Davidsonian, and rests on much the same kind of basic considerations. Since interpretation is nothing but interpretation into more essentially iterable and so unfixed language, that is, since the deferrals are of further deferrals, there are no anchors to fix interpretations even between languages or phases of the same language. Any relation of one discourse to another will have breaks, places where things do not fit. As we adjust interpretation for such a case, another interpretation has to be adjusted. Exactly this kind of situation is sometimes used to illustrate indeterminacy in the construction of truth-definitions, given the interanimation of sentences. Once we have accommodated Jones's remark "Dromedaries have two humps" by assigning to him a desire to test our zoological knowledge, we must reexamine his other zoological remarks, with other expanding consequences. A given indeterminacy thus affects evidence for other cases throughout the interpretation, especially in the cases of pervasive terms of social practice.[32]

Derrida illustrates this kind of infectious displacement in interpreting particular texts. Say that a given assertion somehow does not fit with other parts of a text. The interpretation of that part of the discourse then proceeds to unhinge the prior interpretation of the rest of the discourse. This is not to say that the subsequent reading is now all finalized, any more than pointing out an alternative interpretation for Davidson shows that either reading was correct. If there is no presence behind language, then, as languages and relations between them shift, so do correct interpretations. Even at a given time, there are alternatives. The alternatives at a given time, furthermore, come back to reinfect and displace their point of origin. There is always a gap that cannot be finally filled in.

Davidson's analysis is superior to Derrida's in many respects: the notion of structure, the format of the truth-definition, the detailed analysis of individual locutions to show exactly what *one* interpretation would be are all lacking in Derrida's work. On the other hand, Derrida dwells on some important matters that Davidson does not emphasize. Two such matters strike me as especially important.

First, Derrida extends interpretation to texts explicitly in a way Davidson does not. Interpretation need not be only between languages or total theories as commonly understood, but may also be between fragments of languages or particular discourses.

Second, Derrida expends much more effort on the interpretation of our own theory in terms of parts of it. It is of the greatest interest to Derrida that theories do not fit with themselves, let alone with other languages and discourses. Unless we are divine, the closure of our beliefs under rules of logical consequence (not to mention weaker consequence relations) typically yields inconsistent views. Thus, even in understanding our own views, and in explicating what we ourselves mean, paraphrase will be indeterminate and defensible alternatives incompatible. The project of cleaning up our theories, as Quine has observed, leaves us choices.[33] Since Derrida observes that the possibility of alternative interpretation is essential to a sign qua sign, interpretation and indeterminacy of interpretation must be in principle unending. But exactly this unfilled remainder is also implicit in

Davidson's view that meaning is given by truth-definitions. Words are interpreted by mapping onto words, and what is meant cannot be exhaustively put into words. (Not that there is anything else to put it into.)

Why Writing?

Derridean indeterminacy of interpretation is illuminated by one of Derrida's more famous hyperboles. Derrida claims that writing precedes speech and that all speech is really writing.[34]

This can be understood in several ways. First, writing is the least deceptive form of language in the sense that it is the form least likely to foster a certain illusion. Just as Heraclitus regarded fire as the form of existence least likely to support the illusion of stability, so Derrida views writing as the form of language least likely to support the illusion of pure presence to the self and special semantic attachment to a producer. For those of us raised in the Quinean fold, much of Derrida's discussion will seem directed at mysterious foes. Who believes that speech is special? For Quineans, speech is just inscription with sound waves.

To see what Derrida is concerned with, we have to imagine thinking that speech is somehow more directly connected with full meaning than writing, that somehow speech directly puts meaning fully into sound. The idea gets strong intuitive support from the experience of thinking to oneself, the interior monologue that seems to put meaning directly into something that, if overt, would be speech. But what could this full meaning be?

The real issue here is the notion of an inner sign that directly expresses content, that is, the representations, the signs that are immune to misinterpretation, as discussed above. Speech seems to be inner signs made manifest. How do transcripts of interior monologues differ from their contents? Husserl, whom Derrida takes to be the paradigm metaphysician, struggles to maintain a hybrid notion of "expressive sign" that will be a *sign* endowed with but distinct from its content.[35] According to Derrida, the nature of the sign relation—basically the iterability of signs and their deferral of and difference from what they are signs of—is a force within Husserl's thought that threatens to loosen these interior signs and turn them into indications, things that can stray from the attached thought contents.[36]

For Quineans, of course, it is already obvious that speech and thought are brain-writing, tokenings that are as much subject to interpretation as any other. For our (analytic) tradition, speech is not overtly valorized. Still, non-Quinean circles seem to harbor a covert belief that inner speech is directly expressive of thought. Intuitions of the primacy of speech may contribute to the shocked reaction to Quine's claim in *Ontological Relativity*[37] that translation is indeterminate even in our own case, in how we understand ourselves. This conclusion is a direct consequence of taking thought to be inscriptional and taking inscriptions to be like writing. If inscriptions are like writing, then all we have, even in our inner speech, is a text that can be taken in many ways. Without something besides texts in the brain, there is no such thing as the "correct" interpretation or the one that conformed to the intentions of the author. (The author's intentions, after all, would be just more writing in the brain.)

The notion that everything is a text is a metaphor widely used by hermeneuticists, structuralists, and others. When Derrida combines it with the radical drift of indeterminacy of interpretation and replaces polysemy with dissemination, the metaphor says something very different—the text/meaning distinction goes the way of the scheme/content distinction.

Derrida's claim that all language is writing, then, is a claim that all language is subject to interpretation in exactly the way writing is. Several consequences follow from this. First, the interpreting language is also subject to interpretation, and so on without end in the "regress to a background language." Second, just as writing, because it is a token and iterable in virtue of being a linguistic sign, is meaningful apart from the conditions that produce it and thus has, as it were, a life of its own, so all systems of representation are detachable from their speakers. (Of course, "representation" misrepresents things, since it presupposes a given matched by the words that is better than "'Frogs' represents frogs.") Third, the separation of representing tokens from their conditions of production is essential to their being representing tokens at all. If they were essentially tied to their context, they would not be representations. "By all rights, it belongs to the sign to be legible, even if the moment of its production is irremediably lost, and even if I do not know what its alleged author-scriptor meant consciously and intentionally at the moment he wrote it, that is, abandoned it to its essential drifting."[38] In Davidsonian terms, what is essential to the sign's being a sign is that the sign is actually under the laws of a correct truth-definition, and the law-governed modalities that a truth-definition expresses are independent of particular circumstances. If all representation is like that, then ontological relativity, in its purified and radicalized Davidsonian and Derridean form, indeed begins at home.[39]

Thus, the claim that all language is writing or that writing is prior to speech is the proposal of a model of thought whose consequences dislodge the illusion of anchoring of expressions to meanings provided by the alternative of presence. Only presence would give sense to the notion that an utterance always has a determinable correct interpretation.

For Derrida, like Davidson but unlike Quine, all of our access to the world is impure and subject to drift and separation from its origin. "This structural possibility of being severed from its referent or signified . . . seems to me to make of every mark, even if oral . . . the non-present remainder of a differential mark cut off from its alleged 'production' or origin. And I will extend this law even to all 'experience' in general, if it is granted that there is no experience of *pure* presence, but only chains of differential marks."[40]

The notion that writing is prior, then, requires that we take seriously the *language* part of "the language of thought." If the linguistic model is indeed the way thought is to be thought of, then it too is meaningful in the absence of the producer, and it too is subject to the drift to which language is subject. More accurately, if all language is writing, then the contrast with something by which writing could be anchored to a determinate preferred interpretation is lost. Without a pure, nonwritten, present meaning opposed to writing, interpretation of writing could not be determinate.

2

The Extension of Deconstruction

Deconstruction has for many years been more fashionable than understood. Both practical deconstructors and authors of secondary sources on Deconstruction for Everyman have supplied accounts of the underpinnings of what they are doing—accounts that lead most philosophers to take deconstruction less seriously than it deserves. Basically, less connective argument has been provided than is standard in analytic philosophy.

The peculiar apparent consequences of Derrida's early deconstructive work are partly to blame. Derrida's early texts argued logically that a concern for reaching conclusions on the basis of logical reasoning was unjustifiably narrow. The considerations and arguments that in fact form the rational basis for deconstruction imply that demands for traditional inferential bases are dispensable prejudices. Thus the learner is discouraged from asking after the inferential grounds for the exciting possibilities emerging before him.

In this chapter I will reconstruct the Wittgensteinian ladders of rational argument that can let us ascend to the point from which we can then discard those ladders. I will show a sequence of truth-conditional inferences that lead from the dense argument we find in Derrida's critiques of Husserl[1] to the very different texts of, for instance, J. Hillis Miller on Shelley's poem *The Triumph of Life*.[2] I am primarily interested not in endorsing or rejecting the arguments described but rather in explicating them.

I will start from the relatively familiar "logical" type of deconstruction. This most ancient philosophical genre consists of arguments to the conclusion that a given text or doctrine undermines itself by including or requiring premises that presuppose the negation of the text or doctrine. Two examples of this sort of deconstruction will be exhibited below, one from Quine and one from the early Derrida: I will show how each of these thinkers "logically" deconstructs, in his own way, a familiar picture of language and the world. These deconstructions lead to plausible arguments that the "logical," strictly inferential undermining of the initial examples is but a special case of a more general kind of undermining. I will then demonstrate that daring deconstructions, which discard docile dependence on deductive disparities, are "defensible," meaning that such deconstructions include a plausible traditional inference to the conclusion that drawing traditional inferences is not a privileged philosophical procedure. Finally, I will argue for the legitimacy of applying deconstructive argument to nonphilosophical texts.

Quine and Derrida as Deconstructors: The Death of Meaning

The original pattern of what would come to be called "deconstruction" is the following. A text that argues for a thesis *t* uses essentially a premise *p* that presupposes that not-*t*. The thesis of the text is undermined by presuppositions of some of the premises used to support it. "Presuppose" in the original form of deconstructive argument is defined truth-conditionally. If *p* presupposes not-*t*, then if *p* is true, *t* must be false. Deconstruction directly attacks not a thesis but only an argument for a thesis.

A good example of this sort of undermining is Quine's sequence of attacks on the analytic/synthetic distinction, an assault that Gilbert Harman termed "The Death of Meaning."[3] This distinction consists in the following complex of views. There are necessary truths. All necessity is to be explained as due to meanings of terms (e.g., the substitution of synonymous terms turns all necessary truths into logical truths). Thus, nothing has essential features except in relation to a set of definitions, that is, to an arbitrary choice of language. All questions about what is necessary are questions about what the rules of a language are or how a language is to be chosen.

The basic model behind this account of necessary truth can be set out as follows. Truth, generally speaking, is a matter of a coalition of two factors: the contribution of the world and the meaning of the words. The truth of a sentence such as "Some frogs are green" depends both on "frogs" meaning frogs and on frogs being occasionally green. Since there are these two factors, there are some degenerate cases, in which the meanings alone determine that the sentence is true. Given that frogs by definition are animals, "All frogs are animals" is true solely in virtue of meaning; the facts contribute nothing.

These formulations are linguistic descendants of Hume's statement that all necessity is a matter of relations of ideas. Here, ideas as sense-datum tokens are replaced by the meanings of words, which meanings themselves may be construed as sets of sense data or something similar.

The following pages give a reading of Quine's overall argument from "Truth by Convention" through "Two Dogmas of Empiricism," *Word and Object*, and "Ontological Relativity." On this reading, Quine points out that the analytic/synthetic theorist, in order to explain necessity as due to objective facts about meanings, must be an essentialist either about some kind of linguistic items or about meanings themselves. To be an essentialist is to suppose there are necessary truths about a subject matter that are independent of any linguistic characterizations of the subject matter. The analytic/synthetic theorist thus requires that there be necessary truths that are not explained by linguistic phenomena. Thus the analytic/synthetic theorist presupposes the negation of his thesis about necessity.

Let me set this out in its metaphysical form: A main function of doctrines of necessity is to give an account of the natures of things. What is necessary about a thing would be the features the thing could not lose and still be itself. If there were objects that existed objectively, that is, not just relative to some theory, then there would have to be objective conditions determining when a given object no longer existed. But that would mean that, in the nature of things, the object *could not* survive the loss of those properties. So the object *must have* those properties. Thus the notion of a system-independent necessity is necessitated. If analytic truths are dependent on objective relations among meanings construed as entities, the course of a Quinean deconstruction is clear.

Nor is the doctrine of analyticity as necessity aided by treating meanings as properties. The very notion of a property involves some kind of necessity. For one thing, properties, if conceived as some kind of entity, have persistence and existence conditions just as subjects of properties do. Furthermore, to ground an analytic/synthetic distinction, relations among properties seem to need explanation by the natures of the properties. But natures of properties seem to lead to necessities. If it is the nature of red that makes objects that have it necessarily nongreen, then properties, however they are conceived, involve the same difficulties for the elimination of language- or theory-independent necessities as real objects.

Nelson Goodman's discussions are the most thorough demonstration that "objective" properties are as problematic as "objective" objects.[4] Very briefly, Goodman shows that, without appeals to natures of things, innumerable artificial properties can he constructed that are formally indistinguishable from familiar ones. Goodman also makes clear that, in a theory, objects and properties are determined together, so that what properties exist, according to a theory, determines which objects exist, according to that theory. Turning meanings into properties, then, will not affect the central problem of the replacement of necessity by analyticity.

Since any difficulties with properties correspond to difficulties about objects, let us construe the thesis that all necessity is conventional as the thesis that there are only conventional objects. The above discussion indicates that conventions that appeal to given, natural properties already presuppose essentialism. Also, given that the concept of "real object" involves real necessity, common metaphors of "alternative conceptual schemes" turn out to be incoherent. Since real objects depend on essential properties, the idea of a domain of theory- or language-independent entities of some kind to be carved up into sets, which will then determine properties, is incompatible with the notion that all necessity is conventional necessity. The notion of properties as sets conceals the requirement that the items in the sets have identity and survival conditions, which cannot be arrived at independently of the grouping into sets. The picture of features as sets of objects really requires that the objects and sets be simultaneously constructed.

In claiming that necessity is conventional, the analytic/synthetic theorist asserts that all necessity comes from meanings that are conventionally attached to terms. The two problematic notions here are "meaning" and "conventional attachment."

What are these meanings, if we deny objective necessity? If the meaning of a sentence is established by convention, the convention must have some terms in which to be stated. Such terms can be either purely present objects, such as sense-datum items, or some other kind of unconventional starting point, or another set of conventions. Any kind of objective matrix in which to specify conventions seems to require either the existence of objective rather than conventional entities or a regress to further conventions to fix the items in which the conventions are stated.

The analytic/synthetic theorist assumes the existence of some unproblematic entities, in terms of which the definitions of terms are stated. The unproblematic entities may be abstract entities, sets of sense experiences, or some such. These entities have their own theory-independent natures, and relative to them, the terms of a language are defined. But, if objects and features presuppose some kind of necessity, then the starting point for the analytic/synthetic theorist presupposes what is being denied.

Another side of the same topic is also important. Consider the use of "in L" to distinguish between what is due to meaning and what is merely fact. The analytic/synthetic theorist acknowledges that a *sign sequence* is not intrinsically necessary, but necessary as a *sentence of a given language.* So the idea of a language needed for a set of conventions to define what a person says as true in virtue of meaning requires that the person be speaking language $L1$ in which, say, "Frogs are animals" is a rule of meaning, and not $L2$, in which that sentence is empirical. But this requires that each language have, as its essence, exactly this set of semantical rules. Speakers, in meaning one language rather than another, must intend one of these sets of rules. "Semantical rule" makes sense only as an essential feature of a language. What makes it possible to deny "Frogs are cute" but not "Frogs are animals" in English is the essence of English.

Now, perhaps this essence can be established conventionally, by setting up "rules of language." A rule of language thus is a kind of social contract, consisting perhaps of a promise such as "Let us always believe q when we believe p." Speakers can then intend these promises when they intend to speak L. Such a social contract is either a fiction or a reality. If it is a fiction, it does not solve the relevant problem of how terms really mean. If it is real, it seems to presuppose a representational system in which the linguistic promises are made. But those representations either are themselves subject to determination by interpretation or somehow have intrinsic meaning, so that they mean things by their very nature. But appeal to interpretation just inaugurates a sequence of background languages.

What is needed to end interpretation is some kind of anchor, an intrinsic relation either to a set of stimulations or to a Fregean sense or to some other theory-independent, essenceful object. If the ur-language does not itself have such interpretation-ending anchors, then the drift in the sentences accepted in the ur-language will allow drift in promise-keeping in the constructed language. There can be no ultimate anchors without natural necessities and real essences.

Without essentialism about meanings and semantic rules, there are only the sentences accepted in a given body of discourse. All sentences accepted in the body of discourse are parts of a "theory," which parts differ in various ways in degree, but not in kind. "Objects," then, exist as posits of a theory. What takes the place of objective necessities and essences is the notion of existing according to a theory, that is, ontological commitment.

This Quinean argument shows that the theory that all necessary truths are true in virtue of meanings requires that there be necessary truths that are not true in virtue of meanings. The analytic/synthetic theory of necessity presupposes at least one realm of objects whose natures are not constructs of a theory are constituted by essences, that is, non–language-determined necessities. Any supposed elimination of essences in favor of meanings requires that meanings, at least, have essences.

The analytic/synthetic theorist follows a pattern that characterizes the history of philosophy since Aristotle. Aristotle held that, by a special faculty of the mind, objective necessity and a special kind of certainty coincide. Thus a metaphysical basis exists by which the necessary can be identified with the certain. With Descartes and subsequent thinkers, what had originally been an epistemological side effect of necessity on the mind becomes the criterion for necessity. The necessary becomes the *a priori*. Combine this idea with a certain empiricism, and necessity becomes a matter of relations of ideas. Any intrinsic natures of things in relation, though, would require objective necessities. So the ideas themselves now would have to be Aristotelian substances that have intrinsic natures independently of any relations of ideas. That is, ideas themselves seem clearly to have essential features and accidental features that are not themselves explained as relations of ideas.

Discomfort about such intrinsic natures led to the linguistic turn, which tried to put such relations among mental objects into the secure and more scientific ground of relations among words and their meanings. Where ideas had been the realistic residue, now words and meanings were the unexamined objects in relation. All of these retreats were fruitless, though, since any *objects* in relation commit one to essence and accidents.

By the analytic/synthetic theory, languages could be set up so that various relations of meaning-containment obtained, thus making some truths necessary in those languages. Quine's deconstruction of this last strategy shows in part that this either leaves meanings as substances with their own substantial forms or gives us no notion of necessity different from truth according to a theory.

What both thinkers like Hume and the later meaning-theorists seemed to require was some kind of item whose nature was not only real but also directly and immediately transparent to thought. Only such an item could give an *a priori* necessity that was really a necessity. Such thinkers repressed the requirement that, if this immediacy was to supply necessity, it had to be an immediate grasp of the real, theory-independent nature of something. If the language of thought could not be misunderstood, so that there would exist a level of representation where relations between token and referent could not be misconstrued, then some "present" entities would have to have essential properties. Quine's claim in "Ontological Relativity" that indeterminacy of translation "begins at home,"[5] that we are in the same condition with respect to our own thoughts as we are in relation to any other words with which we are confronted, points out in a particularly striking way the consequences of denying essentialism about conscious contents. Quine thus believes the head contains nothing essentially nontextlike.

Let us now proceed to the "deconstruction" of the analytic/synthetic distinction. The apparent and surface denial that there are objective necessities would preserve necessity, even linguistic, analytic necessity, only by keeping natures. But sameness-defining natures, whether of linguistic items or of sense presentations, presuppose objective necessities. Without objective necessities, neither theory-independent objects nor arrays of those objects exist to be grouped into "the arbitrary collection of sensations" that are chosen as the "defining conditions" for empirical predicates.

Derrida, in his deconstruction of the theories of Husserl, reaches much the same conclusions as Quine does, by much the same kind of argument pattern. The central notion of Husserl's thought is that theorizing should start with what can be present to us in an unmediated way. The necessity that a line intersect parallel lines at the same angle is supposed to be graspable in a primordial intuition.

Derrida shows that the notion of an unmediated awareness, the pure presence of what is, is incoherent with some of Husserl's best analyses. Briefly, Derrida shows two things.

First, since "the present" is itself constructed out of what amount to memories of the past and anticipations of the future, the present is itself not present in a way that makes its complete nature available to us. Part of what is required for any present to be present is absent, displaced from itself.

Second, the distinction Husserl makes between expressive signs and merely indicative signs cannot be sustained. The expressive signs are supposed to carry significance directly, to be invested with meaning, while the indicative signs are merely correlated with the meanings they indicate. As Derrida shows, since any sign must be iterable in order to be a sign at all, or to function as a meaning carrier, expressive signs must be iterable. That is, the being of such a sign as a sign is constituted by a universal, a repeatable element that carries the meaning and would carry the same meaning in another case. A sign has significance in virtue of some aspect of it that can have other occurrences. In Anglo-analytical terms, the type of which a token is a token is what has the semantic properties of the token.

Husserl tries to avoid Platonism and its pure, mind-independent essences by a Kantian-type synthesis of the necessary out of purified present experience. But given Husserl's strategy of constructing universals out of events of intending items a certain way, being a meaningful sign essentially brings in other, future and past possible occurrences of tokens of the same type. Thus, even in the case of an expressive sign, the significance of the sign itself, the meaning it carries, cannot be fully present. The meaningfulness as well as the meaning of the sign are properties whose applicability depends on nonpresent facts. So even in the case of the expressive sign, the meaning intended is separated from the sign itself. Thus there is no basis for the distinction between indicative and expressive signs. All signs are displaced from the meaning they might carry.

Both Quine and Derrida, then, attack the hidden realism built into the kind of present meaning-content that will make the necessary the *a priori*. Whatever has the full presence required either by phenomenology or by logical positivism has to have some objectively real objects, and so some objective necessities. Furthermore, they both see no way to separate the meaning from the sign. Meaning as pure, extracted, semantic content is an incoherent notion.

One illuminating expression for the displacement of all signs from what they are signs of is Derrida's view that even speech is a species of writing.[6] This hyperbole makes, among especially Derridean points, the Quinean point that behind writing or speech can lie nothing but more writinglike or speechlike phenomena. While Quine does not discuss "logocentrism," his treatment of speech and thought as inscription supposes that the model of thought is writing.[7]

If writing is the paradigm indicative sign, having only a conventional and displaced relation to the thought that it communicates, then the hyperbole that speech is a species of writing asserts that all thought and representation is writinglike. Particularly poignantly, thought must be writinglike and so displaced from fully present meaning. But then nothing is fully present, and all talk of "displacement" of meaning is a kind of deception, since there is nothing from which signs are displaced. Every kind of thought is separate from "the thought to be communicated."

In his discussion of ontological relativity, Quine puts this point by saying that radical translation begins at home. A language cannot be explicated in anything other than a language. Without the existence of a kind of language that could not be misinterpreted, we fall inevitably into a "regress to a background language" in interpreting our own speech or the speech of another. A vivid way to express the view common to Quine and Derrida is to say that all thought can be at most brain-writing or spirit-writing, both of which modes of inscription yield texts with at least the hermeneutic problems of other texts. There is no meaning or meaning bearer behind language that is not itself a languagelike phenomenon.

Consequences of This Philosophical Deconstruction

The deconstruction of the contrast between analytic and synthetic truths and between expressive and indicative signs supplies the premises needed for reasoned arguments for the more extravagant, irritating, puzzling claims of deconstructionist thinkers. Even their claim that evaluating arguments ought not to constitute the method of philosophy is defensible from that basis.

As I discussed above in "Indeterminacy of French Interpretation," once language can go back to nothing but language, and interpretation-free anchors for meanings become unavailable, we can no longer escape the possibility of drift, or indeterminacy of translation. Every interpretation is subject to alternative interpretation, since every level is language-like and no interpretation is privileged. The incompletability of analysis into meaning and fact, then, obliterates the possibility of determinacy of meaning. This consequence is central to deconstructive thinking and criticism; many interesting deconstructionist results seem to me to depend on indeterminacy/dissemination phenomena. Further consequences, to be considered below, also flow from the realization that there cannot be meanings if meanings must be ultimate anchors for interpretation. These further consequences likewise arise from the collapse of dualisms of various kinds. The dualisms in question arguably depend on the initial dualism of "real meaning" and "mere sign," the impossibility of separating meaning and fact.

I avoid one common misconstrual of the denial of dualisms. Quine's and Derrida's claim that all representation is languagelike is not the claim that all reality is text or a cultural construct. As I read them, Quine and Derrida assert only the inseparability of the linguistic contribution from the total phenomenon. That is, the world is more than words, but we cannot get at the more in its pure form.[8] To deny a dualism is to deny not one side of the duality but the division.

This is a general philosophical difficulty about getting "pure cases." Generally, dualisms break down because each side of the duality requires the other, making it impossible to pry one side off to arrive at an unmixed half. This means that a certain kind of completeness of account, a kind of finalization and determinacy, is in principle lacking for central metaphysical contrasts.

Let me briefly mention a few parallel cases, without going through the arguments. A famous case of paradoxical lack of final closure occurs in Plato's *Parmenides*. Plato argues that there cannot be a unity, a single thing that is just itself and that is in no way mixed with the opposite character, plurality. This result arises because a unity cannot be without plurality, even as an abstract object. Similarly, Plato argues that what is is inextricably mixed with the Different, what is not. There can be no unmixed cases of being or unity; these are in principle inseparable from each other and from the different. Plato clearly intends this result to be generalized to forms other than being and unity as well, so that all analysis is interminable in principle, lacking completeness. Aristotle's analysis of phenomena in terms of form and matter has much the same structure of never quite finishing. Neither the pure subject that is in no way character, namely matter, nor the pure character that is in no way a subject is a coherent notion.[9]

Both of these lacks of completeness are displacements of natures from themselves, in a way. In the nature of things there is no possibility of getting to the core, just as in radical translation, there is no possibility of peeling off of the language to get to the meaning in isolation but only a succession of translations into meaningful languages. Likewise, in interpreting a poem, there is no possibility of final, definitive interpretation but only deeper and deeper, unending and spreading explications. A poem may always be construed in the light of further poems and texts. Indeterminacy of translation guarantees even that alternatives occur at every point in the deepening.

Now, just as Plato does not conclude that no Unity exists but only Difference, so Derrida and Quine do not suppose that nothing exists but theories or the text. Although it is impossible to say how the world is apart from language, and impossible to isolate a part of what is that is due to language and a part that is due to reality, the world nonetheless is more than text. That "more than text," though, is in principle not specifiable, and is not the foundation for the text.

So what does the incoherence of the concept of pure, present, unmediated meaning entail for other notions and for the dualities they support? A number of notions and dualities that presuppose or rely on that concept simply collapse.

One such undermined notion is that of *intention* as something that has semantic content but is pure and unambiguous. "Having semantic content" means minimally having truth conditions. If intentions have truth conditions of any complexity, then whatever carries the semantic content of an intention must be a structure of components with semantic roles and so must have the same difficulties of interpretation as languages have. Intentions can then no longer provide an interpreter that needs no interpretation behind an utterance or text, since any intention is bound in another text.

Without intentions as unproblematic meaning bearers and meaning determiners, the rhetorical force of a text or utterance is cut loose from alleged anchors. If a question arises about whether any given text is meant seriously or not, the same problem besets any allegedly underlying thought-text or brain-text in which intentions might be embodied as well. The neurological sequence of events that is taken to have semantic content can be taken ironically or seriously, and some further, deeper brain-text will be just as in need of interpretation. The question of what is meant cannot in principle get beyond psycho-quotes if there is no pure present meaning that cannot be misconstrued.

A number of other important dualities that are taken for granted in much philosophical and critical writing are also undermined by construing the attack on meaning as the deconstruction of the notion of a purely present representation that could not be misunderstood. Without meanings as the noninterpretable backing to language, some of the compartmentalizings we practice have no principled basis. I will discuss four of these dying dualities below.

1. *Fact and value, cognitive and emotive content.* If all meaning is given by regress to background languages, then we have no clear way to compartmentalize such parts of meaning as denotation and connotation, or to separate facts from values. If there were nonlinguistic meaning, a kind of language of thought not susceptible to interpretation, then that meaning could have purely factual and purely evaluative parts. For instance, in the classical logical-positivist strategy, the factual content of meaningful propositions is totally specified in terms of sets of sensations that are confirmation conditions for propositions. These nonlinguistic meaning givers contrast with the emotional effects or other phenomena that constitute the nonfactual remainder of meaning.

Suppose we do not have nonlanguagelike meanings underlying language, but always something mixed with more language, so that something languagelike is ineliminable from whatever is taken to be the meaning of some language. Then the division into denotation and connotation would have to be translation into a language that had only factual content and into a language that had only emotional or evaluative content. If "content" is analyzed in a Quinean or Davidsonian way, via the interanimation of sentences, these languages are going to be hard to invent, let alone discover. For a Davidsonian, for instance, the evaluations associated with a term would be a function of the degrees to which sentences containing the term are desired-true, just as the cognitive meaning of a term is a function of the degrees to which sentences using the term are held-true. Since assignments of both desirabilities and credibilities are made on the basis of what is done and said, the assignment of these numbers is indeterminate.

2. *The rhetorical and the truth-conditional.* The same consideration that nothing lies behind sentences that is isolable from languagelike phenomena leads to the conclusion that no distinction can be drawn between the content of a sentence and the form of the sentence. Thus the idea of a feature of a sentence that is "merely rhetorical" is called into question. There is no defensible notion of common content by which to define the contrast between the message and the fancy flourishes with which it is conveyed.

If no principled line can be drawn between what is merely rhetorical and what is part of the cognitive meaning of a sentence, then no such line can be drawn between rhetorical features and "consequences" on the one hand and truth-conditional inferential features of sentences on the other hand. For instance, the tone of impersonal, absolute validity conveyed by the passive voice in an agentless sentence ("it is therefore concluded that . . .") cannot legitimately be separated from the modal quality of what the author is asserting. The "real" consequences of a sentence are defined in terms of truth conditions. But if truth conditions are stated in further sentences, those further sentences themselves need to be purified of the nonfactual. Thus the smearing of the distinction between logic and rhetoric for real language follows from the indivisibility of purely informational, truth-conditional meaning from the total import of a sentence. Unless such a strict notion of truth conditions as "factual" can be specified, the notion of what really follows from a sentence as opposed to what is implied cannot be specified, either. (It is perhaps no accident that words like "imply" deny any dualism between truth-conditional and other consequences.)

If rhetorical consequence cannot be distinguished from logical consequence in a principled way, then we can no longer dismiss the figures, metaphors, and rhetoric of a philosopher as not really part of what is worth discussing philosophically. The notion that the *very same thing* could have been said in plain analytical prose will be indefensible unless a naked, factual-truth-conditional, purely present thought system underlies language. So the image of a philosophical text as an argument in such a thought system layered over with more or less concealing fancy stuff is incoherent if meaning is dead.

Given the above argument, what kinds of critique are appropriate when dealing with a philosophical work? If the argument is not clearly separable from the metaphors and tropes, then, as Rorty has suggested, philosophical critique is literary criticism and philosophy is a genre of literature.[10]

Given this breakdown of borderlines between the rhetorical and the philosophical, we can note one more complication in a preliminary way. The notion of "undermining," which I characterized as "logical" deconstruction, must be broadened. According to the present arguments, rhetorical underminings cannot be sharply isolated from logical underminings and so are also worthy philosophical work. The practice of philosophy, then, will look very different under the Quinean-Derridean-Davidsonian regime.

3. *The metaphorical and the literal.* Having lost the contrast between the rhetorical and the truth-conditional, we should not be surprised that the contrast between metaphorical and literal cannot be sustained. In fact, this breakdown seems to follow directly from the nonexistence of a level of representation that is not languagelike.

Davidson himself has made this kind of point in a widely misread paper.[11] Davidson argues, apparently, that any term or sentence has only a literal meaning. The metaphorical sentence "Wheeler's essay is a quagmire of self-descriptive traps" is to be explained, Davidson seems to say, not in terms of some alternative meaning to which the metaphoric context directs us but in terms of a purpose of the author other than that of alerting the hearer to the drainage problems of my prose. Davidson is widely held to have assigned a special privilege to something called "literal meaning." In fact, given Davidson's participation in the deconstruction of meaning and the (for him) three dogmas of empiricism, his view could not be that metaphors have literal meaning in the "factual" sense. Davidson's claim is that to give the meaning of a metaphor is the same as giving the meaning of any other use of language. A theory of meaning pairs sentences with truth conditions. "Wheeler's essay is a quagmire of self-descriptive traps" is true if and only if Wheeler's essay is a quagmire of self-descriptive traps. Such a sentence gives all there is to give of the meaning of the sentence. The point is that there is nothing behind language but more languagelike phenomena, and any explication of a metaphor will itself have metaphorical as well as nonmetaphorical uses.

All of this discussion is relative to decisions about what sentences are true and when they are true. Uses other than asserting as true depend on such choices, which will not be so clear in many cases of "metaphor." Is this chapter really a quagmire or not? Are problems literally hard, or is "hard" strictly applied only to physical objects? It is hard to see how this question could be answered in a trustworthy way. Is "way" in the previous sentence a metaphorical extension of a physical route? Can a term be literally extended?

Given such problems, truth conditions are generally more determinate than truth-values. To interpret an utterance as literal is to make a choice about whether a sentence is true, from a Davidsonian perspective. The tropes cannot be separated from the straight arrows in any other way than by noting what we are tempted to call "literal." "Literal," then, is like "analytic"—a term without a principled basis.

The notion that there is a nonlanguagelike meaning behind speech is required by the usual explications of metaphor and other exotic tropes. The "meaning of metaphor" requires a language of thought in which metaphors are somehow impossible, so that the real message of a metaphor is transparent when its meaning is understood. If language is always backed up by further languagelike phenomena, then figural understandings abound both in the interpreted language and in the explicating language. There is no unturnable, metaphor-free discourse, and no untropable explication. Freedom from metaphor requires the idle dream of a purely descriptive language of thought, a language in which the satisfaction of "is a quagmire" can be nothing except permanent saturation of earth by water.

If words go back to words, the literal cannot be empirically distinguished from the poetic and tropic, since the words that back up words are themselves subject to poetic and tropic understanding.[12]

4. *Textual essence and accident.* If how something is said turns out not to be isolable from what is said, then features of what is said that would seem to be irrelevant to the philosophical evaluation of a text cannot simply be ignored. The contrast between the essential and the accidental features of a text can no longer be sustained. If part of the rhetorical effect of a given passage of Nozick depends on a reference to Thidwick the Big-Hearted Moose,[13] then other features of a text that are not strictly logical are hard to rule out as irrelevant. The hint that Nozick is not being entirely earnest gives the whole text a problematic rhetorical stance. The possibility that Nozick is advancing his arguments not as theses he believes but rather just as interesting and puzzling hypotheses is suggested by such examples. But then the whole interpretation of what Nozick is doing and what *Anarchy, State, and Utopia* is about is called into question, not by any defect in argument but by mere rhetoric. Similar effects are possible from punning,

double meanings, oddities of syntax that mock contemporary philosophical style, and so forth.

Without meanings, and without a nonlanguagelike backing for language, it is difficult to see how to draw a principled line between features of the language that are relevant to interpretation and features that are not.

Deconstructing Poems?

If the arguments from the Quinean and Derridean destruction of meaning are accepted this far, then the scope of philosophical discussion is much expanded. More than the "arguments of the philosophers" are germane to the philosophical discussion of philosophical texts. So this line of thought treats philosophy as a kind of literature. Still, I have not yet shown how it is possible to treat literature as a kind of philosophy. But the notion of deconstruction of literary works, as this is applied by practicing critics, seems to effect such a transformation. If the poems of Shelley are not advancing philosophical theories, how can they be deconstructed?

The most immediate, intuitive objection to the "deconstruction" of a work such as Shelley's *Triumph of Life* is the view that the poem is not obviously *about* metaphysical issues or the parasite relation. It is a poem, not a treatise. I will work my way up to this question slowly, by first considering what, from a Quinean perspective, we can mean by "about" and "the theory behind the text."

So what is a text about, and what are the conditions for a text to contain a metaphysical (or other) thesis? We already enjoy considerable latitude in determining "subject matter" and "contained thesis," once we reject both purely present intentions that inform the work by determining privileged descriptions, and texts in the world of Forms that lie behind the imperfect expression given by the author's words. Furthermore, from the Fregean point of view and its successors, "about" is at most a rhetorical notion, not one that has to do with truth conditions. That is, in Fregean logic, logically equivalent sentences can be about different things, so that "aboutness" has no role whatsoever.

Let us first consider the kind of models of philosophical interpretation that Quine and Derrida would have to reject. On this traditional model, Aristotle's text, for instance, is only a more or less accurate representation of his thought or of a Platonic entity informing that text. Aristotle's real theory is conceived as something behind the text, more or less concealed by cryptic, careless, or ambiguous expression.

The traditional interpreter, even given a transparent language of thought, or informing Platonic entities, lacks access to either of these sources of textual fulfillment. So such an interpreter falls back on the text as a source of data for constructing hypotheses about the thought or the Form. The devices the interpreter uses consist in various inferences to and from "implicit" doctrines, doctrines from which explicit sentences of the text would follow (given plausible background assumptions) or which (with supplementary premises) are implied by explicit sentences of the text. In this recovery and reconstruction project, such phenomena as rhetorical force are relevant. But a traditional interpreter will consider only those rhetorical relevances and nonlogical connections that he or she thinks may have been the contents of the inner discourse of the philosopher being interpreted. On the traditional model, the goal is the presence behind the text, the meaning of the text that is not itself textlike.

Even on the traditional model, interpreters clearly already go beyond the explicit presuppositions, implied theses, assumptions the author never articulated even for himself, and so forth. But their interpretations are still constrained by the dualities discussed above and the thought that there must be an "intention of the author" determining what about a text is relevant to discuss.

A philosophical interpreter who does not suppose a nontextual meaning behind the text is left with the text itself, but not as data for the construction of some interior or Platonic reality. Since there are only the words, all properties and connections of those words can be relevant to understanding a text. "Understanding" means something different without the final say of the meaning behind the text. Understanding is now an in-principle uncompletable explication, elucidation, and discussion of the text itself.

The interpreter who has abandoned the notion of pure meaning behind the text and has grasped the arguments for the indeterminacy of translation will deny not only the possibility of final understanding but also the existence of exactly one correct account of (for example) Aristotle's views. According to the Quinean indeterminacy arguments and Derrida's discussions of dissemination, all texts are fundamentally drifting and indeterminate, given the multiple patterns of connection with other texts and within a given text. Thus we can find ourselves faced with absolutely un-decidable choices between ironic and straight reading, different families of associated texts, and so forth. Thus, a kind of pluralism arises. This is not to say that any account of the text is as worthy as any other, or that a text can be read as saying whatever one pleases. All that indeterminacy guaran-tees is that there will be ties for best interpretation.

From these considerations it can be argued that deconstructionist readings of poems are legitimate explications as much as other readings are. I must show how *The Triumph of Life*, for instance, can be susceptible to deconstruction even though the text asserts no philosophical doctrines.

As a first step, I will point out that, by the liberal standards of even the conservative philosophical analysts, thinkers often are committed to doctrines that they do not explicitly avow or assert in so many words. A particular view of substance may be presupposed or implied by a thinker's views about logic or ethics, for instance, even though he has no chapters or even sentences devoted to metaphysical questions. The discourse itself can be an especially relevant implicit subject matter. Whether or not the dis-course explicitly mentions itself or discourse in general, the presumptions implicit in what is said can make the discourse self-referential. Paul de Man's discussions in *Allegories of Reading* show how texts can be illumi-nated when regarded as allegories of indeterminacy, and therefore why it is impossible to "read" them, where to "read" is understood as to get total and determinate meaning from a text.

Now, the issue is whether this way in which the text "can be illumi-nated when regarded as" is what the text "really means." To defend decon-structive readings as nonparasitical and as not just formal tricks of mapping the language onto itself, we must consider what the range is of a text's "real meaning" and how texts can be truly self-referential.

Derrida and Quine must construe implicit content to include meta-physical problems. If Quine's argument in "Two Dogmas" and subsequent explications is correct, neither theory and language nor metaphysics and theory are separable in principle. If those dualisms are accordingly aban-doned, then any use of language presupposes metaphysical views, since the language builds in the theory associated with its terms. Any use of lan-guage can undermine itself, not just by explicitly questioning the views it presupposes but by illustrating lack of closure, "mise-en-abîme," and so forth. Since the principles built into the language in fact do prevent a kind of closure and completeness, language can be construed as being "about" the relation between language and the world.

The possibility of legitimate self-referential interpretation follows from denying that anchors in the author's soul select an "intended interpretation" and from the ordinary interpretive procedure of requiring that a discourse fit its subject. While the notion of "interpretation" of literary texts cannot use the precise metamathematical notion of fit as a point-to-point model, a requirement of "fit" broadly construed is appropriate. In common with the famous metatheorems of twentieth-century logic, an "intended interpretation" is relative to arbitrary choices of what refers to what. Thus a well-founded self-referential understanding of a text meets reasonable standards of fit, and the text, under that interpretation, becomes detached from the nonlinguistic world and turns its referring expressions onto itself.

Most interestingly, texts, especially those involving complicated word-play or patterns of metaphor, have an *unavoidable* self-reference analogous to what we find in the Gödel incompleteness and completeness proofs. That is, just as any language adequate for arithmetic must be construable as "about" its calculations and their properties, so a full natural-language text permits being construed as about the text itself.

The mere possibility of modeling texts on themselves does not provide much motivation for doing so. A way of looking at texts is ultimately justified by the illumination and understanding that results. It seems clear that, for some texts, treating them as metaphysics produces illumination and explication otherwise not to be had. Features of the text that had been accidental become integrated into an account of meaning. That Shelley's poem, for instance, can plausibly be read as dealing with metaphysical issues has been shown pretty persuasively by the Hillis Miller article cited above and by Paul de Man's article in the same volume.[14] Texts that are rich and complex can illustrate especially well the self-undermining qualities of language/metaphysics/our theory.

If language indeed has the incompleteness and indeterminacy that Quine and Derrida ascribe to it, then poets sensitive to language would create texts that could plausibly and interestingly be read as about the lack of closure, completeness, and interpretation-ending meaning of language/metaphysics. Texts that are about writing or that implicitly deal with writing, meaning, communicating, and completeness may be especially illuminatingly discussed as metaphysics in this regard. The interpretation of the poet's implicit discussion may hinge on tropes, turns of phrase, patterns of metaphors whose appropriateness is taken back, and on other non–truth-conditional considerations that cannot reasonably be separated from the logic of the text. Such poems under such construals, then, implicitly assert their unreadability and so undermine their own status as texts with a message.

If part of being "about" metaphysics is containing reflection on language and its relation to both thought and reality, the romantic poets, having from the very beginning been famous for special forms of irony, are strong candidates for being closet metaphysicians even without the nudging of Derrida and Quine. That the specifically deconstructionist approach to the romantics is fruitful has been amply demonstrated in the work of Miller and de Man, among others. In many ways, in fact, deconstructionist accounts seem to continue and develop the traditional strategies of the interpretation of the romantics.

I have not tried to characterize everything that could plausibly be called "deconstruction," since "deconstruction" is itself language, and subject to very rapid deployment, dissemination, and drift. "Deconstructive" characterizes kinds of commentary that start with the reflections on language outlined above, and encountered in the texts of Derrida, Davidson, and Quine. Interpreters who accept indeterminacy of translation, the lack of closure and completeness in interpretation, the endless sequence of texts behind texts, and the numerous possibilities of relations of words to other words that are plausibly relevant, share a family of attitudes toward, and approaches to, texts.

My goal was to show that the conclusions of the original deconstructive arguments supported further arguments which expanded the scope of deconstruction both in terms of what "undermining" means and in terms of what objects are appropriate for deconstruction. While there is a great deal more to say about deconstructive practice, and about the justification of the premises on which deconstructive practice rests, the project of this paper is complete.

3

Truth Conditions, Rhetoric, and Logical Form

DAVIDSON AND DECONSTRUCTION

Many of Derrida's deconstructive arguments start from an antiessentialist rejection of a principled line between the cognitive meanings of words and other features of words.[1] Given that the fundamental distinction between rhetoric and logic rests on cognitive meanings, Derrida's denial entails the denial of a principled line between logic and rhetoric.[2] On my reading, deconstruction takes as an early lemma the rejection of a principled line between logic and rhetoric. The basic idea is that the distinction between rhetoric and logic depends on the analytic/synthetic distinction, the fact-value dichotomy, and the cognitive/emotive distinction. Without *logoi*, none of these distinctions will be principled.

As I will show below, Donald Davidson is explicitly and implicitly committed to these same starting points and lemmas. Davidson's thought begins not from Husserl and Heidegger but from the series of reflections leading from Frege to Quine. Davidson discusses the phenomena I characterize as rhetorical in terms of the concept of force and in terms of the distinction between the truth conditions of sentences and the uses to which sentences are put. This chapter shows how, from these commitments and their consequences, the analytic philosophy of Davidson leads to an interchangeability of logic and rhetoric that is equivalent to Derrida's dissolution of that line.[3] As a consequence, Davidson is committed to other startling theses for which deconstruction is notorious. When properly understood, these theses are not so startling and should not be notorious, but should rather be taken as the serious basis for further work.

My argument will be a straightforward one in the analytic tradition, following the spirit of Davidson's investigations into logical form,[4] and relying on his development of the distinction between what is said and the force with which it is said.[5] One virtue of analytic philosophy is its tradition of putting points in transparently simple paradigms. The analytic philosopher will discuss "The cat is on the mat" or "Galileo believed that the Earth moves" rather than the works of Freud and Proust. By following that analytic tradition, I show in a simple way part of what it means to claim that rhetoric and logic are continuous. I hope thereby to remove some of the opacity that has blocked analytic philosophers from seeing what Derrida could be up to.

This result shows something about philosophical problems as well as about philosophers. Derrida and Davidson emerge from traditions that have had little contact over the past century. That they nonetheless reach similar positions on the basis of analogous considerations indicates that from their different traditions a common problem has emerged that transcends the particularities of those traditions.

Most importantly, that these philosophers reach similar conclusions from their different backgrounds indicates that they are getting something right. The consequences of there being no magic language, no language of self-interpreting marks, seem to be forced by some structure that is not peculiar to either analytic philosophy or the continental tradition. If there indeed can be no "magic language" to provide foundations in the ways many philosophers have sought, that is interesting and important. My hope is that by thinking through the problems from the points of view of both Derrida and Davidson, I can see more clearly how to think my own way through or around some of the philosophical questions that have fascinated me for a long time.

This idea that there are "philosophical problems" cutting across traditions contradicts what some have taken to be a consequence of deconstruction, namely, that differing traditions cannot share philosophical problems. Shared philosophical problems seem to presuppose interlinguistic *logoi* in which such questions can be formulated. But just as the indeterminacy of translation still allows that Joe means that snow is white, so deconstruction of the magic language still allows that people can think about the same things. "Same" though, cannot mean "same *logos*." But that means only that "same" cannot be applied if indeed the existence of the magic language is essential to the possibility of thought and speech. That is, to insist that we cannot meaningfully speak of the "same philosophical problem" without assuming a magic language is to assume the very standpoint that deconstruction and Davidson remove. The issue is whether there is something between the perfect sameness that *logoi*, that is, the words of the magic language, permit, and nothing at all. I would argue that we have every reason to think that the terms of a natural language, including "same philosophical problem," function without needing *logoi*.[6] So while there is no "same problem" in the sense that *logoi* would permit, we can still properly say that the disparate discourses are troubled by the same problem. How to think about philosophical problems and distinctions without supposing the foundations that *logoi* permit is in fact one of the major philosophical problems that I hope the joint study of Derrida and Davidson can illuminate.[7]

Logic and Rhetoric

Starting with Plato's war with the Sophists, the properties of words have been divided into two categories.

On the one hand, we have the logical properties, which determine the concept or thought expressed, and constitute the real meaning or content of the term or sentence. These are the features of words that fix the reference of a term and the truth-value of a sentence. The logical properties are thus conceived as the essences of or meanings behind the words. Most important, since the meanings of terms are fixed by logical properties, so are the truth-values of sentences. What are known as "propositions" or the "cognitive contents" of sentences are essentially the abstracted essence of the sequence of words as meant on an occasion of utterance. "Logical properties" are covered under what is categorized as semantics.

On the other hand, we have the rhetorical properties, which are the various other properties of words that can affect how those words function in discourse. Such properties and relations include assonances, pleasant associations, the property of having been used by Shakespeare, and metonymic and metaphoric connections. The rhetorical properties spring from the many material guises (as in the phrase "the materiality of the signifier") in which the same *logos* or meaning can show up. The rhetoric-logic dichotomy is yet another form of the matter-form dichotomy. (This self-referential sentence reminds us that to deny that a distinction can be founded on pure *logoi* is not to say that the distinction cannot be used. So something like the same form has different "matter," and rhetorical connection differs from logical connection. But such differences need not imply that there is such a thing as a logical connection that is in no way rhetorical, any more than there is pure form, or a word that has nothing but the meaning it shares with other words.)

The distinction between rhetoric and logic is then that logic draws logical connections, relations that depend on logical properties; while rhetoric goes from premise to conclusion using rhetorical connections, connections that exist in virtue of accidents of words. Whenever persuasion rests on an expression's effect on a person as predicted from our knowledge of the person's beliefs and desires, the properties at work in the expression are rhetorical. In fact, anything other than "meaning" in the strict "logoi" sense defined below is rhetorical.[8] Note that the rhetorical is defined by negation of the logical, not by any proper feature of its own. This is characteristic of a "binary opposition."

Logical properties are really successors of *logoi*, or Forms, which lie behind the words and which words express. *Logoi* have had many incarnations, such as the "senses" that Frege thought words expressed, the meanings that the logical positivists appealed to, and the intentional entities of Husserl. *Logoi*, in some guise or other, serve as the foundation for many familiar philosophical concepts and distinctions concerning language, meaning, and translation. Our thoughts are supposed to be like *logoi* or to connect directly with *logoi*. When, for instance, we say that our thoughts can be the same whether expressed in Latin or in English, or that some of what we say is true in virtue of meaning alone, we seem to appeal to thought-words that have many of the same properties as Platonic Forms or Aristotelian *nous* tokens.

Logoi have played the dual role of being the real natures of things and of being present to thought. Plato's Forms and Aristotelian *nous* tokens were essences of things and not just magical representations of things. The thought was literally the same as the object, so that things could be in mind, for Aristotle. As essential, constituting features of objects, the Forms that make objects be, *logoi* have diminished in their scope since Plato and Aristotle. Since *logoi* are supposed to be present to thought, and necessarily fit their referents, the logical judgments were necessary truths, truths that revealed the essence of their subject matters. As philosophers lost confidence in intuitions of the essence of external objects, *logoi* became restricted to entities that philosophers thought we could intuit. While the philosophers were trying to be nonessentialist, they retained in one form or another the essentialism implicit in supposing that anything's nature could be directly intuited.

So the British empiricists supposed that Ideas were the tokens of thought that were directly present. An Idea of Red could not be mistaken for an Idea of Yellow. Ideas wore their senses and references on their sleeves. An Idea's reference was fixed by "fitting" its referent; this notion of "fit" ran into difficulties solved variously by Berkeley and Kant. The Idea idea finally yielded, in the phenomenological tradition, to intentional objects, and in the tradition of logical empiricism, to meanings of words. That is, for the logical empiricists from whom Davidson and Quine free themselves, self-revealing essences were restricted to meanings of words, construed as magically represented stipulations of sets of self-revealing experiences.

As meanings of words and so as objects of thought, *logoi* allow a magic language, whose tokens essentially express or are *logoi*. This magic language thus has words that cannot be misunderstood. (We "think to ourselves" in the language of *logoi*, so this perfection of understanding gives sense to alleged tragic inadequacies of language to express our subtler thoughts. The language of thought is perfectly expressive of all properties and nuances, unlike natural languages.) To think the word is to think its meaning directly, to think a term that is nothing other than its essence. While you can be mistaken about what the word *chien* means, you cannot be mistaken about what your thought of a dog is about, or that you intend to speak of dogs. The truth conditions of your thoughts are fixed by their very nature. So a private language is possible with the magic language.

Unlike regular language, the language of *logoi* cannot be misinterpreted, because *logoi* reveal their meaning to the inspecting "I."[9] Or again, the *logoi* are self-interpreting because their meaning is their essence. To be this *logos* is to mean these objects. The history of the magic language has an interesting dialectic on this point: The only genuinely clear candidates for "meaning by their very nature" are items that are in some way identical to the items they mean. Thus Aristotelian *nous* tokens were the entities without their matter. The problem of the magic language has been to make its terms mean by their very nature in some way short of being the very thing. As Berkeley argued, the British empiricist's ideas of red could not be mistaken for ideas of yellow only because they really meant themselves.

Even though both traditions are founded on peculiar versions of *logoi*, neither phenomenology nor Anglo-American empiricism can be naturally comfortable with meanings. These *logoi*, the "words" of the magic language of intention and thought, must be entities that reveal their essences, and thus reveal necessities, to bare inspection. As sketched above, both of these traditions grew out of modern philosophy's attempt to eschew intuited natural necessities. So the empiricists should have been suspicious of the magic language of *logoi*, just because such a language requires that necessary truths and intrinsic natures be there in experience.

Aristotle's lesson, it seems to me, had been largely forgotten by anti-essentialist empiricists who assumed the existence of "given" objects of any kind. Aristotle demonstrated that for any objects whatsoever, there must be a distinction between features the object must have to continue to be itself and features the object could lose and still exist.[10] The very idea of a "given" object, then, presupposes that necessity and possibility are given as well. So the hope of constructing a world from mere non-modal data must fail.[11]

Likewise, the phenomenologists ought to have been suspicious of *logoi*, since these mental words are necessarily repeatables and thus have as part of their nature what is not yet, the past and future possibilities of recurrence. How can such possibilities per se be present? Also, if these words determine an extension, that necessary relation to another object must somehow be totally present in the way a word is. Neither of these features of noetic contents seems capable of being per se completely present to consciousness. (Here I have summarized and simplified some of Derrida's arguments in *Speech and Phenomena*.)

The rejection of *logoi*, and thus the rejection of the basis for the distinction between the rhetorical and the logical, stems from this rejection of the magic language. Such a renunciation entails Derrida's denials of principled distinctions, as well as Davidson's and Quine's denials of dogmas.

Davidson as Deconstructor

On my reading, the basic thought common to Davidson, Derrida, and Quine is that any language consisting of any kind of marks, whether marks on paper or marks in the soul, is no better than words. The marks that constitute intentions, then, are also material, and thus are present to us with something other than just an essence. ("Material" here just means "being something other than pure semantic content.") This "nonpresence" of the true meaning would apply even if further meaningful entities stood behind intentions. If there were a part or aspect of the intention that carried the essence, that part or aspect would itself have a materiality. The difficulty is analogous to Plato's Third Man argument. If thought-tokens are marks, and marks are particulars, then no mark can be nothing but an alleged universal, the essence, that it shares with other particulars.

Thus every mark is subject to interpretation. If we think and intend using marks that are just like words, then the alleged meaning of the word cannot even possibly be an entity that is nothing other than the meaning. Even marks in the soul thus lack a separable essence. But accidental features guarantee the possibility of being misunderstood and of being used rhetorically. So there is no separating these rhetorical connections and features from the logical connections and features. That is, we cannot get to "meanings," entities that have only essential connections, which are related to other things only in virtue of their essence. That is, no entities can bear only logical relations.

The rejection of the magic language is thus the rejection of the coherence of anything satisfying the conditions of being the semantic essence of a word. This amounts to the denial of "meanings" in the traditional philosophical sense. Quine, Davidson, and Derrida in effect work out the consequences of being realistic and physicalistic about thought and meaning. Among the consequences is a radical revision of the notion of "meaning."

The rejection of the magic language implicitly also amounts to a rejection of an absolute or ontological distinction between the logical and the rhetorical aspects of discourse. Let us see how this distinction shows up in Davidson's theory. Davidson, in company with Quine and Derrida, holds that any representation, whether in thought or in words, must be language-like in bearing only a contingent relation to any referent. That is, there are no magical words that interpret themselves, no *logoi*, no meanings in the sense of objects that represent but are not subject to misinterpretation.

The meaning of a word can only be given in other words. Without intermediaries between words and the world, supplied by the magic language, the world is what the language describes, barring a "more genuine" language, sentences of which would *really mean* the world. Briefly, for Davidson, the meaning of a word is determined by what people say and in what circumstances they say it. So meaning cannot deviate from the world. Interestingly, both Davidson and Derrida hold that the issue between realism and nonrealism is a nonissue because the initial divisions, for instance into world and conceptual scheme, cannot be made coherently. Such divisions are dogmas of empiricism or deconstructible binary oppositions.

If there are no magical, naturally referring words, then meaning is nothing deeper than uses of ordinary words in particular circumstances. But "circumstances" are, as it were, precisely fitted to words, in the sense that the circumstances in which "Fred is a frog" is true are precisely those in which Fred is a frog. As Davidson has argued in "True to the Facts," there are no entities making sentences true, so appeal to "circumstances" in which "Fred is a frog" is true adds nothing to saying that "Fred is a frog" is true if and only if Fred is a frog.

I will argue that rhetorical force and logical form must be epistemologically interchangeable in Davidson's accounts of meaning, truth, and interpretation. In explaining or interpreting a particular speech act, a Davidsonian interpreter makes underdetermined choices between explaining a feature as due to logical form and explaining it as due to rhetorical features of the speech act. Davidson's discussions of what I am calling "rhetoric" appear in his papers on force, mood, and convention.[12] In his discussion of force, that is, the purpose for which a sentence is presented, Davidson shows that properties like sincerity, being serious, and being sarcastic cannot be governed by conventions, and so cannot be explained by a "theory" in the usual sense. "Rhetorical force," though, is always part of what is ascribed to a speech act in interpretation.

Force and truth conditions are interchangeable, as I will illustrate below in this chapter by examining the analyses a Davidsonian might give of sentences such as "Only Fred loves Susan." Intuitively, "Only Fred loves Susan" implies that Fred loves Susan. But the implication can be interpreted equally well either as rhetorical or as due to the logical form. So, only relative to an underdetermined interpretation does a sentence have truth conditions. Thus the distinction between rhetoric and logic is an artifact of an undetermined choice of theory, not a reality in the world.

But since a sentence's logical form—that is, its truth conditions— determines whether the sentence is true, it must be that the interpretation of the words is apportioned between truth and rhetorical force, so that truth itself is relative to ascriptions of rhetorical intent. If there are undetermined choices in that apportionment, this is an indeterminacy of interpretation different from those noticed in the analytic tradition of philosophy of science. Such rhetorical indeterminacy is much like what de Man discusses in describing Rousseau's account of predication, in which the rhetorical use of a term as a metaphor becomes a predication.[13] This indeterminacy or, to use de Man's term, "undecidability" between figural and literal amounts to an undecidability between assigning a meaning to a rhetorical connection and assigning a meaning to a logical content. Derrida, who also uses "undecidable," does not want to use the term "indeterminate" because to him it indicates vagueness, fuzzy boundaries, or lack of definition. His term "undecidable," though, would be unacceptable to Quine and Davidson because of its Gödelian overtones. In fact, the phenomena they are labeling seem to me to be much the same: There can be distinct global interpretations, each of which is quite precise. These global interpretations can be seen as centered around the interpretation of a particular term.[14] None of Derrida's deconstructions have quite the form of an undecidability between an explanation by rhetoric and an explanation by logical form, because "logical form" is not a concept Derrida uses. But the assorting of difficulties of interpretation into two more specific categories, namely difficulties about how something is meant and those about what it means, pervades Derrida's discussions in *Limited Inc.*, for instance.

Davidson is committed explicitly and implicitly to the same positions on texts and meaning that Derrida is. For Davidson, truth functions as an analytical interpretive concept rather than as a metaphysical concept. For Davidson, truth is not correspondence in any helpful sense.[15] Most importantly, "true" applies to sentences, not speech acts. Thus a speech act, for Davidson, is the production of a sentence with truth conditions for a reason.

It is easy to get confused about Davidson's theory of utterances and speech acts. For Davidson, sentences are strings of marks in an individual's idiolect at a moment. A truth-definition interprets that string as uttered by the person at that moment. So the fundamental entity being interpreted is an utterance. But within that utterance we can distinguish the truth conditions of the string and the reasons that a string with those truth conditions has been produced. The difficulty is that a sentence at a time may never occur again, or would have different truth conditions if it did. Thus, the only way to make sense of the distinction between a sentence and the reason for producing the sentence is by counterfactuals about what the sentence utterance *could* have been used for in other circumstances.[16]

Given Davidson's account of truth conditions, commands and pronouncements such as "I hereby pronounce you man and wife" have truth-values. So an assignment of truth conditions determines a kind of matrix on which rhetorical force can play. But the same overall result about what a person is doing in speaking can be reached by alternative assignments of logical forms and rhetorical forces. Davidsonian "truth" has little to do with the Hegelian genitive "truth-of" and even less to do with the positivist tradition of taking "fact stating" to be the privileged linguistic function.

Conversational and Other Implicatures

A basic device available to a Davidsonian interpreter is a version of the theory of conversational implicature.[17] Davidsonian interpretation is at bottom just self-conscious application of the rules of thumb we all use in understanding what's up. There is no systematizable theory much more elaborate than the supposition that much of what people do is purposeful. There is no systematizable theory because the interpretation of persons is theory formation, and no algorithm exists for that.[18] Interpretation consists in looking for reasons to explain properties of what is said.

Such properties include the words, of course, and the tone, stress pattern, underlining, and so forth. Sometimes the ascription of purposes goes astray. If your stress pattern is actually the result of hiccups, for example, I can misread an accident as intended. I misread in a different way if you are using the stress pattern deceptively.

So how does this apply in practice? Let us start with some simple examples of "informal fallacies." Suppose I say of my university's president, "He has never been caught stealing university funds," with emphasis on the "caught." This is insulting, and the insult has two kinds of explanation.

First, and formally, the claim that he has never been caught stealing university funds is weaker than the claim that he has never stolen university funds. "Weaker" here means that if he has never stolen funds then it follows that he has never been caught, but not vice versa. Put otherwise, the class of stealers includes as a proper part the class of those caught stealing. Hence, given that the person said something on purpose, and given a general protocol that the purpose was to inform us, the person can be supposed to be saying the strongest relevant things he knows. Thus the remark that the president has never been caught "implies," rhetorically speaking, that he was stealing university funds.

The protocols here are reducible to our (socially learned or, in special cases, individually learned) theories of other people's theories of us, and so forth. Such theories can be then used by speakers, together with what they know about their hearers, about their hearers' knowledge of them, and so on, to say what they want. Thus there are phrases that are almost always used sarcastically.

Second, less formally, much the same kind of interpretation occurs in regard to the stress on "caught." We take this feature of the speech act to be produced on purpose. What could the purpose be? Why accent a word? Numerous explanations may suggest themselves in the indeterminate number of contexts in which stress patterns take place and require explanation. Here, the stress is interpretable as calling attention to the cautiousness (weakness) of the "caught," thus reinforcing the conversational implicature. (Note how the meaning changes with stress on "university.")

Logical Form and Force

What do the above examples have to do with truth and rhetorical force? The commonsense explanations of how we understand the quirks of speech and writing not only seem to leave the relations of truth and rhetoric untouched but, more importantly, seem to require a rigorous line between the meanings of utterances and the maneuvers that are possible only by playing against such meanings. That is, in order even to state an account of how we understand language, sentences per se must have meanings. How, then, do we start to show interchangeability of rhetorical force and logical form?

To begin, this rhetorical use of meanings requires only that an interpretation does take some truth conditions to be the truth conditions of the sentences in question. That is, an interpretation of a feature of an utterance *as rhetorical* requires a decision on the truth conditions of the sentence, which conditions the interpreter construes as presented by the speaker for one or more of any number of different purposes. The interpreter then must choose among these possibilities.

That these choices occur is illustrated by the following elaborated case, which shows the relevance of innuendo to the division of sentential features into the rhetorical and the truth conditional. Consider sentences using "only," such as "Only Fred loves Susan" and "Only the fair deserve the brave."

The tempting analysis of these "only" sentences treats them as backward quantified truth-functional conditionals. Call this "analysis A." According to this analysis, "Only Fred loves Susan" is analyzed as "For all x, x loves Susan only if x is Fred." "Only the fair deserve the brave," likewise, is "For all x, x deserves the brave only if x is fair." (One of the suggestions of the "only if" phrasing of the conditional is that the "only" in "only if" is the same deep-structural element as the "only" in "Only Fred.")

The difficulty with analysis A is that the nicest conditional is the truth-functional conditional. But if the conditional is truth-functional, then "Only Fred loves Susan" and "Only the fair deserve the brave" are true even when Fred does not love Susan and the fair do not deserve the brave, as long as no one else does either. The truth-functional conditional is true when the antecedent is false, so a universally quantified conditional is true when the antecedent is always false. One reason to choose "only" sentences for this illustration is that the "paradoxes" of the truth-functional conditional show up even though nothing especially indicates a connection or "strong" conditional in "only" sentences.[19]

So for these sentences to be true as analyzed, it suffices that no one love Susan and that no one deserves the brave. Thus, the conditional analysis would require us to accept as noncontradictory the sentences "Only Fred loves Susan, and Fred does not love Susan" and "Only the fair deserve the brave, and the fair do not deserve the brave." Most astonishing, perhaps, is that on the proposed analysis, "Fred loves Susan" does not follow from "Only Fred loves Susan," and "The fair deserve the brave" does not follow from "Only the fair deserve the brave."

Most English-speakers find these consequences compelling evidence that analysis A, is mistaken. The typical judgment is that "Fred loves Susan" follows from, is a logical consequence of, "Only Fred loves Susan." Now, "x is a logical consequence of y" means "if x is true, then y is true in virtue of the forms of x and y." Thus if someone holds that "Fred loves Susan" follows from "Only Fred loves Susan," that person must hold that "Fred loves Susan" is included in the truth conditions of "Only Fred loves Susan." The simplest way to include "Fred loves Susan" in those truth conditions is to add that as a conjunct.

Thus the alternative logical form, analysis *B*, for the above "only" sentences is as follows: "For all *x*, *x* loves Susan only if *x* is Fred; and Fred loves Susan," and "For all *x*, *x* deserves the brave only if *x* is fair; and for all *x*, if *x* is fair, then *x* deserves the brave." This analysis is sufficient to make the inferences, and it also exhibits many of the pleasant features of the previous analysis, albeit somewhat less elegantly. The suggestion of connection between "only" and "only if" is maintained, although "only" by itself requires the importation of a conjunct. The "only" sentence is still a backward conditional, since a person who wishes to make "Fred loves Susan" follow from "Only Fred loves Susan" will be inclined to treat most generalities as conjunctions of quantified conditionals and remarks that the antecedent has instances.

Is analysis *B*, then, clearly superior to analysis *A*? Only if there is no other way to explain our intuition that if only Fred loves Susan, Fred loves Susan, at least. Analysis *A* must explain this intuition as a recognition not of logical consequence but of what any writer or speaker producing the sentences "implies," in a rhetorical sense of "implies."

Analysis *A* would be defended along the lines of conversational implicature, as follows: "No one loves Susan" logically implies "Only Fred loves Susan," according to analysis *A*. Since the person is telling us "Only Fred loves Susan," the person is either misleading us or telling us the strongest thing he or she knows about Susan and her relationships. The person is implying that Fred loves Susan, since, although "No one loves Susan" is one way in which "Only Fred loves Susan" could come out true, it is misleading to say "Only Fred loves Susan" because you believe that no one does. In the same way, it is misleading for me to say "I will be teaching either quantum mechanics or philosophy next year," when I know I will not be teaching quantum mechanics, even though what I have said is true. I am trying to impress you by implying, rhetorically, that I could teach quantum mechanics next year.

That is, the only way that the sentence using "only" can be true and not misleading is when the stronger remark, "No one loves Susan," is false. But that means (implies) that Fred indeed loves Susan.

Form and Force: The Indeterminacy of Truth Conditions

There is not much to choose between these accounts. The one is somewhat more elegant, but the other gets the same implications more clearly. So, in the example at hand, how can we tell which of these kinds of implication—logical or conversational—is supporting the inference to "Fred loves Susan"? Notice that this amounts to the question of how we can tell the meaning or truth conditions of someone's sentence from the beliefs we can ascribe to the person by ascribing a normal rhetorical force to the utterance or writing. But in the case of the "only" sentence, the beliefs and desires can be the same: the person believes that only Fred loves Susan and wants us to believe it as well, and so is saying something that will convey his belief. That is, if any difference between rhetorical and logical connections exists in the phenomena, then something in the soul or brain or social structure must select one of these accounts over the other. Otherwise, "rhetorical" and "logical" will be characteristics of a theory presentation; they will be organizational choices rather than reflections of real differences in kinds of connection.

If we have no magic language, looking in the person's head will tell us nothing relevant. Listening in our own heads will tell us nothing relevant. What we will see or hear in the head are sentences in sequence, perhaps. At least, that is what I hear in my own head when I ask "What do I mean by 'guinea pig'?" and get the answer "guinea pig—little eggplants with fur." How will we be able to distinguish the conjunct "And Fred loves Susan" as a logical part of the sentence "Only Fred loves Susan" from the same conjunct as an automatically accompanying belief?

According to Davidsonian interpretation, no distinction can be detected between logical and other connections, since meaning is not translation into a magic language but rather truth-definition. So nothing in the head will fix logical form and distinguish consequences of form from rhetorical consequences. That distinction is relative to a particular interpretation, and is an artifact of the interpretation. To put the point another way, there is just no knowable fact of the matter as to which connections are genuinely logical and which are implications hanging on other features of words, since there is nothing helpfully deeper than words.

Of course, language use involves more than words, since language use occurs in an organism with perception, states, and a brain. But none of these other phenomena are magical in the way the special magic language of the soul was supposed to be.[20]

Davidson agrees entirely with Derrida that logical and rhetorical connection in themselves do not differ in nature. No *logoi* lurk behind logic. Both logical and rhetorical connection are patterns in the behavior or inner causal workings of organisms in an environment. "Logic" and "rhetoric" sort those connections in an interdependent way. Once you choose a logical form and truth conditions, then the rest is rhetorical connection. The difference is entirely relative to the exigencies of a presentation, much like the distinction between axiom and theorem for Quine. Rhetorical force and logical form are two analytical factors between which is apportioned the task of giving a characterization of what people say and when they say it.

Other dichotomies that Derrida attacks are also implicitly attacked by Davidson. Now, Davidson remains committed to the thesis that understanding a language is a matter of having a truth-definition, that logical form is an essential analytical tool. Would this be Derrida's view? Since I have been arguing that Davidson is committed to Derridean positions, the question arises whether Derrida is committed to Davidsonian positions about truth-definition and the importance of form. The answer is a clear "yes." Derrida's whole point in "Speech and Phenomena," for instance, is that the ascription of a form to a sign sequence is essential to taking it as a sign sequence at all.[21] Derrida's "Signature, Event, Context" likewise makes the ascription of form the core of treating sentences as sentences. For Derrida, structure is ascribed rather than discovered in the phenomena intrinsically and determinately, since there are no purely present *logoi*. But this is also Davidson's view about our theories of the other, as I have shown above. While Derrida's interests do not bring him to investigate the details of structure, or to find out how particular forms operate, this cannot mean that he denies logical form. He is just a Davidsonian rather than a Tractarian Wittgensteinian on the nature of logical form.

Davidson is completely committed to undermining the firm foundations whose disappearance is decried by all the denouncers of deconstruction. Davidson explicitly recognizes the revolutionary character of his deconstructions of the various "dogmas of empiricism" and the more general dichotomies from which he has extricated himself. In "The Myth of the Subjective," for instance, Davidson says, "The fallout from these considerations for the theory of knowledge is (or ought to be) nothing less than revolutionary."[22]

On the surface, Davidson seems to oppose much that explicators have taken as central to Derrida. Davidson argues for a kind of shared meanings, against the illusion that objects are "constructed,"[23] and generally speaks with the voice of sober reason. Derrida speaks similarly the impossibility of making sense of "construction" as creating objects out of a given manifold. The discussions of "trace" and "differance" as being "before being," "not concepts and not beings either," in "Differance"[24] and the first section of *Grammatology* reflect some of the considerations that lead Davidson to reject the idea that a "conceptual scheme" categorizes reality. That is, to have a manifold capable of being sorted is already to have applied concepts and thus for there to be truths about how things are prior to anything that could have a truth-definition. Derrida, admittedly, insists on trying to talk about what, by his own account, cannot be talked about. This also manifests itself in his willingness to talk about the world as a context that has alternatives.[25] Furthermore, Derrida does not deny the reality of "shared meanings" in any sense of that term that Davidson would accept. What follows from his arguments is that there are no "shared meanings" in the sense of a magic language.

Davidson and Derrida also clearly differ in their views of the extent to which philosophical notions, for instance the dogmas of empiricism or logocentrism, infect the rest of the culture. Davidson, Wittgenstein, and Quine stand on one side of this issue, holding roughly that philosophical critiques are marginal. Heidegger and Derrida stand on the other side, holding that philosophical deconstructions unhinge notions throughout the culture. So, for Derrida, once certain presuppositions about the notion of "sign" have been deconstructed, we cannot talk coherently about signs, since our words are meaningful only in virtue of their connections to other words. Thus we cannot simply excise "sign" from the network of connections that give it meaning. If philosophical concepts and theories are pervasive, then the consequences of renouncing the magic language are much more widespread. In particular, the self-referential unhinging, which makes the current discussion itself part of the object of critique, only follows if the effect of philosophy is central.

While this difference between Derrida and Davidson is important, and accounts for a good deal of the difference in the tone of their writing, which cannot be accounted for by the difference in their backgrounds, they still share fundamental tenets. They are as close as Aristotle and Plato, for example. Study of these two thinkers jointly is rewarding, especially when they reach astounding conclusions such as that rhetoric and logic are interchangeable.

Davidson, Derrida, and Knapp and Michaels on Intentions in Interpretation

Do you believe in magic . . . ?
—Lovin' Spoonful

In a much-discussed article in *Critical Inquiry*, Stephen Knapp and Walter Benn Michaels attack practitioners of hermeneutics and deconstruction for supposing that "a text can mean something other than what its author intends."[1] Specifically, the authors charge these practitioners with assuming that linguistic conventions determine textual identity; hence hermeneutics and deconstruction are "committed to the view that a text derives its identity from something other than authorial intention. The text is what it is, no matter what meaning is assigned to it by its author."[2]

According to Knapp and Michaels, hermeneutics and deconstruction are closet conventionalist theories, since they reject conventions as determinants of meaning while using convention to identify a sequence of marks as the text it is. Hermeneutics then claims that the meaning of a text is richer than the content the author intended, while deconstruction says meaning is indeterminate and beyond authorial control. But according to Knapp and Michaels, meaning is already independent of convention and is completely fixed by the author's informing intentions. Furthermore, they argue, a text cannot be identified as the text it is apart from the author's intention.

Knapp and Michaels's view is strongly reminiscent[3] of Davidson's view, advanced in many places, that interpretation is primarily of an individual's utterances, to which any public language is inessential.[4] Thus conventions and the "norms" of language are inessential to interpretation for Davidson as well. Davidson's thesis, in preliminary outline, is that interpretation, since it operates by treating a person as a rational agent in a common world, need only treat the speaker as believing mostly truths about the world, and therefore need not appeal in principle to a public language at all. Interpretation is possible in the absence of a public language, and we all are familiar with cases where we abandon the "rules" of the public language in figuring out what an individual means. Therefore, the whole structure of "conventions" and "norms" that so many thinkers have made central to interpretation is not in fact essential to the interpretation of language. Davidson might then seem to be committed to something like Knapp and Michaels's view that the author's intention is the feature that determines correct interpretation. In a certain sense, this will turn out to be true. The difficulty with ascribing the view to Davidson, however, is that intentions for Davidson can be nothing but interior texts, a thesis that agrees with Derrida. Since they hold the same textualist views about intentions, Davidson and Derrida cannot be opposed as intentionalist and anti-intentionalist. The issue of interpretation between Derrida and Davidson, I argue, comes down to the question of how much the determinacy of interpretation results from interpreting these inner texts according to the principle of charity in radical interpretation.

The first two sections of this chapter discuss whether the notion of the author's intention required by Knapp and Michaels, especially the "intention" part of that notion, is plausible or even coherent. In the third section, I examine whether it is accurate to understand Derrida's discussion of "code" and "iteration" as an appeal to "convention" to determine the identity of a text.

In the fourth and last section, I argue that Derrida and Davidson differ in emphasis rather than in core doctrines. Davidson concentrates on the determinacy that ascribing some large body of truths will generate when interpreting an individual. Davidson's paradigm is the individual speaker making utterances. Derrida, on the other hand, is impressed by the indeterminacy that results from removing the *logoi* that intentions would supply. Derrida's paradigm is the text in the traditional sense, and texts in the traditional sense are common property of public languages.[5]

Let me first summarize the role of the author's intention according to Knapp and Michaels. Their position is expressed in two separate claims. First, Knapp and Michaels claim that a thing (inscription, utterance) is meaningful only if it is intended. A sequence of marks can be meaningful

only if it was produced on purpose. Whether these arguments that meaningfulness requires intention are effective or not, they show nothing about
whether the intention determines what the meaning is. Thus Knapp and
Michaels's second claim is independent of the first. This second claim is
that intentions make the marks mean what they mean, that an inscription
has its meaning in virtue of the authorial intention behind it: "Its meaning
is whatever the author intends."[6] That is, the specific cognitive and other
content of a text is brought about by, and is to be explained by, the author's
intention. These doctrines require an account of two notions, namely the
idea of an author and the idea of intentions.

Author, Author

Knapp and Michaels's first claim—that an inscription or utterance is
meaningful only if it is intended—emerges from their remarks about authorial intention. It is specifically the *author's* intention that is required for
an inscription or utterance to be meaningful. But how is Knapp and
Michaels's claim to be understood, given that the very text that expresses it
is a committee document? Even given the possibility of a group mind, a
text or a single line need have no single intention informing it through the
many drafts and versions such documents go through ("An earlier and very
different version of *this essay* served as the occasion . . . ," say Knapp and
Michaels).[7] So, a text as a whole may not have an intention behind it. Biblical texts, which appear to be sequences of blindly glossed collations of
narrative fragments, are not meaningful texts by this account. For example, Genesis 32:22–32, a sequence of redactions, transmissions, and glosses,
would not count as a meaningful text since, as a whole, it is informed by
no coherent authorial intention. A block of text that has been moved in a
word-processed document after its original inscription, and that functions
in unpredicted ways in its new location, would seem to constitute a coun-
terexample to the necessary existence of "authorial intention." Multiple authors and the lack of informing, meaning-determining intentions show
that even if speech acts and text-production acts require actors, and so
must be performed intentionally in some sense, their meaning need not be
a function of the intentions of their producers. That there must be an intention to make something meaningful does not mean that the intention
gives the meaning of the sentence.

But suppose Knapp and Michaels made the limited claim that the author's intentions fix the meaning of the text in the case an author who remembers what she has in mind as she writes, and writes what she means with authority. If intentions can fix the meaning of a text in this special case, that would still be interesting and important. But how does intention provide foundations?

The Marvels of Intending

The second and more interesting claim put forward by Knapp and Michaels concerns the role of intentions: intentions make the marks mean what they mean. What must "intention" mean so that an intention to mean something can fix the meaning of a text or utterance? To begin with, such intentions must have two languagelike features: intentions must constitute an infinite field, and particular intentions within that field must bear logical relations to one another.

Languagelike Properties of Intentions

The considerations necessitating an infinite field of intentions are familiar. Intentions that function as Knapp and Michaels require must be conceptually independent of the language that they inform. Since they must inform sentences in a way that will account for the infinity of meanings sentences can have, the domain of intentions must have a structure at least as rich as the language they explain. Intention must be *more* fine-grained than the language it explains if it is to give an account of the multiple meanings of single ambiguous sentences. That is, to mean only one "reading" of "Fred attends an ugly little boy's school" by saying "Fred attends an ugly little boy's school," one must do something more than have the linguistic intention of saying something meaning "Fred attends an ugly little boy's school." Given the rich infinity of things we can intend, and the grave difficulties of memorizing a list of such things,[8] intentions must have semantically structured contents. The contents of an intention must be organized by means of things analogous to the terms, connectives, quantifiers, and other apparatus that permit an infinity of sentences with distinct truth conditions to be constructed from a finite number of linguistic components. Thus, if intentions are events or states of persons that determine meaning in a way that individuates utterances with distinct meanings, then intentions are sentences in languages or idiolects of thought.

The other apparent languagelike feature of intentions that will serve the foundational purposes of Knapp and Michaels is the required logical articulation of intentions. An intention to meet Fred and Susan involves an intention to meet Susan. An intention to meet Susan is necessarily an intention to meet someone. Such logical relations among intentions require that intentions themselves be compounded of elements in a system of thoughts, and so have the semantic structure of sentences in a language. (Linguistic intentions are even more structured, since they are metalinguistic.) When we intend to mean "meet Susan" by saying "meet Susan," that intention entails meaning Susan. Even if we construe intentions as ethereal "states of the soul," the state of the soul that means Susan must be the same state throughout the various thoughts we have about her for there to be a connection between meaning to meet Susan and meaning to treat Susan.

What Knapp and Michaels mean, then, is that intentions are spoken in the language of the soul, and that intentions to mean are formulated in sentences in the language of the soul. A language of the soul is not an impossible supposition, of course. But a language of the soul, whose tokens are written on psychic slates, seems to have every difficulty that languages of the blackboard have. Interpretation, ambiguity, dissemination, and so forth would affect spirit talk as well as flesh talk. (The intentions need have nothing to do with the physical brain—they could well be states of spiritual stuff.)

Of course, spirit languages can fix meaning relative to an interpretation, just as any inscription can. Thus, when I say "The attack is on" and my words are garbled in transmission and come out of the decoder as "The atman is one," the real meaning of what was said is fixed by the utterance, not by the garbled version. But this fixing is relative. If a question arises about what "the attack" means, interpretation is still called for.

Magical Properties of Intentions

Thus, in order to fix meaning in a helpful, nonrelative way, this language must have two magical properties. Since Knapp and Michaels require that intentions be foundations of meaning, the field of intention they fantasize must have two further, magical properties, which transcend the merely languagelike properties of logical form and infinite, language-matching complexity. Because of these magical properties, the demand that meaning have absolute foundations in intentions turns out to require essentialism about psychic states.

The first magical property of Knapp and Michaels's soul language is that of determining its own interpretation. Without this property, an endless sequence of regresses to background languages of thought and intending would result. To interpret itself, the language of the soul must consist of elements that fix their own semantic properties by their very nature. Some property of a spiritual element must determine what the element means independently of the cultural or linguistic situation of the thinker. The obvious model for such a language would be Aristotle's language "inside" *nous*, whose real tokens are forms of substances without their matter, even though sensible form tokens are used as counters. Such forms determine what they are forms of by their very nature, by what it is to be them. Only such a language will meet the requirements of a genuinely helpful spiritual notation in which to have intentions for fixing linguistic meaning. Knapp and Michaels must be essentialists about the languagelike soul-states in which intentions are realized. A state of the soul, according to Knapp and Michaels, means what it means (has semantic properties) in virtue of its very nature.

The second magic feature of the language of the soul according to Knapp and Michaels is that the meanings of its tokens are what they are independently of the possibility of being iterated.[9] This second feature follows from the first. Knapp and Michaels would acknowledge that, in most cases, a meaningful intention-token would in fact have other possible occurrences. They would deny, though, that a token's identity as a token of a given kind has anything to do with iterability. In principle, a thought token could be totally idiomatic, in the sense that its meaning could be expressed only once. (This would be a little like a magic spell that is exhausted with one use.) If there are terms that have meanings in virtue of their very nature, and not in virtue of their place in some kind of system, then such divine relationships are possible. After all, God has been supposed to make an essence unique to each person, and Knapp and Michaels can follow the medieval philosophers in supposing such haecceities for states of souls.

But the basic requirement for the sort of meaning founding that Knapp and Michaels ascribe to intentions is essentialism about psychic states. The theory advanced by Knapp and Michaels is really yet another version of the "idea" idea, the notion that our thoughts have essences that are transparent to those who have the thoughts. Such ideas, in the guise of the purely present, self-interpreting "meanings" that found analytic truth, are the subject of deconstructions by Quine and Davidson, in numerous works.[10]

Derrida and Iteration

Knapp and Michaels defend intentions as the determiners of meaning by arguing that convention is the only alternative to intentions; hence "any consistent argument against the notion that conventions are essential to meaning turns out to be an argument that what is essential to meaning is intention."[11]

If we apply this line of reasoning to the thought of Derrida, we must portray his attack on authorial control as an argument that conventions overpower the author. Knapp and Michaels characterize Derrida's argument as follows: Derrida claims that neither context nor convention fixes the meaning of a text. According to Knapp and Michaels, the part of the context of a speech act significant for determining whether the act is felicitous is the set of intentions of the actors. Thus Derrida's rejection of context as fixing meaning is a rejection of intentions as fixing meaning. Since meaning cannot possibly be determined by "rules of language" or conventions, Derrida concludes that the meaning of a text is indeterminate, subject to essential drift, and so on. But, according to Knapp and Michaels, one cannot determine what text a text is, or that it is a text, except by appeal to the meaning-informing intentions that, in one stroke, make a sequence of marks into a text and determine what that text means. The text is the expression of the intention with which it was produced.

In this portrayal of how Knapp and Michaels's argument would go against Derrida, the main component is their critique of conventionalism, construed as the thesis that meaning is determined by social arrangements and protocols. But this is not at all what Derrida's argument involves. While Knapp and Michaels have good arguments against the efficacy of "convention" for fixing meaning, their arguments do not touch Derrida's discussion of the role of iterability in constituting meaning and meaningfulness. The main reason for this failure is that Knapp and Michaels miss the generality of Derrida's argument.

Knapp and Michaels's basic arguments appeal to a more fundamental level of meaning that can contravene "conventional" indications of what someone meant. These arguments depend on a kind of privilege that often goes with what people think or say to themselves. Such privileged representations overrule the evidence that conventions give of what people mean. (Knapp and Michaels apply Davidson's demonstration that conventions are evidence for meaning, not constituters of meaning.)[12] While I think these arguments succeed against the efficacy of the social routines and patterns of expectation in fixing meaning, they presuppose that more fundamental level of representation. But Derrida's arguments about the necessity of iteration apply to any kind of representation, and have little to do with "convention."

The issue is the privileged representation, the "what the person meant," which overrules conventions. For Knapp and Michaels, this privileged level is the magic language described above. For Derrida, no such magic language could exist; the language of thought is just another language, albeit one that, in many circumstances, has a kind of privilege. But the privilege is not that of being magical. Deconstruction asks what the status of meaning might be when there is no magical privileged representation that means by its essence.

For Derrida, the issue of iterability is not that of social conventions but rather a question of what it takes to be a token of any kind of text, be it thought-text, intention-text, or written text. Derrida does not allow that any semantic item has an intrinsic semantic nature since he eschews essentialism. A thing is not "of one type" on its own, according to Derrida. There are no natural kinds of tokens. Derrida consistently extends this eschewal to intentions and the tokens in which they are inscribed.

In an important passage that Knapp and Michaels do not choose to discuss, Derrida notes that intentions cannot fix meaning because intentions themselves are marks whose meanings are constituted by iterability. Thus the interpretation of intentions is subject to the same fundamental difficulty as the interpretation of written texts. The semantic features of intentions cannot be fixed in their very nature without the magic language: "The intention which animates utterance will never be completely present to itself and its content. The iteration which structures it a priori introduces into it an essential dehiscence and demarcation. . . . For a context to be exhaustively determinable, . . . it would at least be necessary for the conscious intention to be totally present and actually transparent for itself and others."[13]

So, while intentions are importantly different from written and spoken language, the difference is not a contrast between a foundational, originating magic sentence and the product it informs: "Above all, one then would be concerned with different types of marks . . . and not with an opposition between citational statements, on the one hand, and singular and original statement-events on the other."[14]

Recognizing the impossibility of semantically self-revealing presences that supply meaning, Derrida must construct what it is for an item to be an item in a semantic system by its possibilities of recurrence. He argues that what it is to be a token of a given kind must be constructed in terms of the iterability of that token as of that kind.

Knapp and Michaels miss Derrida's point about iterability by their "social-convention" reading of his text. They construe as a commitment to conventionalism his assertion that a mark must be "constituted, in its identity as mark, by its iterability" so that it is necessarily "organized by a code."[15] Their gloss states, "Because the mark derives its identity from its participation in a code—because its identity is essentially conventional—its meaning cannot be determined by intention alone."[16]

Their gloss of Derrida's view as essentially conventionalistic must ignore passages showing that Derrida uses "code" figuratively when he asserts that every meaningful mark is meaningful in virtue of its place in a code. In *Speech and Phenomena*, especially, it is clear that Derrida is talking about the language of thought, the interior monologues the Husserlian thinker carries on. The notion that iterability is essential is part of an analysis of a "sign" of any kind: "A signifier (in general) must be formally recognizable in spite of, and through, the diversity of empirical characteristics which may modify it. . . . This representative structure is signification itself."[17] In "Signature, Event, Context," Derrida's most compelling consideration against treating iterability as having to do with conventions is that experience itself is meaningful only in virtue of iterability. Three pages past the quotation from "Signature, Event, Context" that Knapp and Michaels cite, Derrida says:

This structural possibility of being severed from its referent or signified . . . seems to me to make of every mark . . . the nonpresent *remaining* of a differential mark cut off from its alleged "production" or origin. And I will extend this law even to all "experience" in general, if it is granted that there is no experience of *pure* presence, but only chains of differential marks.[18]

This passage admits no suggestion of conventions. A "code" by which the person is able to experience the world cannot be conventional, since the possibility of seeing that a convention applies to a case would require an experience to note the properties of the case. So Derrida cannot be supposing that these "differential marks" function in virtue of convention.

Instead, Derrida is noting that the very idea that a thing is meaningful requires that *kind* of thing to have that meaning in other possible occurrences. To claim that an aspect of a organism's sensation means "frog" to that organism is to claim that some other occurrences of the same kind of aspect of a sensation would also mean "frog" to it. Where there is a meaningful but unique use of some expression or mark, that meaning must be understood in terms of some special connection to terms that *are* repeatable.[19]

For Derrida, as an antiessentialist, the notion of "the same *kind* of item" is the delicate part of the analysis. Since no object is by its very nature a token of a type, Derrida must supply another account of what it is to be an item of a kind. He adapts Husserl's account of types as constructed of past and possible future instances, roughly. The result is that an item's being of a given kind cannot be fully present, since to take it as of a kind is to take it together with past and future repetitions. That is, the inscription "read" may be either a present-tense verb or a past participle. To take it as one or the other is to identify it with, and so take it together with, distinct sets of possible other occurrences.

To be taken as an item of a given kind is to be an item of that kind. Given that essentialism is false, an item is of a given kind only relative to having been constructed as of that kind. Since the construction essentially involves nonpresent items, namely past and future occurrences, the meaningful item, as such, cannot be present. Any semantic item is, *as* semantic, nonpresent.

Derrida would certainly acknowledge that the problem of saying what an item means would not arise if there were such natures that could be fully present to consciousness, identifying themselves in the magic language of the soul. His theory presupposes his arguments against the possibility of pure natures that are purely present to the soul. The magic language hypothesized by such neo-Aristotelians as Knapp and Michaels would indeed render otiose Derridean constructions of types to which tokens belong.[20]

These considerations establish that Derrida is committed to nothing about the role of "convention" in fixing the meanings of utterances. In fact, his system allows nothing like a "rule of language," as that term is understood by Saussure and current semantic theorists. Such rules would have to be in a notation whose application was clear by its very nature. (Derrida could endorse Wittgenstein's discussions of rules in *Remarks on the Foundations of Mathematics.*)

Derrida's iterable marks thus are not subject to the kind of critique that Knapp and Michaels deploy against convention. They argue that convention, as a set of social rules, is neither necessary nor sufficient to fix meaning or to fix what a text is. By their arguments, the intention, the "meaning" behind the text in a speaker's brain, makes utterances mean, overriding any alleged determination by conventions. But Derrida's comments about iterability apply just as well to brain marks or spirit marks as to paper or sound-wave marks. Derrida's argument joins Quine's argument in "Ontological Relativity" in pointing to the regress that occurs when magic language is shown to be impossible. Once a person's intentions are realized to be nothing but inscriptions in yet another language, they can no longer provide a foundation for language-meaning.

Derrida does not deny that intentions are real and does not claim that intentions are nothing but inscriptions: "The category of intention will not disappear, it will have its place, but from its place it will no longer be able to govern the entire scene and the entire system of utterance."[21] Only inscriptions read as intentional are read as meaningful. But this does not justify the claim that a meaningful remark can be separated into an intention that informs an inscription and a pure inscription. Such a division would require that the inscription mean something in a special and unproblematic way. But intentions, if they carry the kind of semantic content required, cannot be separated from the inscriptions they inform without being intended in the magic language. So, while intentionality pervades language use, intentional phenomena cannot be analyzed into the intention and the inscription that expresses it. No intention is uncontaminated by inscription, and no genuine inscription is uncontaminated by intention. This is a characteristic Derridean deconstructive conclusion.

Another way to put this is as follows: If essentialism is false, then intentions require language and language requires intentions. Intentions require language in order to be articulate, while language requires intentions to distinguish which marks are texts at all. Since neither can exist without the other, there can be no foundational account that starts with intention-less texts or with textless intentions. But without such a foundational ac-count, the Derridean/Davidsonian indeterminacy of interpretation drifts in.

To resolve this regress by supplying a magic language as the founda-tional turtle beneath the elephant holding up the text's determinacy is pointless. No kind of inscription can exist that is beyond interpretation. As Quine shows in "Ontological Relativity," indeterminacy of interpretation starts at home, with our thoughts and intendings.[22]

Davidson, Intentions, and Private Languages

Davidson's account of meaning, I would argue, agrees with Derrida's in its essentials. Nothing in Davidson's thought would proscribe viewing internal languages as texts, albeit their context strongly shapes their inter-pretation. A person who is being interpreted is issuing sequences of marks, and those marks are interpreted by reasonably ascribing to the person be-liefs and desires that make the person a rational actor in our world. Noth-ing else gives the marks meanings. How determinate such interpretations can be on the basis of radical interpretation could be a matter of dispute.

Derrida and Davidson are committed to theories of meaning that have much the same consequences, but they choose to emphasize different consequences. Davidson is concerned to show that people agree, that peo-ple get a good portion of the world right, and that communication is usu-ally successful. Derrida emphasizes the "indeterminacy" consequences of constructing meaning out of texts, even when those texts have the strongest possible context, issuing from a person with a history.

With his principles of radical interpretation, which demand that meanings be constructed by ascribing truth to utterances by a person in situations, Davidson avoids the "presence" that Derrida criticizes as a pre-supposition of other theories of meaning. Davidson has himself famously denied a "given" manifold either of objects or of meanings.

On the other hand, some of Davidson's writings sound as though in-tentions have some sort of foundational role in language interpretation. In the most famous of these works, "A Nice Derangement of Epitaphs," he as-serts, "There is no such thing as a language, if 'language' is understood as philosopher and linguists have used the term."[23] In apparent support of such a primitive explicatory role for intentions in giving meaning to actions and utterances, Davidson shows that our ability to interpret others who speak in deviant ways means that intentions to communicate can succeed without a public system of representation. Thus, the fact that Mrs. Malaprop meant (intended) "arrangement" by "derangement" is enough to make "arrangement" the correct interpretation. According to Davidson, a person speaking an idiolect as different from any public language as you please can be understood. Thus, no "language" in the philosopher's or in Saussure's sense is required for the fundamental purpose of language, which is communication.

On the other hand, the intention with which a speech act is produced is a matter of the beliefs and desires that are operative in producing it. But beliefs and desires are assigned to a speaker, according to Davidson, in a holistic way, on the basis of assigning intentions to speech acts. Roughly, speech interpretation according to Davidson is action interpretation. A hypothesis about what a person is doing in speaking, namely that he is expressing an intention, amounts to a hypothesis about the beliefs and desires the person has. The beliefs and desires a person is hypothesized to have is the basis from which the truth conditions of utterances are hypothesized. But hypotheses about truth conditions of utterances are also the basis for assignment of beliefs and desires, and so of intentions. No one of the three categories of item—beliefs and desires, intentions, and truth conditions—is an independent basis for the other two. So while Davidson does indeed hold that intention is the basis for meaning, this does not make meaning determined by intention, since meaning is equally the basis of intention.

If hypotheses about belief, desire, intention, and truth conditions provide bases for each other, one could ask what it is for any of these hypotheses to be true. What makes an assignment of intentions to an entity correct? The answer one is tempted to impute to Knapp and Michaels is that intentions are facts about the interior mental states of individuals, and that these are what constitute the truth of claims not only about intentions but about beliefs, desires, and meanings as well.

Such an answer misses Davidson's position on truth. Nothing makes claims true, since truth is fundamental and therefore irreducible. Holistic interrelations among belief, desire, meaning, and intention need not imply that any one of these constitutes "facts," in the sense of referents for sentences. "Joe intends to frighten Sue" is true if and only if Joe intends to frighten Sue. Davidson treats all such claims as empirical hypotheses, but does not hold that empirical hypotheses turn out to be true in virtue of correspondence.

Whether Davidson and Derrida differ substantively can be discussed by focusing on two issues: First, to what extent do intentions, now conceived as "inner texts" that function in the economy of the practical person, fix meaning enough so that communication can take place? Second, is there a conflict between Derrida's ideas about iterability and Davidson's insistence that "there is no such thing as language, not if a language is anything like what many philosophers and linguists have supposed"?[24]

As to the first issue, Davidson does think texts are more "cut loose" from a determining intention than utterances are, so he could be said to "privilege speech." Davidson does think that, by and large, intentions fix the meaning of an utterance or thought, because of the relative richness of an individual's history of speech and action. Texts, as items not tied to particular individuals, are less determinate. The qualification "by and large," though, is important, as is the way we construe "fixed by intentions." Davidson has to acknowledge that interpretation can be indeterminate when no hypothesis has the speaker exactly agreeing with the interpreter.

Texts as public objects, for Davidson, would be tied to intentions, beliefs, and desires, but more loosely and indeterminately, since texts determine less of a unified background of beliefs and desires to filter out hypotheses than do concrete speakers. The farther the text spreads from the speaker or writer, the less determinate it becomes, if "farther" is understood as "more divergent in beliefs, desires, and truth-conditions." That is, language communities, for Davidson, are groups whose utterances are profitably interpreted homophonically. Typically a person participates in several language communities, which differ according to different subject matters. A "text," as a public document, can be reused and thus reinterpreted as coming from any of the language communities to which the originator belonged.

Given the possibilities of reuse and reinterpretation, written texts will be indeterminate in ways that utterances rarely are. "Utterances" of public language communities, that is, sentences that a number of people repeat, will be tied to intentions only to the extent that the language community agrees in beliefs and desires and finds the homophonic hypothesis confirmed. But the divergence of beliefs and desires in a collective is only a more frequent and dramatic case of the divergence that sometimes occurs within a person. Whether one's congratulation to a colleague for his success is ironic, for instance, and whether one's term "impressive" implicitly contrasts with "excellent" may be opaque even to psychoanalysis.

The second issue concerning the difference between Davidson and Derrida may be treated more briefly. Given the possibility of a speaker's making mistakes, and the possibility of idiolectic differences among utterances, are inner texts in fact necessarily capable of occurring in other contexts? Has Davidson given up the idea that a term means in virtue of its role in a system? If that were the case, his view would be that intentional actions are primitive, and form the basis for the ascription of belief, desire, and meaning. Thus the intentions would have the status that Knapp and Michaels attribute to them.

But Davidson's discussion always appeals to theories, albeit passing ones. When a theory ascribes truth conditions to sentences a person produces, it implicitly ascribes truth conditions to a multitude of other utterances that are not produced, including utterances that would include the utterance in question as a part. A theory is a truth-definition, which assigns a role in a potential infinity of utterances to semantically significant components of an utterance. So Davidson's account, even for temporary theories that we actually apply only once, is that meaningfulness requires the possibility of a word's making the same contribution to truth conditions in other utterances. Even temporary codes are codes, and the same considerations about iterability and the interdependence of meaning, belief, and desire apply in such cases as apply when homophonic translation is successful. Thus, Mrs. Malaprop's utterances function as a text (as they in fact *only* do, since she is fictional), and any indeterminacy in interpreting her is not resolved by appeal to her intentions.

Metaphor According to Davidson and de Man

In this 1989 essay, I argued that Davidson has no basis in his own theory for separating the literal and the figurative. After much further reflection, aided by thinking through the consequences of Davidson's "The Structure and Content of Truth," I realize that Davidson's separation of the literal from the figurative arises from his demand that utterances have truth conditions since they always have truth-values. If utterances have truth conditions, then the literal/figurative distinction is guaranteed. The only difficult point for Davidson is that he must hold utterances to have truth conditions and truth-values even though those truth-values are absolutely unknowable. This again is an option made possible by Davidson's taking truth to be primary and irreducible, so that a sentence asserting that another sentence has given truth conditions can be true even though all possible data leave open the question of what those conditions are. Even though there is no "fact" of the matter, the sentence is still true or false, since being true or false is not a matter of correspondence to facts or to anything else.

One way of putting what must be Davidson's view is this: the transition from "obscure" being metaphorical when predicated of pieces of writing to its being literal is like the transition of a slowly melting iceberg from large to small. Davidson is committed to a view of truth conditions like Roy Sorensen's view of vague predicates: vague predications are always either true or false, but for a significant number of cases, the truth or falsity is unknowable in the strongest sense. In the same way, "indeterminacy of interpretation" turns out always to be epistemological. In indeterminacy cases, the utterances have truth-values, but those truth-values are unknowable, not in the sense that they are made true or false by a fact that is irrecoverably hidden but in the sense made possible by the irreducibility of truth.

The irreducibility of truth allows that, in some cases, a given utterance can be either true or false while every other logically independent sentence has the truth-value it has. So the compatibility of indeterminacy of interpretation with every sentence's being true or false rests on the independence of truth.

■

This essay discusses Donald Davidson's account of metaphor in the light of the thinking of Paul de Man and interprets de Man's thinking on metaphor by means of Davidson's conceptual framework. My hypothesis is that to a helpful extent, de Man's discussions of figuration can be understood as supporting and being supported by a Davidsonian account of meaning, truth, and reference. De Man and Davidson share a thesis about language that shapes much of their thought. To put it crudely, they both hold that every level of representation is essentially languagelike. Words are explicated by reference to words, not to magically self-interpreting representations such as thoughts. Although Davidson's view differs from the view that infuses de Man's accounts, they agree about the relation between language and meaning. They both hold that linguistic meaning is not reducible to nonlanguagelike meaning bearers. Other parallels and resemblances follow from this one. For instance, both Davidson and de Man treat the metaphorical as a matter of the force with which a sentence is uttered.

Some of the differences between Davidson and de Man can be understood as arising from their different starting places and traditions. On the one hand, de Man's thought starts from literary concerns, and the problem of figuration and the rhetorical is the central core from which his accounts develop. On the other hand, Davidson arrives at such issues having started from traditional analytic philosophical concerns about the theory of meaning and reference.

The main doctrinal difference, I argue, is one regarding which Davidson can learn from de Man. Briefly, Davidson cannot have a notion of truth that sorts out the literally true from the literally false in a determinate way that systematically keeps metaphorical assertions from being true as meant. By Davidsonian principles, the notion of truth-value ultimately turns out to be quite indeterminate in any areas except the most mono-lithically controlled, even though the formulation of truth conditions may be precise. Thus the way is open to treat the literal as a limiting case of the metaphorical.

But de Man stands to benefit from Davidson as well. Specifically, de Man's arguments on figuration are clarified and strengthened by arguments from Davidson and his tradition. Consider, for instance, Davidson's dem-onstration that no "rhetorical force marker" can be conventional. This an-alytic philosopher's way of describing the uncontrollable disseminating power of figuration supplements both de Man's and Derrida's metaphors in a convincing way.

I treat Davidson's theory of language as the underlying ground for de Man's view. Proceeding to de Man by means of Davidson is my way of making de Man clear to myself and to people with roughly my back-ground of training. What counts as "making it clear" is a question of what texts and modes of discussion are familiar. The more we read in other genres, the wider our notion of "the clear" can become. Thus, a translation into analytic language does not suggest that the patterns of discussion and argument that define the genre of analytic philosophy are the only correct standards. I think those patterns *do* produce depth and illumination. But new modes of argument give startling and valuable views of problems orig-inally formulated and discussed otherwise. In addition to helping analytic philosophers read de Man, this essay may show some ways in which ana-lytic philosophy can be useful to literary thinkers.

Davidson's Theory of Meaning

The Davidsonian insight that determines the rest of his theory is that any level of meaning must be languagelike. Davidson is an antireductionist about words and their meaning: all meaning carriers are like words in being subject to interpretation. "Being subject to interpretation" means that nothing intrinsic to the term determines that it must refer to a given object.

Davidson thus denies the most fundamental element of the standard theory of meaning that has come down to us at least from the time of Plato. The dream of the standard theory of meaning depended on the ex-istence of a level of representation by completely present tokens whose very self-revealing nature determined what they referred to. Such tokens or presences might be thought tokens (the "ideas" of Berkeley et al.) or Forms or meanings, for instance. I call a system of such representations a "magic language." Quine's deconstructive arguments have shown that a magic language that allows meaning to be fixed by the very natures of the signifiers is incoherent with the following three theses: that essentialism is false; that reference is a function of intrinsic features of concepts available to the user; and that necessity is linguistic, if it is anything. Such a magic language would be required by any "foundational" theory of meaning, that is, any theory that demands that interpretation end. Davidson has extended and purified these deconstructions to eliminate Quine's residual essentialist suppositions about observation.[1]

If words carry meaning in the most fundamental and irreducible way possible, then the meaning of some word is a contribution to truth conditions given by some other word or by some formula whose interpretation is as problematic and subject to vagaries as the word whose meaning is being given. If words are as basic as meaning bearers get, then their meaning and truth-value derive from a single kind of phenomenon: persons in a culture using words. The same data determine both meaning and truth. This entails an indeterminacy avoided by traditional theories of meaning, which have interpretation-free tokens. For Davidson, all data both for determining meaning and for determining truth-value consist in what is said and when it is said. That is, speech behavior in concrete situations gives all there is to get both of what terms mean and of which sentences are true.[2]

So an account of meaning can be nothing more than a truth-definition, that is, a finite set of biconditionals about the contributions of individual words to the truth conditions of sentences.[3] Such a set has as consequences all sentences like "'The sea is gong-ridden' is true if and only if the sea is gong-ridden." So neither literal nor figurative uses of language have senses associated with them, if those senses are supposed to be nonlanguagelike meanings. Davidson does not understand "meaning" and "truth conditions" in a way that requires word meaning to be given in some more fundamental elements, such as Quinean stimulus conditions or logical-positivist protocol sentences. Truth-conditional semantics does not describe the truth-values of predications of semantically primitive predicates in more helpful or basic terms.

The dispositions of speakers are affected by beliefs, desires, and other propositional attitudes. The interanimation of sentences based on such propositional attitudes generates *evidence* for a given matching of words to words, but neither the pattern of connection nor the propositional attitudes are the meaning, which is *arrived* at on the basis of the evidence. In the same way, a scientific theory does not mean the data that confirm the theory.

The Metaphorical and the Literal According to Davidsonism

Exposition

A view of meaning such as Davidson's will have some prima facie difficulties with the traditional notion of metaphor as the transference of meaning. The usual explications of metaphor presuppose the existence of a nonlanguagelike meaning that lies behind speech. Without that kind of meaning, two difficulties seem to arise.

First, Davidson's semantics seems to say too little about what metaphor is. In a way, Davidson's prima facie problem in accounting for metaphor is that his *semantics* leaves metaphor untouched.

Second, with Davidson's semantics, it seems difficult to say what a given metaphor means. The meaning of a metaphor can no longer be encoded in the magic language of thought, a language in which figuration is impossible and thus in which the real message of a metaphor would become transparent when the meaning of the thought-sentence was understood. On Davidson's account, language is always interpreted in language. So whatever allowed figural understandings in the interpreted language will also allow such understandings in our interpreting language. Without the magic language, there is no unturnable, metaphor-free discourse. Thus the possibility of understanding the explication as a trope is always present. The fond dream of a metaphor-free language in which the meaning of a metaphor can be given is the idle dream of a purely descriptive magic language of thought, the language in which the very tokens require that they be taken in exactly one way.

Davidson's exposition in "What Metaphors Mean" is primarily negative, and his own account is only cautiously sketched. He shows that accounts of metaphor as compressed simile and as synonymous with simile fail to meet conditions of adequacy for an account of metaphor. All accounts that use the etymological metaphor of the coming through of another meaning, whether a meaning of another word or a meaning from a special poetic realm of meaning for metaphorical language, fall short of adequacy. In particular, Davidson criticizes accounts that take the literal and metaphorical to be senses of words, so that a sentence that can be taken literally or figuratively is ambiguous.

I find these arguments against other views utterly convincing. Here I will briefly consider two points in Davidson's view that differ from the de Manian improvement to be suggested further below.

First, Davidson believes that an account of metaphor must explain why metaphors cannot be paraphrased. This rules out as inaccurate any theory that takes a metaphor to be a compressed simile or synonym of a simile, since for such theories the metaphor would have a perfectly good literal paraphrase. If Yeats's "gong-tormented sea"[4] is short for "the sea that is like something tormented by a gong," then it would have a perfectly clear literal paraphrase. Similarly, any simple "transference of meaning" is ruled out.

Davidson's reason for holding that metaphors are not paraphrasable is the radical one that a metaphor does not *say* anything different from its literal meaning. What makes an utterance a metaphor is not a matter of saying something ineffable, or of saying anything at all. In "What Metaphors Mean," Davidson says, "Paraphrase, whether possible or not, is appropriate to what is *said*: we try, in paraphrase, to say it another way. But if I am right, a metaphor doesn't say anything beyond its literal meaning."[5]

Second, Davidson holds that applying a term literally to a new and unfamiliar case is different in kind from applying the term metaphorically. This tenet is the crucial point on which I disagree with Davidson. In "What Metaphors Mean," Davidson uses the example of a Saturnian learning our language.[6] In accord with his general conception of meaning and language, and his rejection of all three dogmas of empiricism, Davidson notes that learning the language does not differ from learning what the world is like. Learning what "cat" means cannot be separated from learning what things are cats.

The Saturnian has learned to use and understand the term "floor" on Earth, so that he is able to apply "floor" to new and different floors. On his voyage home, taking Davidson along, he hears Davidson characterize the Earth below as a floor, and takes this to be yet another item in the extension of "floor." Davidson, however, was alluding to Dante's "small round floor that makes us passionate," a metaphorical rather than a literal use.

To see more clearly what will be at issue here, suppose that it is the

Saturnian who characterizes the Earth as a floor. According to Davidson, he has spoken incorrectly and made a mistake. He is objectively wrong about what is a floor and what is not. Dante, on the other hand, although he has said something false, has not made a mistake since he was speaking metaphorically. That is, the very same utterance, with the very same meaning, is false on both literal and metaphorical understandings, but constitutes a mistake only as uttered literally.

For Davidson, the metaphorical and the literal differ not in meaning but in the force with which metaphorical and literal utterances are written or said. "Force" is (roughly) the intention with which a sentence is produced. The intended purposes for which one may produce a sentence with given truth conditions vary, for words are versatile and malleable tools. That is, although a sentence has given truth conditions and so a given truth-value, that sentence can be uttered for a number of reasons and can function in a number of different speech acts. A person has made a mistake if something goes wrong with the intended purpose of his utterance, but the sentence he utters is true or false independently of its intended purpose. The truth conditions of a sentence are what make possible the various things that can be done with it, including asserting what is the case and making a point metaphorically. "Metaphorically" describes how an utterance is meant, not what it means. So metaphors are not a class of sentences or phrases but rather a kind of force.

For Davidson, a literal utterance is the plain assertion that the truth conditions obtain. To speak of an utterance as "literally false" is to say that if it were an assertion that the truth conditions obtain, it would be a mistake. According to Davidson, the metaphorical use intends purposes other than telling it as it is. Metaphorical utterances are false, but not thereby defective, any more than are commands that have not yet been obeyed.

The Davidsonian placement of the metaphorical on the level of force rather than the level of semantics is virtually required by any theory of meaning that holds that there are no carriers of meaning more fundamental than words or wordlike phenomena. No other distinctions are available, given that a magic language of thought, in which metaphor is impossible and in which the pure meaning shines through from the very nature of the thought token, does not exist.

Davidson proposes that the distinction between the metaphorical and the literal is one of *force* rather than meaning because there is nothing to meaning (in the sense of "sense") but words, and words do not distinguish the metaphorical from the literal. That is, without the idea of a perfectly expository language that could not be taken metaphorically, the "interpretation" of a metaphor is itself subject to both metaphorical and literal interpretation, because the interpreting language is just a language. Furthermore, interpretation for Davidson renders such trivialities as that "My love is a rose" is true if and only if my love is a rose. When I explain what I mean by "gong-tormented sea" according to Davidsonian semantics, it turns out that "This sea is gong-tormented" is true if and only if this sea is gong-tormented. Nothing in the terms explains what metaphors do, so their function must be a matter of use and the intention with which a sentence is uttered.

I thoroughly agree both with Davidson's semantics and with his appeal to use as what is crucial to the metaphorical. I also agree that a very important part of what some metaphors do is something besides conveying information. As Richard Rorty points out in "Unfamiliar Noises: Hesse and Davidson on Metaphor," the fragment "that dolphin-torn, that gong-tormented sea" is not valued for telling us about gongs or the sea.

Some Preliminary Difficulties

The account of metaphor I will suggest departs from Davidson's account chiefly on the question of whether metaphorical remarks are ever true in a way that differs from the way they are sometimes literally true. To answer this, one must ask whether metaphorical use is really different in kind from the ordinary application of a predicate to a case. And to answer this, one must in turn consider whether metaphor is central or marginal to the philosophy of language.

A fuller argument against parts of Davidson's account of metaphor is given below in this chapter, in the section titled "Amended Davidsonism," which joins features of Davidson's and de Man's accounts of metaphor. For the moment, let me state a difficulty with Davidson's view.

The account according to which metaphors are never true assertions either presupposes a non-Davidsonian notion of truth conditions or begs the question of whether metaphorical utterances might be intended as true assertions. The literal and metaphorical meanings of "He was burned up" are identical. The utterance is true if and only if he was burned up. Now, Davidson would say that this sentence is false on occasions when the referent of "he" was angry but not incinerated. But what are the grounds for saying it is false? Davidson must hold that incineration is the literal meaning of "burned up," and that a surfeit of heat under the collar is always insufficient for incineration.

But an alternative account is that being burned up sometimes involves combination with oxygen and sometimes does not. Unless Davidson has in mind an account of meaning in which meaning is given by privileged webs of belief, he has no more basis for claiming that all cases of being burned up are oxidations than for claiming that all plates are crockery, or that all pain is a sensation. It is no objection, either, that you can be burned up one way but not the other, since you can have your armor plate but not have a dinner plate.

So the appeal to "literal truth" and to the literal falsity of metaphorical utterances begs the question. If metaphorical remarks are sometimes true assertions, then the truth conditions of those remarks do obtain.

The key problem here is that the notion of literal truth is quite obscure and indeterminate on a Davidsonian (or Derridean) conception of language. Although the truth conditions of "Fred is burned up" are quite clear, the truth-value may not be. "Fred is burned up" is true if and only if Fred is burned up, but the question of the truth or literal falsity of a metaphor is whether Fred is actually burned up.

Since there are no tokens that determine sets by their very essence, that is, no senses expressed that determine by their very nature what objects fall under them, there are only patterns of what people say, and when they say it, to fix extensions of terms and thus the truth-values of sentences. As Davidson notices, such truth-*values* can be indeterminate, since patterns of what people in a culture say and when they say it can be mapped onto complete linguistic systems in numerous ways with different ascriptions of truth and error to particular sentences. Not all contents of assertions will be either true or not true, except relative to some arbitrary choices.[7]

A related problem is Davidson's account of the death of metaphors. Metaphors die slowly, and whether they are alive or dead is sometimes indeterminate. "Indeterminate" here means not that we cannot tell whether the metaphor is still alive and thus false by Davidson's lights, but rather that there is no fact of the matter.[8] Metaphor slides insensibly over into the literal, but it is difficult to imagine that falsity could slide insensibly over into truth.

In a subsequent section, I will consider a Davidsonian account that avoids this kind of difficulty.

De Man's Discussions of Metaphor: Rousseau's Language Learner

Preliminary Remarks and Cautions

De Man discusses many of the philosophical questions about metaphor in his chapter on Rousseau in *Allegories of Reading*, entitled "Metaphor (Second Discourse)." In this section I will translate de Man's discussions into terms that connect with analytic philosophy and Davidson's discussions of metaphor. I do not pretend to carry "de Man's authentic view" over into the new terminology. The supposition that there is a common thought or set of problems that can be expressed indifferently in one group of predicates or another is contrary to the thinking of both Davidson and de Man. The terms in which these two figures think of language are mutually alien, with no simple term-to-term equivalences.

Yet a deep similarity joins these thinkers: both deny the standard logocentric view of the relation of thought and language. The logocentric supposition is that thought takes place in a magic language, a way of representing that cannot be mistaken, by means of terms whose very nature reveals what they are terms for. Such self-interpreting terms would be Hume's ideas of the contents of our intentions with respect to the use of language, according to Carnap.

Two further cautions remain. First, the rhetoric of de Man's text makes some parts of "de Man's account" questionable, since he presents important theses through expositions of other thinkers or in texts in which it is not clear whether de Man is speaking "in his own voice." Given the views I will ascribe to de Man, though, "in his own voice" is always a problematic notion.

Second, developing a philosophical account in the vocabulary of "analytic philosophy" requires giving genre-appropriate arguments or argument sketches for the theses being translated. In the translation to follow, I will supply such arguments. But since arguments can be supplied in more than one way, the thesis that these will be "de Man's arguments" would take long defense.

So the translation I will propose as the thought of Paul de Man will be surrounded by indeterminacy on even the best account. We have here, in fact, a good case of indeterminacy of translation in Quine's sense, or indeterminacy of radical interpretation in Davidson's sense. There is just no fact of the matter as to what exactly de Man means in "our terms." There is no way to say exactly what de Man said except in de Man's words, or words that have the textual and theoretical connections his have.

De Man's Account of Metaphor and Meaning

I will present de Man's account as a theory of the nature of language, while commenting on his commentary on Rousseau. I will supplement his discussion of Rousseau with some remarks from his article "The Epistemology of Metaphor."

According to de Man, Rousseau says two apparently incompatible things about the relation between naming and conceptualization. In the *Discourse on the Origin of Inequality (Second Discourse)*, Rousseau takes naming to be the primitive linguistic act, whereas predicating is an articulation, a division into categories, of the named objects. Since predication or, in de Man's words in *Allegories of Reading*, "conceptualization, conceived as an exchange or substitution of properties on the basis of resemblance, corresponds exactly to the classical definition of metaphor,"[9] Rousseau's account seems to make nomination literal and to divide language into the literal and figurative. In the *Essay on the Origin of Languages*, on the other hand, Rousseau supposes language to start with an expression of passion, specifically through the use of a general term. ("Start" here should be taken logically, not temporally. De Man reads this narrative as an allegory of linguistic dependencies.) De Man's reading attempts to make these two doctrines constitute parts of a single view.

In the *Essay*, Rousseau takes the first use of a general term—which occurs when a person applies a term more or less translated as "giant" to a fellow human—to be an expression of fear.[10] In *Allegories*, de Man surprisingly, not to say bafflingly, calls this application metaphorical and metalinguistic.[11]

As a first approximation of de Man's point, this utterance of "giant" is metaphorical because an outer item, the man, is called by a term proper to an inner item, the fear; thus the utterance meets the conditions for carrying across meaning. But for de Man, figuration is essentially a matter of rhetorical force. He even speaks of the fear felt at the approach of another human as a "figural state" because that fear is a *hypothesis* of future harm rather than a known fact. Propositional attitudes, or "passions," are to be thought of as different rhetorical forces with which propositional contents can be entertained or uttered. Rhetorical force will turn out to distinguish the literal from the metaphorical for de Man in a way precisely analogous to Davidson's account.

De Man calls such deviations of force "figural," the notion being that figural representations turn away from direct descriptions of reality. Such representations mean something else. De Man identifies the rhetorical explicitly with the figural. Meaning is a feature primarily of speech acts, for de Man, so a turning of meaning is a turning of a speech act. A troping is a use of a representation for something other than direct reporting of what is the case. An untroped representation, purely and literally true, would be an assertion that is literally and strictly the case, with no admixture of representing what is not the case.[12] Thus, "giant" is a metaphor, even in this narrative in which such a word is being uttered for the first time in a stimulus situation.

For de Man, then, rhetoric begins at home, in the interiority of the person who has the various attitudes toward contents of sentences. A person in relation to her own representations is in a rhetorical situation. Since on de Man's view the representations themselves have a dubious rhetorical standing, the special status of a person in relation to her own utterances begins to be erased. That is, the representations themselves already have rhetorical histories, owing to their use of general terms. These contaminated histories raise the same questions about their relation to some originating intention that the utterance has to its originating intention.[13] The "giant" case has other important features as well. For instance, de Man says that this metaphor "disfigures." This is de Man's paradoxical term for the change that takes place when a figural state is put into words. The figural state, when put into words, can be taken literally, so the metaphorical expression, qua expression, falsifies something. The idea seems to be that a "literal" reading is the prima facie force of whatever is put in a declarative sentence.

To put this in other terms: as an utterance, "giant" cannot carry a "rhetorical force marker," a sign that would say how it was intended. As Davidson has argued in "Moods and Performances" and "Communication and Convention," a rhetorical force marker, a token that could be attached to an utterance to fix its rhetorical force, would, in virtue of being a mark at all, allow being used with different rhetorical force. This permanent possibility that rhetorical force can be misunderstood relative to the "intentions of the speaker," or can be indeterminate at a deeper level of analysis, is a main source of the instability, indeterminacy, and unreliability of language, according to de Man.

This point is crucial to de Man's whole conception of language. Suppose we have the following marker for sincere assertion: "Hey, I really mean that . . ." Now, when I say "Hey, I really mean that you're my type," we do not know whether I am kidding. Iteration does not help either: "Hey, I really mean that I really mean that you're my type" can still be used to lie or to give an example in a philosophy paper. Force cannot be put into words, because words, by being words, are detached from any necessary connection with an intention. As soon as intention is expressed, it must be expressed in something that need not carry that intention.[14]

On my reading of de Man, his talk about "meaning" being misrepresented, or language being deceptive about what we really mean, is a necessity of exposition that does not commit him to holding seriously that there are intentions that are epistemologically more reliable than language.[15] De Man needs the old logocentric notion of "intention" to describe the indeterminacy of language, but that old notion is then abandoned and replaced by an "abyss," the continental alternative to the metaphor of "regress to a background language." At ground level, there are no intentions apart from language and no language without ulterior rhetorical force, that is, undirected by intention. This pattern of mutual presupposition, which is repeated in the discussion of Rousseau on the relative priority of denomination and predication, points up a kind of groundlessness.

This is not to say that consciousness is nothing but language, but rather that the conscious intention behind language cannot be separated out from the language. There is no such thing as the pure intention informing the pure language.[16]

The "falsification" in the metaphorical use of a term, then, is twofold. First, the inner state, a passion, is ascribed to the external world—the object is characterized by something representing the passion. I argue later that this misnaming is really to be understood, along Davidsonian lines, as an utterance produced for purposes other than saying how things strictly are. Second, by being put into words, the representation loses its privileged tie to a particular rhetorical force, that of a hypothesis, and is turned into what can legitimately be read as an assertion of what is the case.

The nature of rhetoric also can explain why de Man calls metaphor "metalinguistic." If the rhetorical force with which something is thought is something like the intention with which a sentence is said, then saying something sarcastically or ironically presupposes a consciousness of and a representation of the sentence said. So the rhetorical use of language requires that the user have a metalanguage in which sentences of the object language can be represented.

How much of language is affected by this kind of dislocation and disfigurement? Here we need to turn to the passage from the *Second Discourse* that de Man discusses in *Allegories of Reading*.[17] This is the passage in which, apparently, acts of denomination are the primitive linguistic operations, rather than uses of the kind of general term that expresses passions. Rousseau's picture there seems to be that first, objects are named, and then, on the basis of resemblances among named objects, a general term is applied that labels distinct things as the same. Distinct objects are all called by the same name "tree," so that a transfer of meaning from one case to the next takes place. That is, "conceptualization, conceived as an exchange or substitution of properties on the basis of resemblance, corresponds exactly to the classical definition of metaphor."[18] This is metaphor, since, when a new entity is to be labeled "tree," it is called by a term previously applied to something else. So for Rousseau, the use of predicates, what de Man calls "conceptualization," is essentially metaphorical. The crucial argument for de Man shows how this process is always analyzable as a turning of rhetorical force.

De Man accepts Rousseau's narrative of conceptualization but does not suppose that "natural resemblance" will fix the language into a system. For de Man, there are multiple "natural" bases in "resemblance," hence the metaphors that constitute the predicate "system" will not be a system.[19]

De Man resists the usual interpretation of this passage as contrasting the literal, denominative stage of language with the conceptual, figural stage. Rousseau says that denomination depends on noticing difference, so that individuals are given distinct names only when they are noticed as being distinct. But "different" is a concept, which would have to have been applied to new pairs on the basis of the metaphorical extension that was described earlier and that will be explicated in detail in the remainder of the present section. Thus Rousseau takes denomination to presuppose conceptualization.

De Man's reading thus both makes denomination presuppose conceptualization *and* makes conceptualization presuppose denomination. It also makes metaphor, the calling of something by the name of something else, part of every use of language whatsoever. Since a metaphorical utterance introduces a rhetorical indeterminacy into a figural, rhetorical situation in which *that* indeterminacy had not existed (although perhaps other indeterminacies did), language itself turns out to be intrinsically unreliable. Metaphor corrupts any "direct" naming of what is the case, and metaphor, calling something by some improper name, is required by any conceptualization, which in turn is required by any language whatsoever.

Figural displacement is fundamental to language in two ways, according to de Man. First, language is figural in the sense that it involves disfiguration, the misrepresentation of the force of a propositional content. The gap between an intended force at a particular level and the liberation from any necessary connection with that force when the utterance is produced makes every level of representation subject to misrepresentation.

Second, de Man holds that all predication is a calling of a thing by a term that is not by nature appropriate to it. Here is the crucial point at which the assimilation of all metaphor to rhetoric needs to be justified: this characterization, which is used to label predication as metaphorical, sounds like the typical definition of metaphor as calling one thing by another's name, as de Man notes. So de Man seems to deploy two notions of figure: the figural as intending a different rhetorical force, and the figural as using a name for an object to which it does not properly apply. The first is his general conception of figure, whereas the second is used to describe metaphor, a special case of figure. De Man needs some account of how the second notion is really a special case of the first, in order to maintain the identification of the rhetorical with the figural.

How is meaning some other referent than what is said a matter of rhetorical force? How does de Man assimilate the account of conceptual extension as metaphorical to the rhetorical analysis of saying something other than what is meant? Surprisingly, the account turns out to be Davidsonian.

Conceptualization, de Man says, is calling one thing by another's name. Consider the situation in other terms: When Charles is discovered to be a frog and said to be a frog, and Albert and Bertha are familiar frogs, the term "frog" at that point has the set (Albert, Bertha) as its extension (barring the "natural division" of things, which would make Charles *already* in the extension of the term).[20] So when Charles is said to be a member of that set, that is, to be a "frog," the remark is not strictly true and is not strictly "meant." The speaker or thinker does not seriously believe that Charles is identical to Bertha or to Albert.

The rhetorical force involved in the predication is, then, exactly like the force Davidson ascribes to metaphor: the sentence is uttered not to assert a truth but to point up something. It is recognized as being not literally true but said for some other purpose. In this case, the purpose is to bring out a felt resemblance or to illuminate Charles by calling him an element of the set (Albert, Bertha).

When one says or thinks "Charles is a frog" the utterance is now freed from any special attachment to the complex metaphorical intention. This "disfiguring" amounts to a kind of literalization, so that Charles is said to *be* a frog. Then the "extension" is "in effect" the set (Albert, Bertha, Charles), and the feeling that something about Doris makes it appropriate to call her a frog sets the narrative on another cycle. (Given that every frog is thus labeled, none of the predications are "strictly true" by some Platonic standard of "true.")

In short, Rousseau's narrative as transcribed by de Man and read here pictures ordinary predication as involving exactly the kind of rhetorical force that Davidson takes to be characteristic of metaphorical utterance, a force conveying that the utterance should not be understood as strictly a description of how the object really is. In both cases, utterances turn from direct assertion in a way that is to be understood in rhetorical terms, that is, in terms of how sentences are used rather than what they mean.

Thus, de Man and Davidson agree that metaphorical remarks are never strictly true, as meant. The difference between them is, rather, that for de Man, given the exigencies of extending predicates to new cases, predications are never strictly true, in the required sense of "strictly true," while for Davidson, they sometimes are. More specifically, the only point of doctrine separating de Man from Davidson is Davidson's view that not all utterances involve this turning; there is a kind of application of terms, the regular literal assertion, in which the subject of the predication, the new candidate for membership in a set, is *already*, by its nature or by the nature of the thought, a member of the set of objects to which the term applies. This is a difference the last section suggests Davidson should dispense with.

On this issue, de Man draws inspiration from Nietzsche's "On Truth and Lies in the Extra-Moral Sense." Nietzsche points out that there is no such thing as truly proper application of a term to an object, since words are nothing like their referents. Thus, *all* predication is metaphorical, in the sense that one thing is called something else. Fear is called "fear," which is nothing like it. I read this Nietzsche passage as an especially vivid denial of magic language and so of anchors in the nature of things to keep a term stably connected with its referent.

The main difficulty in accepting de Man's view is his use of the notion of unreliability. Nietzsche's position, after all, seems to be little more than an excited response to the arbitrariness of the signifier, or a descendant of Berkeley's thought that an idea can only resemble another idea. De Man's understanding of "unreliability" is not really contrasted with anything *reliable*, since no language or representation system is possible without these "defects" of arbitrariness and dissimilarity to what is represented. In the same way, for Rousseau, on de Man's reading, no pure language of denomination is possible. This part of de Man's thinking may annoy analytic philosophers, since "unreliable" seems to suppose a standard of reliability that something logically could meet. The objection would go: "Nothing could be 'reliable' by de Man's standards of telling it like it is, so it is hyperbolic to say that language is fundamentally defective."

But there *could be* a kind of representation that yields a reliable, determinate language, namely, the magic, self-interpreting language of thought that makes intention clear and provides the background of determination by which to anchor interpretation, translation, and meaning. The remarks about unreliability are a way of denying a magic language and of asserting that these slippages relative to the dream of such a language are forgotten consequences of its unreality

"Unreliability" and "indeterminacy" for de Man are expressed in his Wittgenstein-like suspicion that accounts of the world will never be complete, that practices have no "system," in a strict sense. This view depends on the arbitrariness of the signifier, as well as on considerations of rhetoric. A view of language and the world that supposes natural connections between words and things, as Aristotle supposes for the magic words of *nous*-ing, would derive its systematicity from that of the world. A system without such ties, which recognized the "arbitrariness of the sign," might try to achieve system by convention, by somehow fixing what means what. But then the rhetorical observation that words can possess no force markers eliminates the possibility of a conventional determination of how things are meant. So the indeterminacy, for de Man, has two sides. First, the determinacy produced by a natural connection between word and referent is unavailable. Second, the determinacy that might be established by a fixed set of conventions, rules of language for extending terms, is unmanned by the unconventionality of force.

That this is de Man's view, and not just the view he ascribes to Rousseau, is borne out by other de Manian texts, especially "The Epistemology of Metaphor." Here de Man observes that, in the empiricist tradition, the extension of general terms is difficult to control by means of the natures of the entities they refer to, since we have access only to the ideas of them. Control of extensions of general terms by definitions will not achieve stability because of simple ideas, whose extensions are irremediably subject to troping.

The project of getting our ideas to correspond to real kinds in nature, or even of securing them as a fixed arbitrary collection of ideas, is undermined by the possibility of meaning things otherwise, that is, of troping. Regarding Locke's condemnation of arbitrary ideas that do not correspond to real natures, de Man says in "The Epistemology of Metaphor" that "the condemnation, by Locke's own argument, now takes all language for its target, for at no point in the course of the demonstration can the empirical entity be sheltered from tropological defiguration."[21] The basic view on which de Man's analyses turn is that the ideas of the empiricist tradition always threatened to function as words, since no necessary connection obtained between features of the idea and the nature that gave rise to it. So ideas could not be trusted to correspond to the same things in nature. The wordlike quality of thought-terms tended subliminally to undermine the magic of the language of thought.

Ideas as words had features that could connect them with each other in virtue of their accidental properties rather than in virtue of the underlying realities they represented. The language that expressed these ideas was subject to the same difficulties, so philosophers nervously sensed that their derogatory remarks about the unreliability of language would also apply to ideas. Thus, the distinction between legitimate representation and misleading tropological representation cannot be made a distinction of kind. Owing to the contingency of the connection between idea and thing, no reliable basis is available for grouping ideas according to their corresponding underlying realities. "In each case," de Man states, "it turns out to be impossible to maintain a clear line of distinction between rhetoric, abstraction, symbol, and all other forms of language. In each case, the resulting undecidability is due to the asymmetry of the binary model that opposes the figural to the proper meaning of the figure."[22]

De Man's reading unpacks an aporia in the tradition's notion of the thought and its relation to reality: the thought was supposed to consist of magic words that would reveal by their very nature what they were true of, much like Aristotle's *nous* words. But the tradition needed to find some medium we could actually be said to think in, and "ideas," which were basically sensory particulars like Aristotelian phantasms, seemed to be the only candidates. But the ideas that were the only appropriate candidates for the tokens of such a language turned out to be irremediably wordlike. They were not magic, but had characters unconnected with the real natures of their referents. Those characters supported tropic, inappropriate connections and thus allowed misinterpretation. (If the child's idea of gold, by its nature, leads him to apply "gold" to a flower, the misapplication of the idea is formally the misinterpretation of a word.)

De Man believes that the wordlike features the philosophers found threatening are always present in any thought; that is, that thought is wordlike. Thus the permanent possibility of troping, and the indistinguishability of the trope from the straight, means that the instability and indeterminacy feared by the tradition are actual.

Davidson with de Man

In this final section I show two things. First, I show that Davidson's account of metaphor could be amended by the addition of de Man's insights to repair exactly the difficulties we found with Davidson's account. (The amendment here is symmetrical, since I take this whole essay to indicate some of the ways Davidsonian considerations can supplement the argument and exposition of de Man's account.) Second, I argue that the main amendment, to the conception of predication, is in fact already implicit in Davidson's thinking.

Amended Davidsonism

The most easily stated difference between the accounts of Davidson and de Man concerns the truth-status of metaphorical utterances. For Davidson, such utterances are always false, as meant, except accidentally. For de Man, metaphorical remarks are as true as any predication ever is.

Amended Davidsonism takes up Davidson's suggestion in "What Metaphors Mean":

When we read, for example, that "the Spirit of God moved upon the face of the waters" . . . "face" applies to ordinary faces and to waters in addition [but] all sense of metaphor evaporates. If we are to think of words in metaphors as directly going about their business of applying to what they properly do apply to, there is no difference between metaphor and the introduction of a new term into our vocabulary: to make a metaphor is to murder it.[23]

To summarize in advance: amended Davidsonism questions the notion "properly apply to" and the existence of a "sense of metaphor" that distinguishes the metaphors from the literal assertions. Metaphorical uses of sentences are sometimes true assertions—applications of the very same terms in the very same senses as literal uses. But although waters have faces, they do not therefore have noses.

On the amended account, the literal and the metaphorical would be separated as follows: A sincere, "literal" assertion is intended to be automatically interpreted, making the routine connections to other predications and taking all the routine evidence and consequences to be relevant to the predication. The metaphorical assertion is proposed as true, but those automatic routines of interpretation are intended not to be followed. The metaphorical assertion intends that a routine group of connections and generalizations be suspended. The metaphorical assertion is a claim that the predicate applies to the case, but that some other predicates that are often connected with it do not apply in this case.

"Interpretation" as it is used here is not just the simple deployment of Davidsonian truth-definition clauses so that sentences of the interpreted language can be understood in terms of the interpreting language. "Interpretation" here is understanding the other as "rational." On the broad notion of Davidsonian interpretation, so understood, people try to maximize agreement with their interlocutors holistically.[24] Given a prima facie strange remark, such an interpreter can attribute error to another on certain topics, decide that the other person is using words differently, or reinterpret the rhetorical force with which the remark is made. All such judgments are evaluated holistically, without any guarantee that there will be a single optimal solution.

One important device for treating our interlocutors as rational by our lights is that of reading the rhetorical force of their remarks as other than assertive. This is the strategy Davidson holds to be correct for all interpretation of metaphorical remarks. But strategies of radical interpretation other than making the force nonassertive sometimes enter into the interpretation of metaphorical remarks. Let me begin by characterizing interpretation.

To simplify a great deal,[25] the "interpretation" of another's ascription of a predicate always involves ascribing beliefs to that other. When I hear Fred say, "There is a dog," my decision that by "dog" he means "dog" is my ascription of an ill-defined array of my beliefs to the other. For instance, I ascribe the belief that dogs are animals, that no dogs are Saxons, that my friend Pam has a dog named Jeff, and so forth.

The interpretation strategy to be followed in understanding someone's remark as a literal assertion ascribes all or most of the interpreter's "important" general beliefs involving the terms in the sentence to the other person being interpreted. The rhetorical force of a literal assertion that a predicate applies to some new case includes the intention that all "important" general beliefs be applied to the case.

In a metaphorical ascription of a predicate to a new case, the intention is that some important general beliefs not be ascribed to the speaker, that the adjustment be elsewhere in the maximizing of agreement. When the metaphor is familiar, some adjustment may already have been made, and there may be different sets of generalizations more or less in place in the theory of the other. When a person is (metaphorically) crushed, I might believe that a shopping trip would be therapeutic, a change from my beliefs about those crushed by boulders rather than by life itself. Such a metaphorical use, with its own generalizations, begins to rate its own entry in the dictionary.

That is, if the metaphor is taken as a true assertion, the modified beliefs and the adjustments in surrounding theory ascribed to the speaker are adopted by the interpreter. Where a metaphorical remark is taken to be a true assertion, the interpreter of a metaphor may maximize agreement by suspending or dropping some of her own general beliefs and adding others. If the crushing metaphor was new to her, and the remark about the crushed person seemed true, the interpreter would qualify her own beliefs about the physical damage crushing entails in order to understand the remark that I am crushed.

A new metaphorical application of a term X supposes that there are more kinds of X's than we thought. There are not different "senses" of the verb "fly," denoting or not denoting the flapping of wings, which apply to birds and airplanes, respectively. These are just two *kinds* of flying, and were proposed as such on the first extension of the term to flying machines. This extension of the understanding of a term by an interpreter is like the realization that "some dinosaurs were protected by plates" is not a remark about an early use of crockery. "Plate" as it occurs in "tectonic plate" or "armor plate" may be taken to be metaphorical by the naive. It is not "really" metaphorical, though, since most people already believe that there are many kinds of plates, and that different things are true of tectonic plates and dinner plates.

All such plates share a certain flat configuration, but the necessary and sufficient conditions for meeting that configuration (i.e., for being some kind of plate) are specified only by the condition of being a plate. So "plate" is unparaphrasable in the way a metaphor is unparaphrasable. This appeals to Wittgenstein's concept of "family resemblance" from the *Philosophical Investigations*, which rests on the observation that without Platonic meanings as outside constraints, language need have no standards for the application of a predicate in other terms.[26]

Unamended Davidsonism, by making the typical metaphor false, solves one problem I should address: an utterance that is true if taken metaphorically but literally false would seem to make some term both apply and not apply, on amended Davidsonism. That is, when I am (a) crushed by the princess's refusal but (luckily) (b) not crushed by the boulder her servants drop from the castle wall as a parting gesture, Davidson says that (a) is false and (b) is true, whereas my amended account makes both (a) and (b) true applications of the same predicate. The amended account must characterize such cases as *kinds* of crushing, aspects with respect to which one is crushed, or *ways* in which one is crushed.

When both literal and metaphorical understandings of an utterance are possible, a relativization can explain how the two understandings can coexist. There are familiar arguments that relativizations can save us from multiple homonymy.[27]

We still have to acknowledge the cases to which Davidson assimilates all metaphorical interpretation. A metaphor is often not a serious claim about reality, and the consideration that the sentence might be true is meant to be amusing, or has some other purpose than pointing out an unnoticed kind of case. At other times, the metaphor is serious, but its point is not to convey anything that could be called "information" in any separable sense.[28]

Some interesting metaphors are cases of serious intentions other than that of information transmission. These are the kinds of metaphors that change the way we think and feel. They are understood not in terms of isolable "cognitive content" but rather in the way Davidson describes. However, on Davidsonian as well as Derridean grounds, the whole notion of "cognitive content," as a separable aspect of what we see and feel, is suspect. Worthwhile "learning" is not just the ingestion of propositions but rather a whole complex of states that cannot be divided into the cognitive and "other." A metaphor that requires very radical interpretation, and that one eventually takes to be true, is one of these life-changing metaphors whose effect is described better in terms of insight than in terms of packets of data.

The process of understanding a "deep" metaphor is of a piece with coming to see that a term applies in an unsuspected case. Suppose someone I respect says that Wittgenstein is a very ironic philosopher. I may come to agree by thinking about Wittgenstein and irony, perhaps changing my mind about both. My coming to understand "what she meant" will not easily be put into propositional form, but is a mix of attitudes on these and related topics. This inseparable mix of the "cognitive" with the "other" is characteristic of learning generally, not just of the kind of learning we derive from poetry. (I think I learned this from Davidson.)

Let us see how amended Davidsonism deals with two problems: the movement from live to dead metaphors and the distinction between a metaphorical use and a new application of a term.

First, the de Manian supplementation deals with the transition from live to dead metaphor, given that all predications are founded in metaphor. On Davidson's view, "Celeste is an eggplant" is false until people call guinea pigs eggplants often enough that these animals become part of the extension of the term. At that point, "eggplant" is a dead metaphor that can be part of a truth-definition clause. That is, a sentence such as "Celeste is an eggplant" has become literally true, and guinea pigs have become part of the extension of "eggplant." But the death of a metaphor is an insensible drift from the novel to the old hat. No sharp line divides such dead metaphors as "My heart is broken" from the still-live ones. Truth, though, cannot have degrees. Thus we should not say that dead and live metaphors differ in truth-value, the live being always false and the dead sometimes true. Amended Davidsonism, by viewing routine predication and exotic metaphor as end points on a continuum, fits well with the lingering illnesses of metaphor.

Second, the failure to reflect some intuitive line between the metaphorical and the literal is justified. In "What Metaphors Mean," Davidson objected that if metaphors are extended applications of terms, "all sense of metaphor evaporates."[29] This evaporation seems altogether fitting and proper, since the "sense of metaphor" does not give clear results. On a revised Davidsonism, the notion of genuine metaphor has no rigorous theoretical definition. We apply "metaphor" in ways that resist systematization and seem to admit of degrees.[30]

When a metaphorical utterance is produced that one is inclined to accept as true, how does one know what to keep and what to abandon among the general beliefs associated with the terms of the utterance? Performing the kind of interpretation intended by the utterer of a metaphor is like creating a scientific theory in response to data that make the old theory impossible to retain. Just as there are no rules and no algorithm for the creation of scientific theories, so there is no algorithm for the interpretation of metaphor. In both situations, we have "recalcitrant data" that exert pressure to become part of our thinking. In this case, the "recalcitrant data" are the proposed new cases in which the predicate is to apply. The "adjustments in theory" are changes in connection and inferences that must be made to accept the new cases as cases of the same predicate.

So how is metaphor to be interpreted? There can be no prior absolutely controlling guides, nothing like an algorithm, because such an algorithm would be language that was itself subject to interpretation. There can be no determining guides to a project of, essentially, changing language, because there is no system of meaning bearers prior to language to provide such controls. We cannot take an "outside" point of view from which to oversee or evaluate our adjustments in beliefs and language. There is no point of view outside our beliefs, desires, and other propositional attitudes and so no point of view outside our language. Adjustments in propositional attitudes are inseparable from adjustments in language if there are no meaning bearers prior to language, since the contents of propositional attitudes must then be languagelike.

In interpreting a metaphor, then, we may well find no single answer, especially when the figure is really interesting. We can produce wrong answers, however, and criticism can point them out. Getting a metaphor right does not mean following the intentions of the utterer. The utterer of the metaphor does not control how the metaphor is rightly taken. The first person who extended the steam-boiler expression "all fired up," for instance, may have thought that a team that is all fired up is angry, since that connection is there in the words. The metaphor as applied to sports teams came to have something to do with enthusiasm rather than anger, as is the case with other heat metaphors. A metaphor is a text.

Coming to accept original metaphors as true, then, is changing language and theory. If no semantic bearers exist below the languagelike, then changing and adapting language cannot proceed by an algorithm or a routine. Without Platonic Forms or the like, there is no prior code in which the meanings of words exist, and thus no foundation that can provide the basis for changing language to adjust to the Truth. Platonic Forms or their like are required for there to be a general background language from which changes of language can be plotted. Given that there are no prior meaning bearers, the extension of predicates demands creativity, since absolute outside constraints are lacking. This does not mean that such interpretation is groundless, just that the grounding relation lies not in external absolutes but rather in practices. In a phrase, the theory is Wittgensteinian.[31] Only if nothing but impossibly rigorous rules could control practice would the lack of standard-providing Platonic Forms mean chaos.

There are no algorithms or genuine rules more helpful than "Call all and only roses 'roses'" for extending predicates. The kind of interpretation that applies to live metaphors applies in attenuated form to predication generally. The *routine* for extending predicates in any new case is not fixed by an outside standard, because there are no meaning bearers more intrinsically connected to what they fit than language. Thus every application of a predicate is an extension to a new case that is not fixed either in the nature of things or in the language.

"Nonmetaphoric" interpretation is just routine, in more generally following old patterns. It is not essentially different from the "creative" interpretation required of original metaphors. After all, some old generalizations are falsified and some new generalizations come true whenever a new case of a predicate is discovered. The discovery of a frog in my bed falsifies the previously believed generalization that my bed harbors no frogs. Whenever it is fitting that a term be applied to a new case, some adjustment of old belief is required. The more radical the adjustment, the more the utterance seems metaphorical, other things being equal.

So extensions to new kinds of cases, if such extensions are controlled not by the very nature of things but by a combination of conceptual equipment and the world, are not essentially different from extensions to new cases of the same kind. That is, the very notion of a kind of case is something in part shaped by the linguistic practices. Routine categorization is thus not a matter of just fitting the raw facts, either.

Why Davidson Really Already Believes This

The main amendment borrowed from de Man is a change in how the use of general terms is conceived. In this last section I argue that this conception of predication is implicit in Davidson's thinking. (Of course, this also amounts to a kind of defense of de Man's ideas as reconstrued here.)

For de Man, metaphor, which in analytic philosophy has been treated as a marginal phenomenon, is made the paradigm of the most central operation of saying things, predication. Normal predication, which has always been treated as property ascription determined by the presence or absence of an external control, namely, the real language-independent property, is on this account a degenerate kind of metaphor. Metaphor, which has always been treated as a deviant exception to the correct use of language, a fallen misuse justifiable only for aesthetic effect, is made the central model of how language functions. On Davidsonian grounds, metaphor and ordinary predication ought to be cases of the same phenomenon.

What, after all, are the bases for extensions to new kinds of cases? For Aristotle, such extensions take place on the basis of real analogies in the natures of things. The basis for taking "broken" to apply to hearts when a person is emotionally crushed is obviously that crushed things are broken, this heart is crushed, so this heart is broken. Here, this "natural" connection itself depends on another metaphor, since "crushed" does not naturally apply to the heart of a person who still survives. That is, the basis of this analogy is partially linguistic, or more dramatically, "contaminated by the linguistic." The fact that crushing things lowers or depresses them does not help either, unless something in the nature of things connects depressions and depressions. These are not raw facts of analogy isolable from the background of language in which they are thought.

Our world, although connected with the truths about things, is not based on a given. From a traditional realist point of view, this means that our conception of the nature of things is "contaminated" by the merely linguistic. There is no pure exposition by terms that have exactly the one property of referring to their referents. In explicating the analogy by which a metaphor is justified, we have either an endless trail of metaphors or a case of catachresis. In either case, the analogies are mediated by the language in which they are framed.

If the analogy could be stated in terms that permitted no metaphorical extensions, then we would be extending terms to new cases on the basis of the raw facts, the facts that exist prior to any conceptualization. But Davidson has argued that there can be no such level of fact (see "On the Very Idea of a Conceptual Scheme"). The linguistic varnish cannot be removed from the raw facts.

The de Manian account of metaphor is thus implicit in the antifoundationalism required by the complex of views about necessity and language that Davidson shares with Quine and Derrida. Part of this complex is the denial of purely natural analogies, analogies that exist independently of any way of looking or thinking. Such analogies would require a nature of things capable of being a pure external determiner of meaning. In effect, such prelinguistic analogies would be features of the "manifold" that exists prior to any conceptual scheme and that is organized by that conceptual scheme. Davidson's rejection of "the very idea of a conceptual scheme" is thus a rejection of the purely natural analogies that could found metaphorical extensions of a basis independent of the language. If all analogies are mediated by language, then all metaphor based on analogies is mediated by language.

The picture of the relation of language and the world can no longer be that of a code or algorithm. If all external anchors for the analogies that support metaphors are contaminated by the linguistic, then we have little reason to expect the analogies to form a system. There may be no single system of connections, so a given term may connect with other terms in contradictory ways. As de Man's investigations of figuration show, typical systems of metaphor are nonsystems, patterns of connection that assign central terms contradictory roles.[32] The impossibility of purifying our access to the extensions of our terms, of separating it out from the linguistic shaping of what we say, means that our words cannot rawly reflect the real. Without a foundation in something guaranteed to be coherent, such as a single world or the magic language, the patterns of connection and association among words and texts have nothing to force them into a unified system free from contradiction. The model of metaphor as the primary linguistic operation removes the misleading metaphor of the algorithm or world code as the basis for what we say.

Thus, on Davidson's principles, predication is essentially figuration. In the absence of pure natural kinds uncontaminated by language, any extension to an *old* kind of case is a leap not determined by the nature of things. Predications of the most elementary sort are very dead metaphors, metaphors, perhaps, by etymology alone. The most exotic metaphor is continuous with the most fundamental operation of language.

6

True Figures

METAPHOR AND THE SORITES

The following essay can be regarded as a working-out of the consequences of not taking truth as primitive and irreducible. That is, if we follow Quine and take "indeterminacy" situations to be ones in which a given ascription of truth conditions has no truth-value, then indeterminacy of interpretation means that the utterance in question has no truth-value except relative to an arbitrary interpretation.

In the case of metaphor, Davidson's theory is that a metaphor is an utterance that is literally false but is produced for a purpose other than asserting that the truth conditions obtain. To my mind, the problem with Davidson's theory arises from the fact that metaphors pass insensibly into literal truths. For example, "easel" was originally a metaphorical extension of "ass," but now, "easel" is used literally to mean the artist's stand. According to Davidson, in the sequence of utterances of "easel" in Dutch and English, some particular utterance, perhaps "I just set up my easel," was the first such utterance to be true. (That utterance, from that speaker, could be true while contemporaries continued to speak illuminating falsehoods with the same words.)

To accept Davidson's view of metaphor, which must incorporate the literal/figurative distinction, we have to accept that utterances can be true or false but necessarily undetectably so. A Davidsonian position on the death of metaphor is like Roy Sorensen's position on vague predicates: "*A* is a tall man" always has a truth-value even though in principle nothing could determine the line between tall and not tall.

Davidson's view that truth is irreducible accommodates this result, but still I cannot shake the feeling that making truth a magical phenomenon without rigorous connection to the physical world is not a good idea. On the other hand, the notion of "truth" that one is able to generate along the lines discussed below in this chapter seems deeply unsatisfactory.

In this chapter I also take for granted the primacy of public languages over truth conditions that could be ascribed to private, individual languages. Unless truth is primary and determinate independently of every "fact of the matter" stated in terms of objects, properties, or other "correspondents," an individual's utterance can have a truth-value only relative to the distinction between utterances that agree and those that do not agree with some standard of what to say and when to say it. That is, a Davidsonian version of Wittgenstein's private language argument would seem to show that, if the truth-value of an utterance is a function of an individual's dispositions to apply terms, then whatever an individual said would be true, since it conformed to his dispositions. Davidson would reject the argument by insisting that truth-value is not a function of anything. That is, truth-value is not reducible to any facts about anything else. So Davidson can reject the private-language argument.

As a final corrective note, I would add that it now seems clear to me that Davidson would accept something like Sorensen's analysis of sorites paradoxes: That there is no empirically determinable line separating a tall man from a man who is not tall can mean that the line is in principle unknowable. In the same way, the indeterminacy of interpretation can be taken to mean that the truth conditions, and so truth-values, of some utterances are in principle unknowable. If truth is irreducible, such unknowabilities are to be expected.[1]

■

Friedrich Nietzsche, in his essay "On Truth and Lies in an Extra-Moral Sense," makes the following comment:

What then is truth? A mobile army of metaphors, metonyms, and anthropomorphisms—in short, a sum of human relations, which have been enhanced, transposed, and embellished poetically and rhetorically, and which after long use seem firm, canonical, and obligatory to a people: truths are illusions about which one has forgotten that this is what they are; metaphors which are worn out and without sensuous power; coins which have lost their pictures and now matter only as metal, no longer as coins.[2]

What is the criticism in this passage? Truth, the set of true sentences of a human language, is or uses a mobile (changing, shifting, inconstant) array of figures of speech. These figures—metaphors, metonyms, and anthropomorphisms—are defective on many counts: they are enhanced, transposed, and embellished to produce an appearance. They seem to be something they are not. A figure is thus a kind of lie. A metaphor transfers a meaning from one thing to which it properly belongs to another to which that meaning does not properly apply. A metonym names an associated item in place of the proper item itself. Anthropomorphism humanizes objects, giving clocks faces, tables legs, and hurricanes eyes. More generally, anthropomorphism conceives things in human terms, relative to human interests and considerations.

So how are words, the foot soldiers of the mobile armies, lies? The words of a human language are pretenses of being something else because they are mere words. "Red" has nothing in its nature that connects it with or makes it be red. "Red" is not an authentic name, not a term that really means red. Nietzsche's denunciation of truth despairs of the sorts of connections that, according to his deluded predecessors, could make words authentic. Words were supposed to gain a kind of magical connection with things by a connection with "ideas," something authentically referring. Nietzsche realizes that no such ideas "before the mind" or "before the brain" would be better than words. Marks on neurons, brain-tissue lesions, or ghostly tokens would have all of the distance from genuine naming that words have.

But then, Nietzsche has given us a very odd derogation of metaphor and the "truth" of human speech! Consider the criticism that metaphors are like worn coins, without the pictures. What would freshly minted coins be like? To speak of an empty or washed-out metaphor presupposes a contrast with the sensory fullness of things, or the sensory fullness of a kind of thought uncorrupted by the languagelike, a kind of thought in which terms directly and transparently mean the sensory experiences or realities that they mean.

Alas, Nietzsche says, nothing attaches words or thoughts to things except human relations, and human relations, as referential equipment, are necessarily deceptive and defective. But Nietzsche has noticed that, in principle, nothing better than wordlike marks could exist. This bewailing of a deficiency that is a necessary deficiency of every case, and so a deficiency only relative to an impossible dream, can be termed "nostalgia," the longing for what is past and thus inaccessible. So what is Nietzsche (perhaps pretending to be) nostalgic for?

He is nostalgic for some version of Plato's vision of Souls and Forms. The Forms can be present to the Soul, according to Plato. The Form then functions as a word that can have only one interpretation. Thus Forms would constitute a kind of magic language of items that are their own meanings, and so by their very nature determine which objects fall into their extensions. Other versions of this model are the ideas of the British empiricists, sense data, and intensions. Regular human words, which are all we have, according to Nietzsche, fall short of this authentic grip on the real and on meaning. But what exactly must the relation be between a spirit blip and an extension? And how could metaphors, our empty words, fail to live up to the literal without the possibility of something to live up to? That is, without the possibility of Platonic or Cartesian spirit tokening to be the full-fledged "literal"?

What would a theory of language be that was Nietzschean, but without the nostalgia? The following essay is an attempt to sketch an account of truth and meaning which is not nostalgic, which recognizes that words are nothing but a sum of human relations, and that they could be nothing better in principle.

This essay is midrash on Davidson and Quine, with supplementation by Derrida, de Man, and Foucault. The general account of language, which will be described but not argued for in depth, is Davidson's and Quine's. The main additions to Davidson's sophistication of Quine's picture of language are two, as follows.

First, I try to incorporate some account of how power relations affect what is true. I do not pretend that this chapter is a full account of how "power" affects language and reality. Nor do I suppose that there is nothing going on but politics. What we say is affected by aesthetics, by laziness, and by other considerations besides power and interest.

Second, I argue that the *unanimous* "cultures," "(scientific) communities," and "forms of life" that have been assumed by analytic philosophy are deceptive fictions. Thus "community" does not support the philosophers' notion of language as a unified system of rules. Cultures and communities are more or less disunified coalitions of more or less disunified groups of more or less disunified individuals.

In the last sections, I show how metaphor and the infamous sorites are accommodated on this modified Davidsonian-Quinean account. Important metaphors show the relevance of power in an especially transparent way. Sorites paradoxes demonstrate the need for an account of truth that lets truth be adjudicated rather than fixed in advance. A struggle over literal truth illustrates in an especially transparent way how persuasion and power affect truth-values.

What Language Is Not: Some Premises for a Nietzsche Without Nostalgia

The Platonist picture of language and truth requires one of two possible foundations: first, a "magic language," as described below; and second, a natural segmentation of the world so naturally well-founded that any plausible language would have to have terms whose extensions matched that segmentation. The fundamental premises of a Davidsonian Nietzscheanism are the denial of the magic language and the denial of natural segmentation.

Magic Languages and Magic Arrows

To deny the possibility of a magic language is to say that no representing tokens have natural semantic natures. Nothing intrinsic to g-u-i-n-e-a-p-i-g gives that sequence of types an extension that includes my late pet Celeste. But thoughts and their components are no better than words. There is no "magic language of the mind" whose terms, by their very nature, fix an extension. A magic language is one whose terms directly and necessarily express Fregean senses. Fregean senses themselves, as objects before the mind, would constitute a magic language.

Alternative magical connectors between terms and things are the magical arrows presented in Wittgenstein's *Tractatus*. On a *Tractatus*-like account, there are no mental terms that by their own nature attach to an extension, but the mind can "intend" extensions for its thought-terms. Theories that call on such magical apparatus need to explain how a term can have magical bonds of affinity with items in its extension. There are too many relations among thoughts and objects, even if we restrict attention to causal relations, so a theory must privilege this spiritual-intentional grasp as a *magic* bond.

A magic language or arrow would allow a clear notion of literal truth independent of culture and convention. With a magic language of interior meanings, truths could be formulated privately, in thought, whether or not an external language existed.

The relevance of "politics," broadly construed, to extensions of terms follows from the denial of the separability of fact and value and the denial of the analytic-synthetic distinction. These denials in turn follow from the absence of a magic language and from the consequent absence of an epistemological given.

The absence of a magic language means that there is nothing more purely meaningful than words. No kind of representation can carry the purely factual component of a word and keep it separate from the "value" part of a word. That is, if facts and values were genuinely theoretically separable, there would have to be representations that were purely factual and representations that were purely valuational. But since all radical interpretation is *action* interpretation, and since action reflects belief and desire, all intentional tokenings express belief and desire. So there is no "purely factual" meaning.

The lack of an epistemological given follows from all representations being wordlike and nonmagic. As Davidson has often pointed out,[3] without a magic language whose terms carry meanings by their very nature, the determination of what sentences mean and what is true, that is what the facts are, rests on a single kind of data: what people say and when they say it. Thus, without a magic language, learning a language cannot be separated from learning about the world, and therefore the analytic cannot be separated in a principled way from the synthetic. If this is true, "contingencies" of what we say and might have said are likewise indistinguishable from contingencies about what the world is or could have been.

So changing language is continuous with changing the facts; and changing the facts is continuous with reevaluation.

Natural Fixation

A sort of Platonist truth that will sustain an invidious distinction between genuine truth and conventional construction can be constructed from the hypothesis that, while there are no "magic terms" whose very nature determines what they mean, there is a privileged "partition" of the world relative to which "labeling behavior" can be matched to natural kinds. Such a partition would consist in either a naturally given set of properties or a naturally determined array of "real essences." So although nothing about "dog" connects it to dogs, charity of translation dictates that the term fit the only candidate kind. With a naturally selected "partition," supposing that "partition" can be made sense of, only a limited number of extensions are available, so nature will supply enough purchase to get reference and truth and falsity.

I have argued against the possibility that objects whose natures were fixed by natural necessity could provide a determinate interpretation of terms. If there is an objective segmentation, it does not divide the world into people, medium-sized physical objects, or personal relations. In several discussions of sorites paradoxes, I have argued that, since it is arbitrary where we draw a line between a tall man and a man who is not tall, "tall" is not a genuine natural property.[4] That is, "the nature of things" does not select the extension of "tall." The presumption of such arguments is that, for objects whose essences are fixed by natural necessities, every thing will either be one of those objects or not, and this determination is made in advance. Thus, the intuition that, for instance, if one hair is removed from a non-bald man's head, the man will still be non-bald, conflicts with the supposition that baldness is a feature that is determined naturally, by the combination of nature and the meaning of the predicate "is bald." Exactly what we must say about such predications must wait until we have discussed metaphor, in the last section.

Arguments similar to the ones constructible for "tall" can be constructed for such predicates as "is a person," "is a table," "is alive," and virtually every other term for things and properties of the lived world. Only mathematical objects and perhaps microparticles have "essences" in the sense required to give nature a chance to determine a genuine segmentation into preferred objects and preferred groups.[5]

For instance, no *set* of entities is determined by "is a person." For borderline persons, often there is no fact of the matter about whether a given entity is a person or not. If there were, then nonpersons would be separated from persons by one-second intervals in developments from fertilized egg to child. Most importantly, we know that there is no "hidden fact" about whether a given entity is or is not tall. The inability to apply the predicate is not a lack of information.[6]

So, even if there were a privileged "segmentation" into properties and objects, nonetheless, persons, tables, and tall men could be neither parts of that segmentation nor definable in terms of parts of that segmentation. If medium-sized objects were so definable, the nature of things would show exactly which objects were persons, tables, and tall men. But no such general answers are available, and all such borderlines drawn in other terms are arbitrary.

I do not conclude that, since no sharp line distinguishes dogs from nondogs, there are no dogs. The only conclusion justified is that there are no dogs if being a dog is determined by natural necessities. The sorites paradoxes show, not that there are no dogs, but that dogs are not a natural kind, not a kind of object fixed by an array of natural necessities such that whether an object is or is not a dog is determined by the nature of things. What to say about borderline dogs must wait for the last section, after we have seen how metaphors can become true.

Sorites paradoxes show that, in the sense of "natural object" in which to be an object is fixed in advance by natural necessities, no medium-sized natural objects exist. Tables, heat, justice, persons, and reason have an existence and essence that rests in part on who says and does what and when they say and do it. These contingencies about what we say are not "merely verbal" but also "substantive decisions."[7]

Part of what it is to be a person is determined by culture, not by natural necessities. While nature has a lot to do with whether persons exist, no systematizable relation obtains between what is really happening, as a configuration of microparticles, and persons and other familiar objects.[8] Natural kinds and natural laws are relevant to the language of social existence and medium-sized objects, but their influence on what's what is mediated and diffuse.

"Social constitution" is not a simple derivation from a "cluster theory of reference" that makes the reference of a term a function of the beliefs associated with the term.[9] Cultural constitution involves more activities than just the cognitive. A concept is a complex of desires, actions, beliefs, things known, and every other social phenomenon that involves "propositional attitudes."

Such "socially constituted" entities cannot be "artifacts" of the culture, even though their reality and nature depend at least in part on contingencies about us and what we do. "Artifacts" are objects made from something. But the only objects not subject to sorites desecration are objects that could not supply the material for a construction. Only microparticles and mathematical objects could have sharply defined "good essences" that would provide well-defined sets as extensions. Hence, whether or not the world is or could be partitioned in an ontologically privileged way, the objects of the lived world are not constructed *from* anything.

For the languages in which we think and speak, as opposed to the mathematical constructs we might fantasize, the very items that are to be elements of sets are not given by the nature of things. There is no truth-value- or reference-bearing manifold prior to conceptualization, that is, prior to language or the languagelike. So there are no items of any kind waiting to be grouped into sets. Without a manifold of epistemologically given objects, no alternative "conceptual schemes" can be formulated as "constructions" or "artifacts."

If what we are to say in which circumstances is not fixed by nature, then by what is it fixed? We also do not want to say that what is the case is fixed by our wishes or by our mere decisions about what is to be called what. Let me begin to deal with this by two examples.

First, suppose our mothers and fathers had all applied the same term to both cats and dogs. Would cats and dogs have been the same kind of animal? It seems that nonnostalgic Nietzscheanism must say "yes," since what a thing is depends on this sort of training. But how do we construe the counterfactual question? We should not construe the question as being about what we would have judged if *our* parents had done this. We describe what is going on in the imagined situation in *our* (actual) terms. And in our terms, cats and dogs are two kinds of animal, not one. We, after all, believe that what we say is true. So, cats and dogs would have been two kinds. (However, we can recognize that nothing much hangs on what we say about cats and dogs being two kinds or one kind.) So the question must be about what other people would judge.

Second, consider the question "If there had been no cultures, would there have been dogs?" Of course there would have been. If no people existed, the world might well still be full of dogs. Once again, *we* are describing the situation. Now, would the statement "There are dogs" have been true? No, not if by that statement we meant that the sequence of shapes T-h-e-r-e- -a-r-e- -d-o-g-s would express a truth if it occurred in a situation with no culture. On the other hand, our statement, "There would have been dogs in that eventuality" is true of that way that things could have been.

So, finally, what does depend on us? Even though we are trained as we are, we have to recognize that that particular training is contingent:[10] we could have been trained otherwise, and then other things would have been true. Apart from other stage-setting, we are imagining that a single change in what we say has occurred, while everything else stays the same. Such alternative training is like learning French rather than learning English as babies; it might be "merely linguistic." But that kind of "different training" cannot be distinguished in a principled way from substantive differences of opinion.

How, then, do our terms end up being "fixed by the culture?" As a first, vague, and familiar approximation, let us say that the extensions of terms are fixed by "practices in a culture."[11]

A Practicing Culture

Well-armed, hostile native Americans have surrounded the Lone Ranger and Tonto.

> Lone Ranger: "It looks like we're in deep trouble, Tonto."
> Tonto: "What do you mean 'WE,' white man?"

Suppose we start with the following: What we mean depends on what we say, do, and write in which circumstances, and how what we say fits in with our lives and relations. But how does this work, and what are these "practices"? Well, practices involve, among other things, norms. Norms are what we do, as in "We don't bite other children, do we?"

Now, for a pattern to be a practice rather than a natural necessity, the practice must be "unnatural." The practice might not exist, and people have a tendency to fall away from it. So the practice continues to exist only in virtue of activities that keep it in existence. That is, norms and thus practices are enforced against some opposition. Since norms are enforced, and enforcement involves some kind of forcing, power relations are essential to the existence of practices, and so of cultures.

Anything cultural, then, requires at least token resistance on the part of at least the draftees to the culture, the children. The very unnatural nature of norms, then, assures that authority will always be resisted and that no culture will be unanimous. In this minimal sense, then, a culture is necessarily built on power and coercion. There is no pure, unanimous culture.

The only question about coercion and repression in a culture is how much there is of it and who gets to coerce whom, not whether the culture is repressive and coercive.

So why do we call these objects "dogs"? Well, because they are dogs. It is tempting to divide the question: what we call the dogs is up to us, we might say; but which things are really dogs is fixed by nature. The dogs are already there, waiting to be called something. But this view supposes that something like "choice of language" or "stipulation" is up to us. And stipulation requires both that what is merely linguistic can be separated from the factual and that a magic ur-language is available in which stipulations can be formulated. So what the dogs are is set by what we say and in what circumstances we say it. According to Davidson, the "circumstances" are not a world that we "organize." There are no pre-conceptual neutral terms in which we contemplate choices about whether this is a dog and this is not. Both the world "as artifact" and as "given" presuppose a given.

But who says which items the dogs are? Some want to call things dogs when they are not, and vice versa. Practices and norms prevent or inhibit such deviation. Now, the practices that constitute language can be matters of contention. Some speakers resist practices. Such speakers go along with practices only because they must think and talk, even though their language serves those who say what is what. Resisters and reluctant collaborators are, as it were, trapped in alien practices of thought and speech. Since there is no magic language, there is no private language, so people learn language by finding out what to say and when and where to say it. But learning these practices, like learning table manners, can require more or less punishment. Also, habits of applying terms can fit or fail to fit something that could be called interests, whether of classes or of genders.

Linguistic norms can serve or disserve interests. Two ways in which this can happen are as follows. First, entrenched connections of terms may serve or disserve interests in an application to a case. An obvious case is that of fetuses: If fetuses are properly called persons, then, given what we are inclined to say about persons, other practices will be brought to bear; for example, the women will be proscribed from disposing of their unborn. What are fetuses really?[12] Second, the underdetermination of what we say in a new case by previous practices guarantees the continued occurrence of opportunities to be pragmatic (by our ruling lights). Given a new borderline case, such as a fertilized egg in a divorce settlement, whether it is a property issue or a custody issue is a matter of moment. The issue turns on who is in charge. Of whose lives are these practices forms? Who gets to decide which forms of life shall exist?[13]

I want to assert two theses about interest and language: first, the language in which the underlings, those lacking power to decide, formulate beliefs and desires can work against their interests, and second, the underlings can be aware of this. Both of these theses are difficult to construe, given that we think and desire in a language. The underlings cannot have any clear idea of alternatives, since all clear ideas are formulated in a language, and the underlings have learned to think by learning to speak and think in the "masters' language." Thus the underlings cannot formulate the exact better pattern of what is said and when it is said before a change has been made, since that is a position from which they must think within "the language of the oppressor." (The oppressor has a similar problem of thinking his way out of his situation.)

In order to proceed, we need to purify ourselves of two nostalgic prejudices. For one, we need to avoid thinking of language and interests as premeditated. By the premises above, premeditation supposes that we would already have a language in which to contemplate how to talk in various situations. Also, we should be post-romantic about power relations and the fact that someone says what is what. Mom, after all, is our authority on many topics. Language, culture, and therefore thought disappear if everybody gets to decide for themselves (so to speak) what to say and do. A culture essentially consists in differential relations of authority and power.

By the very nature of norms, a culture is not a unified "we." This means not that some class or group must dominate others on all topics at all times but just that some class or group has to be authoritative on each occasion in which something comes up. Hence, "What do you mean 'WE'?" I think "culture" has to be construed much as we would construe "language." That is, given both the social nature of language and the fact that no two people have exactly the same pattern of what they say and when, "speaks the same language" must be construed holistically, with nothing guaranteed to be the same from speaker to speaker. If languages are artifacts of cultures, the same will hold true of "is in the same culture."

What happens when a coalition of groups has more than its fair share of power? "We" can serve the interests of those who have authority or who may be able to appropriate authority. "We" sometimes implicitly recruits the hearer, getting me to acquiesce in what we say and do. "We" sometimes innocently undermines the illusion that the hearer is included.[14] "We" is often a coercive or self-deceptive "we," a fiction that supposes a unanimity of interest and decision, that projects a hegemony into a unanimity.

What is hidden by our use of this term "culture"? I am in my culture along with people who watch *The Cosby Show* and care about the Red Sox. "Culture," especially in what some wishfully call "late capitalism," hides a diversity of incompatible groups. Has there ever been a culture that fit the "philosophical" notion of a culture? Or is this always a masking term, referring to a loose assortment of coexisting, overlapping, and interacting groups and individuals? Just as Davidson has suggested that the philosophical notion of a language does not fit anything real in the case of idiolects, so the same applies to "culture," given that a public, shared language is a function of culture.[15]

The important question, for those who want to rearrange or preserve the power distribution and the differential accommodation of various interests, is how much those games cohere, both within and among themselves? The picture of a typical "culture" now is both more hopeful, since the culture is too loose and diffuse to keep the alienated in line, and more ambiguous, since the alienated are also products of and thinkers within the culture from which they imagine themselves alienated.

Thus a disunified concept of culture shows how "we"s who are not heard as having authority, who do not get to decide what is said and when, still get to be heard, to a degree.[16] This is a tricky notion, given that there is no language helpfully more transparent in meaning than the one in which we speak, think, and write. The various "we"s themselves exist only in virtue of a somewhat ineffectively constituting culture. That is, the groups in a culture are constituted as groups by that culture, not by natural divisions alone.[17]

Why can't a hegemonic discourse keep people in line? On the one hand, we have something like reality interfering with a construction imposed by the dominant. The dominant ideology is supposed to be cognitive, a theory. On the other hand, and just as importantly, such a cultural "theory" is an organization of pleasure and pain, of what is valuable and despicable. But the "data" in this case, though not independent of the hegemonic conceptual scheme, yet resist it. Things just are not working out very well for the underclasses. Pleasure and pain, in practices, are like "observation" in science. There is no "pure data," but the world troubles "theory" nonetheless. Such accounts, in this broad sense of "account," can run afoul of the others who are subordinated.

So this hegemonic discourse is analogous to a kind of theory, and fails to fit the world of the underlings in the very way that Aristotelian physical concepts fail to fit the world, as Kuhn describes.[18] This is to say not that any general views are mistaken in their own terms but rather that the system as a whole gives bad results.

Likewise, if a culture's "theory" is always and at every level of representation a mix of value and fact, the "account" does not contain any "mistaken values" but gives bad results for the underlings. "Bad," but not in the sense that there is an alternative ready to be articulated. The underlings are faced with a bad result rather as Michelson and Morley were faced with a bad result in the measurement of the Earth's speed through the ether. They had no indication of what exactly was wrong—things just were not working out. When "theory" is generalized to be adequate to practices, an analogous "incommensurability" still must allow for differences in "success," defined, now, truly pragmatically.

In a sense, everyone's interests are being served. That is, culture is not *ignoring* alternatives to the dominant conception of "true interests"; rather, no thinkable alternative yet exists for culture. Similarly, on a Kuhnian account, Aristotelian physics did not *ignore* Newtonian principles; rather, the new conception did not exist as a thinkable alternative for the earlier system. The alleged would-be "interests" that are excluded from language games are thereby excluded from clear thought, as well.

But the very incoherence of the "culture" and of the "hegemony" leaves room for discontent. "Culture" comprises not a single discourse but a variety of competing attempts to say what is what. As it were, many regions of "what is to be said and when it is to be said" are up for grabs, or, more politely, under discussion. That "culture" is an oversimplification does not necessarily mean that no interests are in charge; it means only that the charge cannot be total. There is a kind of hegemonic "we," even though it is not a single, totally coherent "it." Not all of us are members of it, although most of us professors are on a subcommittee. (I mean "us professors.") The powers that be do get to say what is what, and this is not a bad thing, really. At least from our point of view.

Metaphors, Dogs, and Truth: Extending Terms to the Limits of Their Extensions

Metaphor

The application of figural speech is especially clearly underdetermined by practices and nature. The periphery called "metaphor" is a particularly revealing illustration of the Nietzschean-Davidsonian position on truth. Nietzsche's assimilation of predication to figuration is justified in this section.

What happens when one of us says something such as "Celeste is an eggplant"? In particular, is what we have said true? "True" means, we might start by saying, that the facts fit the rules of what is to be said. Now, the facts are the truth conditions of true sentences. By the rules of the language, "Celeste is an eggplant" is true if and only if Celeste is an eggplant. Notice that without a magic language, there are no facts as mediators fitting our language to the world.[19]

Any "conversational" or "rhetorical" rules of what is to be said are equally unhelpful. In appropriate circumstances, the rules would tell us to say "Celeste is an eggplant" if and only if Celeste is an eggplant. The "rules" that are enforced in determining what we say in what circumstances cannot be *linguistic* rules. The question of the proper application of a term, at least for public languages, must come down to this: Who is in charge here?[20]

When a term is being contested, as "human being" is now, "true" is out of place, as is "false." "Language," we might say, is being challenged. But there is no principled distinction between challenging language and challenging an account of what is the case, since without a magic language there is no principled distinction between the analytic and the synthetic.

The philosophers' notion of "true" and "false" seems (almost) to fit when the practices are (almost) completely fixed, so that one can (almost) tell in advance, for every possible object and kind of object, whether that object or kind is in the extension of the term.[21] A full-blown philosophers' language would have determinate extensions for its terms. Each term would determine a class, whatever happened and whatever the world turned out to be. We could expect efficient application of "true" and "false" in the case of totalities that we can figure out in advance, such as the numbers and the sets of grammatical sentences in first-order quantification theory. There, we can prepare for every eventuality, in those terms. But the objects in those theories are given in advance, and a language already exists for stating the possibilities.

In natural languages, however, the very items that are to be elements of sets are not given by the nature of things. There is no manifold prior to conceptualization, that is, prior to language. Without a manifold of given objects, no alternative "conceptual schemes" can be formulated as "constructions" or "artifacts."

So what about metaphor? Davidson is almost right, as always.[22] But he retains the redundant term "literal," by which the claim that Celeste is an eggplant is "literally" false. His analysis is that "Celeste is an eggplant" is proposed for other reasons than saying what is the case; it functions rather as a device to get us to see Celeste in a certain light, as an eggplant. And this analysis is right about many metaphorical uses of terms.

But Davidson has no basis deeper than thinking that Celeste is *not* an eggplant for rejecting the claim that Celeste is actually an eggplant, or for generally rejecting metaphors as literally true. In theory, there is no problem whatsoever with truth-definitions and true metaphors: the consequence that "Celeste is an eggplant" is true if and only if Celeste is an eggplant certainly goes through. Notice that "true" here functions solely as a kind of semantic linking concept between sentences and their truth conditions. And the truth conditions of "Celeste is an eggplant" are quite clear.

Davidson denies that Celeste is an eggplant because of such prior commitments as that all eggplants are vegetables. But this new case is not in principle different from the case of swans: people used to be disposed to say that all swans are white. Besides, guinea pigs are vegetables, in their way. Adjustments in other things we say have to be made in any case where we find unusual cases in which a predicate applies.

Davidson is surely right about many metaphorical speech acts. In this case, in fact, I called Celeste an eggplant not to inform anyone but to tease her. But sometimes our intention in saying such things as "Criminals are victims of their environment," "Fetuses are persons," or "Wildernesses have rights" is to *urge* that the statement be true. This verbal urging, especially when the topic matters, is not just observing the obvious, but it is not sharply distinguishable from literal predication, either.

Davidson's view gives no account of the drift from live to dead to literal. Most importantly, it gives no account of political struggle to make live metaphors literally true. What happens when ideas become literally thought-objects, or when thought can become literally clear? A theory that has abandoned culture as monolithic and coherent must account for the figural becoming literal.

Davidson notices that with no magic language, and so with nothing better than words, there is no place for metaphorical meanings or for literal meanings, as items communicated by words. Hence, any difference between the literal and metaphorical has to be a difference in "force," in how something is said rather than in what is said. So is "Celeste is an eggplant" true or false? False, but amusing. How about "victim" in "Jones is a victim of AIDS" or "Martha is a victim of a society's sexist pattern of child-rearing"? "Victim" is clearly being extended metaphorically, at least at this moment (except that to call something "metaphorical" is, in this context, itself a political act of derogation), but the metaphor may soon die. A lot hangs on this categorization. If you are a victim, you have been attacked unjustly, there is an attacker, and compensation is owed. Likewise, if alcoholism is an illness rather than a character defect, then treatment rather than condemnation is in order. If a strong desire for unusually frequent sexual activity is an addiction, then we should try to cure it. What are the "facts" of literally correct statements versus mere metaphor?

If truth is a matter of norms, of what "we" say and when we say it, and there is a struggle about what is to be said, truth is loose. We should not think that somehow the truth is already there, waiting to be discovered. "Is true" is like "is a turning point," "is the winning run," or "is a decisive play." Such concepts can only be applied retrospectively. The question of whether respect could be literally deep had to wait for the outcome of a cultural development. Remember that apart from the declaration "This is what we say here," nothing *makes* our application of "table" to a clear case of a table fit the literal meaning. That is what it is to be a table. Metaphorical application is continuous with "regular" application of predicates.[23] Exactly analogous remarks pertain to metonymy and other figures.

This is not to deny a difference between the figural and the literal but just to say that the difference is not a principled distinction of two kinds of use of language. We can still say that "Fred is a heroin addict" is more literal than "Fred is a sex addict." That a particular theoretical division is not supportable does not mean that the distinction, vague and loose though it may be as a normal part of a natural language, is not valuable.

If a term or a region of discourse is being struggled over, or perhaps just quarreled over, and if the sides are well matched, nothing avails us a concept of preexisting truth. No godlike presence, no Moira, has determined a winner in advance. No secret fix is in. At the moment, and at every moment, whether a controversial figural utterance is true or not depends on what happens. So, for now, the utterance is neither true nor false. Natural languages are unlike logical theories, since no natural language has a *natural* interpretation that assigns truth-values to all of its sentences.

The Solution to Sorites Problems

What should a Nietzschean-Davidsonian say about borderline dogs? Such cases are undetermined, neither dogs nor nondogs. Borderline dogs have much the same status as metaphorical applications of terms. Before such cases are in dispute, nothing is true about them. When such cases come under discussion or dispute, then they are decided one way or another.

The solution to the "logical" paradox of sorites arguments is equally simple. Given the above account of the extension of predicates to new cases, the crucial premise of the sorites paradox is that if a is a dog, and b differs from a only by magnitude c, then b is a dog. But this premise is false when we are applying predicates on borderlines. In disputed or disputable areas, the principle would be read as follows: If it were adjudicated that a is a dog, and b differs from a only by magnitude c, then it would be adjudicated that b is a dog.

But this is false of human adjudication. The next case may have different contestants, and the other side may have more persuasive arguments. "Precedent" is always subject to interpretation and thus is only an unpredictable constraint on new cases. Besides, the adjudicators may change, and "good reason" may subtly shift in its application. The important point, as I argue below, is that the unpredictability of adjudication does not mean that the application of "dog" in borderline cases is "unobjective."

The question of exactly which objects the dogs are has no answer now. The borderline cases have not yet been discussed, so their status must await actual adjudication. Also, there are no items that *must* be borderline, or that are guaranteed by the nature of the case always to be borderline.

In cases where our practices do not already strongly predispose us to make certain predications, we have no guarantee that we will decide one way or another. In most uncontested cases, we simply do not care, and consequently the cases are left undecided. Briefly, natural languages are not systems in the way philosophers have often imagined. In some ways, "logic" does not apply to a real language.

Borderline cases differ from metaphorical extensions of terms in that they seem to require something like continuous variation. But some extensions of terms may strike us as both metaphorical and borderline.[24] For instance, the "borders" in "borderline cases" are not actual boundaries, typically. Here I must gloss over numerous considerations: With a predicate such as "tall," exactly one dimension is relevant.[25] We are convinced that, even if it were important to be tall, there would be nothing "objective" about an arbitrary line between the tall and the nontall. Our conventions about "tall" make any such distinctions arbitrary.

Predicates determined by more than one feature or "dimension" differ from predicates like "tall" in several ways. First, for such predicates, more than one kind of case can be "marginal." A "borderline" case of personhood, for instance, may well be a metaphorical extension of "person." Certainly we could describe the extension of "addiction" to sexual desire equally well as a metaphor or as the extension of a vague borderline. Second, a predicate such as "person" or "bald" does not yield an ordering such that for all x and y, either x is more F than y, or y is more F than x, or x and y are equally F. Third, a multidimensional concept is subject to "factual changes" and "reevaluations" in many more ways than is a one-dimensional term, since a dimension may itself have disputed borderline cases.

Multidimensional concepts are concepts with many connections in our webs of belief and desire. For the same reason that a statement like "Bachelors are unmarried" seems merely verbal, so a decision that only those people six feet or more in height are tall seems purely verbal. For richer concepts, there is nothing "merely verbal" about an unpredetermined application of a predicate.

Since any predication always involves both facts and values, an adjudication of a borderline case can be "objective" even though competent speakers could disagree. Without a "unanimous culture," we have no single standard of the rational or the objective. Nothing more fundamental than the claim "This is what we do" governs adjudication. Consequently, the apparent "irrationality" of deciding that a is a person and b is not, even though a differs on dimension D only by g amount of dimension D, need not be "unobjective." So an actual adjudication that we agree on is a result that is more than "merely verbal."

For some predicates, the single-dimension ones, decisions are more arbitrary. For others, the decision is more substantive. For multidimensional predicates—predicates connected to many other determinations and judgments—a judgment, for instance, that this is a dog, can be objectively correct. That truth, though, is not already there in the position; it must await the outcome of a struggle or discussion. The borderline dogs are not already one or the other. Retrospectively, they will always have been dogs, if they are judged to be dogs. (Those future language-users are speaking from their position, using their language.)

Consider two stories about a borderline dog: Suppose that a special tax is levied on dogs but not on any other kind of animal. A ruling must be sought in a borderline case. Now, if nothing but the tax hangs on it, we may say the outcome is "merely verbal." That's all right, if "merely verbal" is not taken to contrast in a principled way with the "genuinely factual." For only a bit more involvement of "dogs" is needed to make this substantive:

If dogs have rights, and dog-ownership brings on special obligations to care and train and nurture, then there will be a more serious battle about a given borderline dog, with lawyers and scientific testimony. With more connections to belief and desire, the issue is what the real dogs are, not merely verbal, even though last year's clear nondog can be today's clear dog.

Truth

What is truth? At every point in these sequences of changes, the homophonic truth-definition holds, while disagreements about surrounding sentences continue. However, nothing about the truth of individual statements follows from the truth of the biconditionals. That is, we can continue our discussion of whether "Celeste is an eggplant" is true while agreeing that "Celeste is an eggplant" is true if and only if Celeste is an eggplant. In the same way, once baldness becomes punishable by death, we can discuss whether Fred is bald while agreeing that "'Fred is bald' is true if and only if Fred is bald. As liberal men, we would be eager to limit applications of "bald," of course.

A sequence of symbols is not just true *tout court*, but "true in L," where "L" names a language, with rules of application. What "nous" means depends on whether it is French or Greek. That "." is conjunction depends on semantic rules. Our question "What is truth?" thus is "What is it to have an L?" Of course any L is only as illuminating as its explicating language, which states what is what—so we can expect nothing much from application to our own case.

In a real language, the "L" is in dispute. That dispute is not about which meanings to attach to which words, but rather about what is to be said and when to say it.[26] All such disputes take place in a particular concrete situation that makes some predications suitable. That is, the particular pattern of interconnections that is taken as more or less fixed determines which further determinations of the not-yet-fixed serve which concerns.[27] Truth is "a mobile army of metaphors, . . . metaphors which are worn out and without sensuous power." More exactly, truth is the momentary balance of power in a many-sided war among various guerrilla bands.

▓▓▓▓▓▓

A Rabbinic Philosophy of Language

This paper reads a famous passage of the Talmud as an allegory of how we should think of truth, nature, and the contingent. In the light of an allegorical discussion of the passage, I derive a way to think of language and the world without adopting either the idealist's or the realist's fantasies. I argue that, on the view of language implicitly adopted by the Rabbis of the legend, what we say can be true even though it is not entirely dictated by nature.

It Is Not in Heaven

The Bava Mezia (the Middle Gate, a tractate in the order Nezikin, Damages) records the following well-known anecdote.[1] Let me say first that the rhetorical force of many passages in the Talmud is not entirely clear. That this passage appears in the Talmud does not mean that the apparent moral is official Jewish doctrine. Orthodox commentators differ on what to make of this passage.[2] The anecdote in question arises in the discussion of a Mishnah passage on wrong done by words, from a chapter on commercial harms and their rectification, from this tractate on transactions. (At the end of the story, the point is connected with verbal harms when Rabbi Akiba informs Rabbi Eliezer in a very delicate way that he [Eliezer] has been excommunicated.)

The case (on one interpretation) concerns a kind of stove made of sections that are put together. One such stove had become unclean, but was then broken apart. Now, a broken utensil is not subject to uncleanness, so the broken stove at that time was not unclean. But when the stove is reconstructed with fresh sand, is the (new?) stove now clean or unclean?[3] Rabbi Eliezer says clean; other Rabbis, led by Rabbi Yehoshuah, say no. The other Rabbis wind their arguments around Rabbi Eliezer like a snake; Rabbi Eliezer presents numerous replies. The majority go along with Rabbi Eliezer's opponents. Now, Rabbi Eliezer says, "If I am right, let the carob tree indicate it," and the carob tree does so. The majority reply, "You cannot prove by means of a carob tree." Rabbi Eliezer appeals to two further miracles, both of which occur and both of which are rejected by the majority Rabbis as not valid forms of argument. Finally, Rabbi Eliezer says, "If I am right, let a voice from heaven declare it." A heavenly voice[4] says, "Why are you disputing with Rabbi Eliezer? The halakhah is in accordance with him everywhere." Rabbi Yehoshuah rises to his feet and says, "It is not in heaven," quoting Deuteronomy 30:12.[5]

The Gemara goes on: "What does 'It is not in heaven' mean? . . . That the Torah was already given on Mount Sinai, and we do not pay attention to a voice, for you already wrote in the Torah at Mount Sinai: 'Incline after the majority.'" Sometime afterward, Rabbi Natan met Elijah[6] and said to him, "What did the Holy One, blessed be He, do at that time?" Elijah replied, "He smiled and said: 'My sons have defeated me, my sons have defeated me.'" The story goes on to say that the things Eliezer had declared clean were burnt, that Eliezer was then "excommunicated,"[7] that Akiba volunteered to break the news, and so on.

Let me make a couple of preliminary points. First, the argument that the Torah says one should incline after the majority rests on an appeal to Exodus 23:2, which says, "You shall not be after the majority for evil." The Mishnah on Sanhedrin procedures (Order Nezikin, Tractate Sanhedrin 2a) argues: "It is said, Thou shalt not follow a multitude to do evil. I infer that I am to be with them to do good." Behind this argument is the overall interpretive principle that the Torah, and so Exodus 23:2, is the word of God. So the words "to do evil" are a qualification that is not inserted accidentally.[8] Rabbinic interpretations are based on an understanding of the origins and purpose of the text.[9] The point is that these citations and applications of Torah are interpretations, not something transparently there in the text. It is not obvious that Exodus 23:2 contains a general instruction to follow the majority in rulings, and that the majority will be correct.

What Does This Have to Do with Language, Truth, and the World?

The question this passage raises for me addresses interpretation and truth. The Talmud is the record of interpretation of Torah, both written and oral, especially the imperative content of Torah, the halakhah. The important issues are how the truth conditions of commands in Scripture and Oral Torah apply in kinds of circumstances. For instance, what does it take to obey the command to say the evening prayer? How late can you be? The above passage suggests that the Rabbis regard such commands as binding but as having truth conditions that are either unknowable or indeterminate until the Rabbis make a judgment.

I will make five of points about the above anecdote.

1. The account of language and its relation to reality implicit in the passage is a position that is not a traditional realism nor yet an idealism. Truth is regarded as contingent on human decisions to some extent, but not thereby relative. Specifically, the account of language and truth implicit in the anecdote of the Stove of Aknai is a version of the accounts of language that one finds in Derrida, Davidson, Wittgenstein, and other naturalisms that renounce magic languages and a given. The Rabbis, at least in this anecdote, deny magic language and assert that their decisions can make truth.

Without magic languages, the extensions of terms are indeterminate in the sense that situations can arise in which everything about the previous application of the term, together with the facts, is insufficient to determine the truth-values of predications using the term. When we confront such situations, according to the Rabbis, we make a judgment. Those judgments are not necessitated by anything in the situation, but are not for that reason invalid. The result of such judgments is that the application decided upon is true. One could ask whether it was always true. Davidson and the Rabbis would say "Yes" but would add that no one could know that the judgment was true until the judging process took place. Davidson, however, might deny that a decision, even in a case where all the facts are in, does not guarantee truth. Wittgenstein, it seems to me, would agree with the Rabbis that the sentence is now true, but would reject the claim that the sentence had always been true. Derrida would regard the indeterminacy as giving grounds for saying that the very concept of truth does not apply in this case.

The general analogy between the Rabbis' argumentative context and our secular philosophical one is that the Torah plays the role of nature, the true beliefs we start with in confronting new situations that require judgment.[10] The Rabbis are us, the "interpreters of nature." The halakhic rulings of the Rabbis are our judgments of what is what. According to this anecdote, then, Torah, at any given time, underdetermines when predicates apply. In particular, Torah (both written and oral, up to the point in question) underdetermines whether this stove is unclean. So it looks as though part of what exists is either unfixed or unknowable even by God until the Rabbis (that is, we) decide what is what. But that does not mean that the question has no answer, or that there is no halakhah on the issue. It means only that no answer or halakhah is determined by anything else that is the case yet. The answer is decided by the Rabbis, according to the rules of the Torah itself. If we remember that the Rabbis declared unclean everything that Rabbi Eliezer had declared clean, it turns out that the Rabbis apply their judgment retroactively. Of course, what rules of interpretation are specified by the Torah is also subject to interpretation. Thus at no level whatsoever are the decisions dictated by something fixed for all possible situations.

The Oral Torah does not fill out the written Torah completely, since those to whom Torah has been passed can disagree. That Rabbi Eliezer has had the Oral Torah transmitted to him but can disagree with Rabbi Yehoshuah and be wrong, shows that no simple interpretive algorithm is available.

2. For many texts, one would think, we can in principle determine what the meaning is in principle by asking the author what was meant. If I write "Reading is obscene," you can, at one unproblematic level, tell whether I mean the practice or the city by asking me, by asking me to read the sentence aloud, or by biographical research. These practical possibilities of clarifying ambiguities and identifying truth conditions have led to the illusion that implicit in any act of speech or writing is a complete specification of the set of possible worlds meant. (Such miraculously complete words are the Greek *logoi* discussed below.)

In the case of the written Torah, no such illusion is sustainable. For the most important parts of the written Torah, nothing like the author's intention is available, on a historical account. On the Rabbis' account, an author's intention is available, but it is limited just as words backed by words are limited, as I will argue below. The author's intention cannot be complete in the sense of specifying a set of possible worlds, because the author's intentions are words, even if they are words of God.

According to modern scholarship, the most authoritative texts, the Pentateuch, have no author. (The Rabbis, of course, would ascribe both a human and a divine author to the text. But they still succeed in abstaining from the view that intentions are formulated in a magic language. For us moderns who are not Orthodox Jews, the lack of an author makes it easier to avoid the usual move to "the author's intention" as definitive and magical.) The standard text is the result of a series of redactions, adaptations, and compilations of hymns, genealogies, regulations, ancestor tales, folk stories, and traditions. At every stage, it seems, the "authors" more or less correctly regard themselves as transmitters. At every stage, the "authors" interpret, edit, and annotate. Thus there is no "authorial intention" to give the illusion of a foundation for the text.

3. Given that the Mishnah has been ruled to be "Oral Torah," and given that this very ruling is incorporated in the Mishnah, Torah is completed by the Rabbis. Oral Torah, which the Rabbis are adding to by providing interpretations, is Torah; so the historical composite of the rulings is a good part of Oral Torah. If the Rabbis determine rulings by their deity-independent majorities, even on the basis of the divine text, then the Rabbis are making Torah. The Rabbis' contribution is inseparable from the Divine contribution, since the Rabbis in effect get to say what the Divine Word means. The connection between Torah itself and the rulings, which are interpretations of Torah, becomes complex.[11] In fact, it begins to seem that there is no line between text and "ruling based on text." The very character of the text is shaped by the Rabbis' discussions, since what the text is about is shaped by how it is taken, and what texts it is taken together with. Thus the text and the whole procedure of deriving halakhah from the text is thoroughly mixed with interpretations, procedures, and practices that are underdetermined. At every point, the sequence of consonants could have been taken otherwise, in some sense. That is, cultural contingencies intrude at every level of the relation of the culture to the text.

The fact that interpretation—that is, contingency, what is not "forced by the text"—plays a role at every stage does not mean that Torah consists of nothing but interpretation. It means only that the "construction" put on the text cannot be separated out from the text itself. Of course, some Rabbinic interpretations are more loosely tied to the text while others are tightly tied,[12] just as some statements are more empirical that others, even though the contribution of experience in such statements cannot be separated out from the contribution of linguistic rules, according to Quine.[13]

But Torah *does* mean what the Rabbis say it does, in the precise sense that their determinations of truth conditions are correct. The "majority rule" criterion claims truth for the majority judgment. So those contingencies about what might have been are no more threatening to the correctness of their interpretation than the fact that we might have called paws hands threatens the truth of "Dogs have paws, not hands, on their front legs." The truth of "Four home runs were hit yesterday" is likewise not threatened by the fact that we could have decided that a ball is a home run if it would have gone over the fence had the fielder not interfered (i.e., great plays would be "goal-tending").

4. To continue this line of thought in a slightly different way: Suppose we take "logos" to mean a word in the sense of a very special word of thought, a Fregean sense. Such a word has every detail of application already worked out; it would be a David Lewis word, one that selects a set of possible objects in this and every other possible world. In the case at hand, a God issuing instructions about what is clean would speak *logoi* that contained, for every possible object and situation, a sorting of that object into the class of clean things or the class of unclean things. The Greco-Christian God, the God of the philosophers, is a God whose creative words in Genesis and elsewhere[14] are *logoi*. If God's words were *logoi*, cases not already covered in the original speech act would be an impossibility. God's sentences would be complete specifications of sets of possible worlds in which they were true. God would already have thought of the stove of Aknai, and His words would cover that precise case. The "meanings" in the Platonic sense, which God had in mind (in His thoughts/words) would have covered every possibility. (David Lewis thinks we talk like this but mean large disjunctions.)

The God of the Rabbis (and even more clearly, of the Hebrew Bible) has no such intentions and speaks no such words.[15] If we read the words that God says as like the words of regular people (so that "vayomer" means "and He said" in the sense of said *words*, the plain sense of the text), then God's thoughts are like our thoughts in that they are not complete in every detail.[16] When God says "Let there be light," He does not specify a set of possible worlds. It is important that God actually speaks. That is, if His intentions are not Platonic, then something is left indeterminate, no matter how complete an explanation God makes to Moses to be passed down, as long as that explanation is in words.

Such a conception does not make a finite God and does not make a finite Word of God. Even if God's words are infinitely detailed, that does not make them necessarily complete. If I say "Bless all the numbers," my words would express an infinite intention, but if I have not thought about the fractions, the irrationals, and the imaginary numbers, some items may be left out. Did I mean those, too, or not? If my words are mere words rather than *logoi*, there is no answer that is not implicit in my relations to the world. (And even infinitely rich relations over infinite time can still leave unanswered questions.) The word does not reach out and decide every possible application in advance.[17] The Platonist thinks I had to have meant one or the other; the Quinean and the Rabbis think no such thing. What we mean is what we say, and while language may be magic in some ways, it is not complete in this Platonic sense.

Words have been credited as magical in two ways. First, words are magic in the sense of having a *natural* (as opposed to conventional) relation of reference, a natural correspondence, to what the words name. God's words have such relations according to both the Greeks and the Rabbis. Second, words are magic in that their use somehow fixes their extension in every possible future case, leaving no question undecided. These latter are the magic properties of words that the Greeks and Christians seem to ascribe to divine words and that some philosophers ascribe to human words as well. (Wittgenstein is not one of these philosophers. In *Remarks on the Foundations of Mathematics*, Wittgenstein joins the Rabbis in insisting on words being words, and not magical Greek *logoi*.)

5. Heidegger apparently believes that the Christian conception of God incorporates the features of the Greek notion of Being, the infinitely detailed (neo-)Platonic mind in which every detail of every possible circumstance is already implicit. Every bit of reality, in the words of God's mind, is like the completion of pi, which is determinate all the way down

to the finest detail. Heidegger's view is also, apparently, that Western philosophy has adopted this onto-theo-logy, even when it has renounced God: That is, the laws of nature are Greek-God-like Platonic words. The nature that is brought about has every possibility already worked out.

Heidegger is wrong if he refers to a *Judeo*-Christian God. While Rabbinic Judaism is certainly monotheistic, and certainly regards God's Word as in itself creative (and thus like the *logos* in being magic in the sense of having a natural correspondence to what the word names), we have no reason to read the word of the philosophers, let alone the God of the philosophers, into the Word of the God of the Hebrew Bible or the Rabbinic discussion. It must be admitted that Heidegger is right about what happens when Judaism adopts the God of the philosophers via Maimonides' adaptation of Islamic meditation on the properties of the One God.

I claim that the Rabbis' procedure is essentially right, especially in the case of predications that are subject to sorites paradoxes: We need not conclude that, since there is no sharp or uncontroversial line between dogs and nondogs, therefore there are no dogs. The only justified conclusion is that there are no dogs if being a dog is determined by natural necessities. The sorites paradoxes show, not that there are no dogs, but that dogs are not a kind of object fixed by an array of natural necessities.

Nature is textlike in leaving some questions open, no matter how complete the laws of nature are, unless nature is a possible-world-specifying text with a yes or no answer to every possible question in every possible language. Just as there is no fact of the matter about whether Huckleberry Finn had an odd or even number of moles on his right arm, so, prior to a social decision, there is no fact of the matter about the precise point at which a fetus becomes a person or a nontall man becomes a tall man. "No fact" here means that nothing about the situation determines in other terms what is the case.

To make the parallel with texts more complete and precise: Just as a text, even an infinitely long one, may not say anything about certain topics, so nature (or God's demands) does not answer certain questions. Given an understanding of *Huckleberry Finn,* we can reasonably argue about whether Huck ever believed that it was his duty to return Jim to his owner. If the issue were to become important—because, for instance, we were writing a sequel or expanding certain chapters—then we could argue about what is the right way to go on. Once we had added the sequel or expanded the chapter, that would put further textlike constraints on further questions. Insisting that nature has decided every question because nature has decided some questions is not more appropriate than insisting that, because the number of consonants in a given chapter is definitely decided by the text, so are the questions about Huck's moral opinions.

Some things are not strictly determined by the text but are reasonable implications of the text (in some sense): we can reasonably infer that Huck has two fibulae, for example, even though it would not be impossible for these to be missing. Likewise, it is clear that using your word-processor as usual is prohibited on the Sabbath, though that is not said either in the Mishnah or the Gemara. Backing up your hard disk when it starts to crash just before sundown of the Sabbath and continuing to let the machine back up files during the first half-hour of the Sabbath would be a debatable case, since it would be a kind of emergency, and the machine is doing the work, sort of.

Most texts are unlike nature in that they clearly include some basic, definitive passages on their topics, even if we get to add on. The Torah is not one of these texts, which is what makes it so useful for my purposes: The Torah contains no ur-text; rather, it has revision and decision all the way down, just as we have with nature and the medium-sized objects of our world.

The reason why neither the laws of nature nor Torah cover in advance all the things to which we require answers is that in both cases, the objects, acts, and people the laws apply to are subject to continuous variation. They are not themselves precise objects, acts, and people. It cannot have escaped notice that the problem of the stove of Aknai is the philosophical problem of defining the unity of a single object. When is an object one thing? When is it one thing of this kind? As is well known, such questions have only formulaic answers, and these only in special cases. Numbers, geometrical objects, perhaps some well-governed physical particles have identity conditions that can be stated generally, conditions on being what they are and on being the same thing. For any medium-sized objects, borderline cases will always be constructible, as I have argued in numerous papers on sorites paradoxes.[18]

Granted, perhaps nature determines all the facts in some terms, just as the sequence of consonants does. The number of alephs in Genesis is there in the text in as firm a way as the positions of the microparticles may be in nature. But important things are left open once all such phenomena are known. In particular, the truth-values of many important utterances are left open by a total knowledge of all such phenomena. As I argued in the previous chapter, such questions as whether a person exists, whether an object is of a given kind, of whether an object is tall or just, are incompletely determined by nature.

Finally, one might ask why it is of any significance that some ancient Rabbis seem to have had views about language and truth that make truth contingent on social decision but nonetheless objective. It seems to me important because that is the correct view, and it is of some interest that the view is intuitive enough to fit with some people's intuitions about what truth requires. Briefly, the Rabbis show that the traditional notion of truth as fit between what propositions express and truth-makers in nature is not necessarily the only notion that fits deep intuitions. There are alternatives.

Deconstruction, Cleanth Brooks, and Self-Reference

In the 1940s, a group of critics known as the "New Critics" became influential in American literary criticism. The New Critics includes such figures as John Crowe Ransome and Cleanth Brooks. They approached texts as literary works of art, much as compositional analysis in the visual-art tradition approached paintings and sculpture. Texts were objects to be studied for their intrinsic features, apart from relations to the world and human edification. In particular, the referential aspects of literary works exterior to the text were deemed secondary considerations at best. For instance, in discussing a Donne poem, Brooks shows little interest in whether Donne's description of love was accurate with respect to seventeenth-century English lifestyles, but is fascinated by the ways that features of the poem function together. Brooks focuses particularly on the traditional aesthetic value of unity, and a constant theme in his analyses is showing how the various features of the art object as such exhibit surprising unities in the diversity of elements that constitute a text. Brooks is especially interested in the aesthetic phenomenon of making a conceptual unity out of a prima facie paradox, as in the examples in his essay "The Language of Paradox."

One particular compositional feature contributing to this holding-together fascinated Brooks: the way the poem itself instantiated the theme of the poem. Self-referentiality as an aesthetic device was not new in literature, but to my mind, Brooks was among the first to use appeals to self-referentiality in very persuasive and deep ways, especially in *The Well*

Wrought Urn, in order to demonstrate the sort of aesthetic unity that appealed to him.

The very notion of taking the poem itself as an art object opens questions about the reference of a literary art object. Since Brooks's interest was in the text as such, he and the New Critics rediscovered that interpretations that treated the text as self-referential were illuminating. The interest in the text itself led to explorations of the possibility that the figures and structural features of the literary works constituted systems of thought, much like theories. The examination of literary productions of various sizes, from individual poems to life works, produced something plausibly like such literary-world-systems in the verbal objects that constituted the literary texts.

Deconstruction, I will argue, continues the text-as-text work of Brooks and the New Critics. However, the deconstructionist critic looks for ways in which partial systems fail of coherence and completeness. That is, both Brooks and the deconstructionist critics examine "systems" implicit in literary works, but they seek different results. The literary deconstructionists' aesthetic found contradictions and other incoherencies under a facade of unity in works of literary art. Thus, the aesthetic of unification of diversity is challenged by an aesthetic of tension between a sought unity and the incoherencies being masked. From the point of view of this chapter, that difference conceals a broad agreement in the conceptions of language and texts.

Brooks and deconstructionists share a concern for the text as such. But they also, I argue below, share a conception of language that substantially departs from the tradition both in literary criticism and in philosophy of language. Roughly speaking, both kinds of critic are committed to the view that language is as illuminating as forms of meaning get; that there are no meanings communicated by language that are more directly meaningful than language itself. This resemblance is striking enough to justify regarding deconstructionist criticism as more closely allied to Brooks and New Criticism than to any other style of literary criticism. That is, while it is true that deconstructionists depart substantially from the New Critical aesthetic of unifying implicit "theories," the underlying conception of what literary criticism is working on is the same, and is, in literature, the innovation of the New Critics.

Once one starts to think of texts as aesthetic objects, one realizes that the components of texts—words and sentences—have a dual nature. A word indicates something other than itself while also being a thing among those others, and so can itself be designated by a word. When it happens that a word or text is the object of its own pointing, the word or text is self-referential.

The possibility of self-referential words and other signs illuminates the nature of systems of concepts both in mathematical logic and in literary theory. The mathematical results are the object of much dark reference in semi-popular writing on deconstruction. Self-reference is indeed the device by which the famous paradoxes as well as the fundamental results of twentieth-century mathematical logic have been achieved. This is not to say that self-reference *accounts* for the phenomena, but rather that the phenomena turn out to be demonstrable by the use of self-reference, at least in the earliest formulations of the proofs. The original proofs of the famous metatheorems depend on criteria of interpretation that expand self-reference, so that texts that are not obviously self-referential turn out to be so on interpretation.

Deconstructive literary theory uses terms like "unreadability" and "undecidability" to describe features of literary texts thought to be analogous to mathematical undecidability.[1] It supports this figural extension of mathematical concepts by considerations about figuration, narrative, and other aspects of texts that have been taken to constitute systems. The explicit appeal to self-reference supports more intuitive deconstructive demonstrations, for particular texts, of the lack of meaning-fixing foundation, lack of systematic coherence of metaphors and imagery, and lack of narrative coherence.

"Self-reference" in literature and literary criticism has a long history. A text can talk about itself specifically, as a sonnet may call itself "this paltry tribute," or about texts generally, as when Plato condemns writing; or it can "break frame" and comment on its own fictionality, as does Calvino's *If on a Winter's Night a Traveler*. Perhaps most famously, Pope's *Essay on Criticism* partially consists of lines such as "A needless Alexandrine ends the song, / That, like a wounded snake, drags its slow length along."[2] Much self-reference of interest to critics is less transparent. The text has a "surface" reading that makes it about something other than textuality, poetry-writing, or poems. But the subtle reader sees that it is really about these very topics, that it is self-referential. This sort of allegorical reading of poems is a tradition among Cleanth Brooks and his colleagues, for instance.

"Surprising," "non-surface," allegorical self-reference is also a specialty of deconstructive critics such as Geoffrey Hartman and Paul de Man.

The metaphorical extensions of the metamathematical notions of self-reference, undecidability, and incompleteness by deconstructive literary theorists are defensible, but in rather limited ways. Briefly, mathematics is a best case, with a clear notion of and criterion for incoherence and a completely syntactically transparent language. If mathematical theories of a certain richness are incomplete, then the plausibility of the idea that theories generally are probably complete is undermined. Ordinary language and the theories implicit in ordinary language would be expected to be even less likely to be complete. Of course, just as in mathematics, restricted theories can be complete, so, perhaps, very simple fragments of ordinary language might be complete and coherent as well, except for their role within the larger theory of which they are in fact a part. What the metamathematical results show is that one can expect to find incoherence in rich, that is, global, theories.

Literary theory of the New Critical and deconstructive kind, like metamathematics, treats texts as objects and focuses on intrinsic features of texts. Specifically literary-aesthetic rather than mathematical arguments reach analogous results because of analogous phenomena. That is, the famous paradoxes and metatheorems support the results of deconstructive literary theory in the negative sense that the mathematical systems investigated by metamathematics are best cases—if they lack completeness, then nothing better could be expected of less organized systems such as systems of tropes. Both mathematical and literary texts lack a magic-language anchor to prevent self-referential interpretations, and in both cases those self-referential interpretations reveal a failure in principle of certain formal dreams.

The difficulty in applying metamathematical results in any direct way to literary texts is that the notions of coherence, contradiction, demonstration, and theory, among others, are much broader, vaguer, and looser in literature and indeed in language generally than in mathematics. So the deconstructor needs to do distinctively literary work, using the looser and broader demonstrations that his subject matter requires.

Underlying the literary arguments about grounding and self-reference, I think, is an attempt to work out the consequences of the widespread literary insight that words are the fundamental meaningful items.

Literary studies, after all, studies words qua words. The thought that the words are what matters, not something behind or above them, is a characteristic motif of critical writing. This insight is expressed famously in Brooks's denial that paraphrase of a poem is possible.

Literary theory is not a kind of language but rather a rhetorical take on a text, the "literary reading." We can read the Bible, the *Iliad*, or the Constitution as literature. So literature is continuous with other kinds of discourse. Part of what is special about "literary reading" is that it makes alternative rhetorical forces stand out more obviously. Thus, many conclusions in literary theory (the philosophy of literature) apply to the philosophy of language generally.

I proceed by three stages in the following discussion.

First, for readers who need an informal explanation of the metamathematical results themselves, I have included a section sketching some of the metatheorems, including Alfred Tarski's result and Kurt Gödel's completeness and incompleteness results. This section may be skipped by anyone already familiar with these famous metatheorems and by anyone offended by presentations of results without proofs.

Second, I describe a line of literary argument that removes the privilege of the "literal," shows a kind of multiple reference Derrida calls "dissemination," and provides a framework for establishing how and why languages and texts may fail to form systems. The argument that constitutes the second part of the overall argument of this chapter contains two premises, as follows.

A. One premise is Brooks's insight that works of literature cannot be paraphrased in a way that captures what they say. I argue that this in effect eliminates meanings in the magic-language sense and makes words the most fundamental level of representation. So the unparaphrasability premise undoes the hierarchy of literal base-meaning and figural extended meaning in literary works. Thus the various "figural" readings of a text will be correct readings, including the reading that makes the text a figure for itself or for writing. The impossibility of paraphrase eliminates an ideal realm of meanings, nonlanguagelike presences standing behind texts, which could fix the kinds of analogies and resemblances that arise among words and texts and thus restrict figuration and allegory. Thus, too, the coherence and systematicity that such an ideal realm could impose on language is unavailable.

B. The other premise, needed for the argument throughout, is that the objects of our world come "theory laden," that is, language laden. The natural world of objects, like an ideal realm of meanings, is a source that could impose its structure in order to privilege the "literal," keep the wanderings of metaphorical extension of reference within the bounds of natural analogies, and force coherence on language and texts. But if the objects of our world are already theory laden, then, to put the matter in a Davidsonian way, there is no "given," no uninterpreted, prelinguistic presentation of the world. This is implicit in the idea that language is the bottom level of representation. If the best we can do in giving the truth conditions of "Fred is a frog" is to say that "'Fred is a frog' is true if and only if Fred is a frog," then contingencies of our language are contingencies of the world. "Nature," then, cannot provide a privileged literal meaning that prohibits self-reference by itself being a unified system. So "nature" cannot control figuration, and cannot guarantee that the language or textual system can or does form a single complete and coherent system.

From premises A and B it follows that language is constrained neither by the ideal realm of senses nor by the world of natural objects. The inadequacy of constraint to a coherent system is manifest in three related failures: failure to establish a privileged meaning for terms; failure to restrict the wanderings of figuration; and failure to guarantee coherence in a total system.

This first stage of the argument establishes that there is nothing special about literature that could save literary language from the restricted application of metamathematical results described above. That is, nothing fixes literary reference in a way that makes reference helpfully more externally determined in literature than in mathematics. Literature and mathematics alike, for instance, necessarily lend themselves to allegorical or metaphorical mappings.

The argument moves from considerations about "disseminations" to the question of the coherence and completeness of the formal structures that have been alleged to characterize texts and language. The two external sources that would guarantee that texts and languages should be complete, coherent systems fail. Without the guarantee, one can hold either that interpretations of texts form internally coherent systems or that they cannot do so. I discuss some of the ways Paul de Man has supported the thesis that textual systems are incomplete.

The second stage of the argument demonstrates that the thesis that texts can and will usually fail to form coherent complete conceptual totalities is made plausible by the metamathematical results. The arguments leading to and using self-reference are as well-founded in literary theory as in mathematics. Thus the failure of closure and completeness illuminated by self-reference shows something important about literature and human language generally.

The units of this literary allegory of mathematical logic are rather poorly defined. Roughly, texts, single works, can be construed as like a mathematical theory. In fact, as I will eventually conclude, nothing is quite like a theory in the mathematical sense of a set of sentences. The larger units of language—such as an oeuvre, a discourse, and a culture's whole set of language games—correspond for some purposes to a logical language. Now, since nothing really fits "theory" and nothing really fits "language" in the logical sense, all that the distinction between text, discourse, and language will amount to is different degrees of diversity of authorship, beliefs, regularities of language use, and so on. Thus I will generally use these terms interchangeably.

The idea of applying mathematical results to literary theory has usually been taken backwards: For metatheorems to apply to literary texts, it is thought, such texts need to be enough like mathematical languages that the mathematical results will apply. But literary texts lack such features as being closed under logical consequence. "Consequence" itself in ordinary language and in literature is vague and broad and not precisely definable. "Coherence" is thus a much looser and richer notion in language and literature than in metamathematics.

The metatheorems in question, as noted above, are negative—they are claims that completeness and coherence of various kinds are lacking. Relative to a literary text, a mathematical theory is a "best case." If incompleteness, groundlessness,[3] and lack of system occurs in the formal languages of mathematics, then we have no hope that a perfect and complete system could underlie a literary work. Whether this negative result from mathematics holds of literature depends on whether something saves literary language from the Tarski paradox and the incompleteness results.

To be saved from Tarski, literary language needs to be able to isolate self-reference and thus to isolate the lack of groundedness that self-reference indicates. That is, the global collapse demonstrated by Tarski holds only for systems that are closed under logical consequence. Since literary texts and languages are surely not systems in that sense, it could be thought that the self-referential problem areas resulting from the universality of the truth predicate could be isolated and thus restricted to some odd areas.

Similarly, one could claim that the mathematical incompleteness results hold because mathematical theories are not tied to "intentions" or to real-world objects and thus allow arbitrary assignments of expressions as "meanings" of numerals.

The third stage of the argument demonstrates that exactly those special features of literary languages are lacking. Self-reference and lack of groundedness are ubiquitous, and cannot be isolated precisely because constraints on reference either from intentional idealities or from the natural world are lacking for literary texts. That is, the dislodgment of literary reference from ties to intentions or to natural objects shows both that Tarski's discussion applies to natural language and that Gödel's incompleteness results undermine the possibility of total systems in literary texts.

A Sketch of Some Metatheorems: The Use of Self-Reference in Metamathematics

The question of reference in mathematical arguments can be addressed in two ways. The first way takes terms to have references by "definition," stipulation, or "intended interpretation." In the first subsection below, I offer some reasons why this postpones questions rather than answering them. The second way, adopted whenever reference is an issue, takes the terms of a mathematical discourse to refer to a set of objects just in case those objects model that discourse. By the Skolem-Loewenheim Theorem, there will be multiple equally good assignments of references to mathematical terms. Among those multiple references, for interesting languages, are the very expressions themselves. So self-reference is unavoidable.

The semantic paradoxes and the set-theoretic paradoxes reveal the groundlessness of reference most clearly.[4] Tarski argued against the very possibility of a consistent use of "true" for languages that contain their own metalanguage: "A characteristic feature of colloquial language . . . is its universality. . . . These antinomies seem to provide a proof that every language which is universal in the above sense, and for which the normal laws of logic hold, must be inconsistent."⁵ This chapter argues that Tarski is deeply right.

Numerous objections have been leveled against this remark about natural languages. Natural languages are not going to collapse under the impact of isolated contradictions, because the principle needed for such collapse, that a theory contains all logical consequences of its components, does not apply to texts or discourses of natural languages. We can tolerate inconsistency in our beliefs precisely because we do not believe the consequences of what we believe. So, someone might argue, since many portions of our language are all right, and we are not always talking about our very sentences, the untoward consequences of taking our truth predicate to be a theory can be ignored. We can still use that predicate when talking about truth and falsity, without worrying about the problem cases.

I will argue that both the Tarski paradox and the Gödel incompleteness result do apply to literary language. Such language is in fact ungrounded in exactly the ways needed to upset attempts to isolate groundlessness and self-reference. Groundlessness is in principle everywhere. Nonstandard yet legitimate interpretation, including self-reference, is ubiquitous, and the lack of groundedness that such nonstandard interpretation reveals likewise infects every part of language.

Stipulation

The familiar solutions for the semantic and set-theoretic paradoxes restrict self-reference by constructing hierarchies of levels of objects and levels of languages with terms denoting those objects. My problem with these solutions, construed as accounts of how actual languages, formal or not, can avoid paradox, is that the notion of "setting up" such a language requires a background language (in which the stipulations are made) whose coherence, univocity, and lack of capacity for metaphor has to be assumed. But if Tarski is right, those metalanguages, for example, the English and German of my logic books, are corrupt.

The hierarchies designed to solve the semantic paradoxes assume that the references of terms and predicates of languages are subject to acts of will or fiat, what is called "stipulation." In order to avoid the semantic paradoxes, a hierarchy of languages is constructed so that the place of a language in the hierarchy is defined by the level of objects referred to by terms in the language.[6] Hence the Liar Paradox, "The sentence on this page in quotation marks is false," cannot be formulated in any language that is a member of such a hierarchy, because that language is semantically fixed such that there can be no reference at level n to objects at level n.[7]

Formally, "semantic fixing" is just the selection of a mathematical function.[8] Reference relations are defined as functions from expressions to objects, so the hierarchy exists in virtue of being a mathematical structure, a complex set. Consequently, the solution to the paradoxes via hierarchies says that a mathematical structure exists that could be the reference structure of a language without paradox.

But how do we bring it about that any actual language, whether mathematical or "natural," embodies such a structure? The sincere promises of the stipulators take place in a language subject to interpretation, to a determination of what function is in fact the reference function for that language. Stipulation therefore fixes only a given function relative to a metalanguage in which the references of terms are already fixed.

Appeals to "intended interpretation" are essentially appeals to another background language in order to fix which function is the reference function for the language. If the intentions that determine "intended interpretation" are semantically structured, then every difficulty with interpretation of languages obtains with the interpretation of intentions. It makes no essential difference even if intentions take the form of spirit-stuff notation. The only kind of intention that could absolutely and in a non–question-begging way *determine* which function we have in mind would be an intention formulated in a magic language of thought whose tokens fix interpretation by their very essence, as Aristotelian *nous* tokens do. That is, if we lack a given, it is not much help to be told that "By 'plus' I mean plus."

Models and Reference

Failing a magic spiritual grasp of essence, the criterion for reference or "aboutness" of a mathematical discourse must be a formalization of the "fit" of a discourse with what it is about. This mathematical concept of "aboutness" or "fit" is defined by model theory.

Very roughly,[9] model theory decrees that an interpretation of a language is an assignment of entities to terms and classes of such entities to predicates. A "theory," as a mathematical term of art, is some subset of the sentences of a language. A model of a theory is an interpretation in which all the sentences of the theory are true (relative to a metatheory). A model is given in a metalanguage, so that *which* objects are in question is only as clear and unproblematic as the referents of terms in the metalanguage.

The model-theoretic notion of aboutness amounts to a precise account of the criterion that a theory is about what it fits. A theory is about whatever the theory would be true of. By the Skolem-Loewenheim Theorem, more than one array of objects can be a model of any theory. That is, the criterion of "fit" will not select a single referent for a given theory. Thus, the references of terms of a theory are always relative to a choice of interpretation, with no particular assignment privileged by "best fit." Similar remarks apply to the terms of the language in which the interpretation takes place. By the criterion of fit, such "regress to a background language," and the consequent expansion of what can refer to what, relative to alternative choices, cannot stop with a founding language whose references shine through transparent terms.

This multiplication of what refers to what is made plausible by the "abstract" character of mathematical discourse, which isolates it from sensation and from likely candidates for causally fixed references for mathematical singular terms. For mathematical aboutness, as both Paul Benacerraf and Hilary Putnam have pointed out, all that matters is the structure.[10]

The Completeness and Incompleteness Results

Given this account of what it takes for a theory to be about a subject matter, it turns out that mathematical theories of a certain expressive richness are unavoidably about themselves, among other subject matters. This necessary self-reference can be used to show a kind of completeness and a kind of incompleteness.

First, the completeness: The Gödel completeness theorem for first-order functional calculus is a proof that the consistency-testing procedures of the first-order functional calculus will show a set of sentences to be consistent if and only if that set of sentences in fact has a model, a way of understanding the terms and predicates according to which all the sentences in the set are true. Theorems, sentences whose negations test *in*consistent, thus correspond to logical truths, sentences true in all models.

The proof that this is the case works by taking the expressions generated in the consistency proof as the objects to which those very terms in the proof refer and generating extensions of predicates from occurrences of sentences in the consistency proof. The result is that the proof sequence itself provides a model of the set of sentences being tested for consistency. The expressions of the language themselves constitute a domain of objects for that very language of exactly the right number of items to go with the predicates and terms required by the consistency proof.

Second, the incompleteness: The Gödel completeness result showed that theoremhood coincides with logical truth and, more generally, that the results of syntactic symbol manipulation correspond with semantic notions. "Logical truth" differs formally from ordinary truth in that for many sentences, neither they nor their negations are logical truths. In richer languages, ones "adequate for arithmetic,"[11] one might hope to establish that theoremhood coincides with arithmetical truth. Arithmetical truth, though, is like ordinary truth, since we suppose that for any arithmetical sentence, either it or its negation is arithmetically true. "Completeness" for languages adequate for arithmetic means that proofs exist for each of the truths of arithmetic, that is, half the sentences formulable in the system.[12]

In a theory adequate for arithmetic, an interpretation of the numerical terms can be given such that, under that interpretation, some numerals also refer to expressions themselves. A mathematical relation can then be defined that holds between numbers A and B, systematically paired with expressions a and b, just in case a is a consequence of expression b. That relation "represents" consequence. The condition of being adequate for arithmetic guarantees that the language will have predicates that represent the logical-consequence relation and thus represent "_____ is a proof" and the open sentence "There exists a proof of _____."[13] So the numerical terms really mean expressions as well as numbers. Systematically, the numerical relations obtain if and only if the relationships among expressions hold; hence the expression means each one, equally.[14]

Gödel's proof shows that, for any axiomatization of such a theory, sentences expressing their own unprovability from those axioms can be expressed.[15] Such sentences are unprovable in that axiomatization. Given that the theory contains only truths about arithmetic, such sentences must be true. For any system whatsoever, therefore, some arithmetical truths are unprovable within that system.

Thus the paradoxical self-referential sentences are unavoidable, in the sense that their existence is guaranteed by the mathematics. As long as the mathematical relations exist and the relations among expressions obtain, the mathematical language will contain these sentences.

Self-reference for such languages, then, is not an accident that can be repaired by ruling out such sentences, because the subject matter of the sentences, by the very criterion that determines what sentences are about, must also be those sentences. To put things differently: The possibility of a language's turning back on itself is built into the expressive powers of the language. The lack of completeness with consistency, the lack of total systematization, depends on such possibilities of self-reference.

. . . And Literature?

The argument for the relevance of mathematical results to claims about the existence and significance of ungroundedness and unavoidable self-reference in literature requires that some apparent disanalogies between literature and mathematics be shown not to exist or not to matter.

Literary theory treats texts from natural languages whose approximation to "systematization," "proof procedures," and "isomorphisms" are extrapolations from social practices of what is said and when it is said. Such social practices reflect power relations, probabilistic organisms, and so forth. To say the least, any analogues of mathematical notions are not so sharply defined as in mathematics. Thus, for instance, the correspondences (e.g., between characters and sets of virtues and vices) that justify construing a tale as an allegory may not be analyzable as mappings of term to entity and predicate to class. Mathematical languages are formalizations of such natural languages, which formalizations can be imagined to involve perfectly regular speakers talking about a perfectly intelligible, well-defined subject matter.

I need to defend applications of two metamathematical results to natural language and literature: the Tarski result and the incompleteness result. In the application of the Tarski result, the difficulty is that the dire consequences seem only to hold for formal languages. In the incompleteness result, the argument seems to work only if reference is determined for natural languages in much the way it is for mathematical languages. Both difficulties are dealt with by the same considerations about reference.

First, with respect to the application of Tarski's remarks, it seems that the nonformality of natural languages would protect natural-language texts from the consequences that mathematical theories suffer from the existence of contradictions. In nonformal-language texts, where there is no demand for closure under logical consequence, perhaps contradictions need not ruin an entire text. A contradiction need affect only the claims with which it is directly involved. In fact, the existence of hidden contradictions is the most usual state for a set of beliefs, construed as a text.

For protection from Tarskian groundlessness, natural languages would need two things: first, a way of isolating the effects of contradictions that arise from the universality of the language, and second, a way to keep control of what is self-referential, so that stable, well-defined areas can be maintained that are clearly not about themselves or about discourse. More generally, natural languages need a coherently traceable reference relation.

The isolation of contradictory elements seems possible because parts of natural languages seem to be tied to intended senses and to natural referents. Thus these parts seem to be true and false independently of relationships with the contradictory sentences. For example, the fact that "My hair is blue" follows from a contradiction that I happen to believe does not mean that "My hair is blue" is included in the text of my beliefs. Real belief is just not closed under logical consequence, unlike formal theories. Contradiction does not generate global incoherence in systems of belief, as it does in formal theories.

Intended senses and natural referents would also keep self-reference in control, since they themselves are clearly not self-referential, being well-grounded in the world and in concepts. Furthermore, they would provide natural grounds with which to maintain coherence in trails of reference.[16] So the dire effects of Tarski's strictures on universality need not undermine an author's text or a language, a culture's text, if reference and sense can be tied to unified and clear grounds in intentional idealities or natural objects.

Second, with respect to the incompleteness results, the formality of mathematical languages seems to make application direct. While the application of a positive result, such as a completeness result, would require showing that natural languages were, despite appearances, relevantly like the formalization, the application of a negative result requires no such adherence to a form. That is, if incompleteness and lack of system infect even the formalization, so also must natural languages lack totality, unless some natural-language property forces the devices in the formalization to fail.

Such a natural property would be a tie to referents that blocked the self-reference arguments by privileging the "real meaning" and "real referents." Natural-language texts, it might be argued, are not incomplete since they really do not talk about themselves, except in rare cases. Both the senses of natural-language terms and the world to which natural languages apply include more than structure, it might be held. Unlike mathematical languages, natural languages seem to have intentional meanings and ontologically privileged designations for many of their terms and predicates. Thus their meaning might seem hierarchical, stable, and coherently whole because of the stability and reality both of the idealities themselves and of the referential ties of concepts to the real world with its preconceptual relationships and properties.

To apply Tarski and Gödel to literary texts, then, we must establish that literary texts are not sufficiently tied to ideal meanings or independent real-world referents and that therefore self-referential outbreaks of this ungrounding can always be expected. Without those ties, the ability to keep self-reference isolated and to maintain clear areas where none of the metalinguistic effects can undermine groundedness would be destroyed, since nonrelationally determined senses and referents are the only way to preserve isolation and prevent self-referential interpretations from making paradox in new places. Thus Tarski's criticism of natural languages, though perhaps not borne out in detail, given that natural languages are not *closed* under logical consequence, is borne out in spirit.

Weakening the apparent privilege of the natural tie of natural language to ideal senses and natural referents is essential to making the reference of terms of natural language texts multiple so that texts can generally be read as self-referential and thus necessarily incompletable and resistant to total systematization.

Even if we had some reason to accept a kind of given without a magic language—that is, if we had a causal theory of reference that determined real reference by natural relations between given physical objects and words —the problem would not be much improved. Any causal constraints on reference are weakened by the remoteness of the topics of conversation from objects with plausible essences by nature. A theory that holds that there are "essences by nature" ascribes to entities criteria of existence (i.e., a line between accidental, survivable change and essential change) in virtue of their own nature. But "essences" amount to natural necessities, and natural necessities are natural laws. So the objects that have essences are the microparticles of physics, not the medium-sized physical things of the lived world. Without essences, there cannot be the sort of strict natural kinds of well-defined objects that could determine well-defined sets. In view of considerations about borderline cases such as those I raise in "Reference and Vagueness," the medium-sized objects of the world would turn out to be fictions whose details differ within and among different cultures. Thus, "medium-sized objects" would be vague constructs even if a causal theory of reference were true at some level. This means that the world of objects cannot function as independent sources to fix references, at least for literary works, which tend to deal with persons, horses, houses, and other kinds of objects that are not candidates for fundamental particles of physics.[17]

Numerous *metaphysical* arguments for a loosening of the "natural" reference relation have been devised, for instance by Quine, Davidson, and Derrida.[18] But I would propose an argument with a clearer connection to literary concerns that gives a better explanation of why important literary theorists began to think in different ways about language and meaning. The next four subsections present this argument.

The argument uses two strategies. First, Cleanth Brooks's thesis in "The Heresy of Paraphrase" and other essays in *The Well Wrought Urn* is shown to entail the thesis that concepts in the philosophical sense do not exist. Thus, such concepts impose no constraints upon what words and texts can mean. Second, objects are not given, and therefore are not the same or different in kind by virtue of nature alone. Thus nature does not fix the way things can mean, either. This is not to deny that there is more to the world than words, but rather to claim that the world of medium-sized objects we live in is always already meaningful, that is, contaminated with the linguistic. Thus, I argue, "natural analogy" and "natural referents," since they are not outside language, cannot provide systematic limits on allegory and figure.

The Heresy of Paraphrase: The Loosening Ties

In the articles collected in *The Well Wrought Urn*, Cleanth Brooks argued that the meaning of a poem cannot be given by a paraphrase. A rendering of the poem into any other language would create an object with a different meaning. As Brooks says:

The poem communicates so much and communicates it so richly and with such delicate qualifications that the thing communicated is mauled and distorted if we attempt to convey it by any vehicle less subtle than that of the poem itself. . . . If we are to speak exactly, the poem itself is the *only* medium that communicates the particular "what" that is communicated. The conventional theories of communication offer no easy solution to our problem of meanings: we emerge with nothing more enlightening than this graceless bit of tautology: the poem says what the poem says.[19]

Sensitive readers throughout history have had intuitions similar to Brooks's. Those who, with Wordsworth, hold poetic language to be "an incarnation of thought"[20] rather than clothing for thought endorse essentially the same view of the relation of the particular language of the poem to the meaning of the poem. I regard Brooks's thesis as a clear expression of *the* central literary insight, whose consequences are absolutely incompatible with all philosophies of language that postulate meanings as magic-language entities expressed by words.

Some accounts of the "unique meaning" of a poem imagine "poetic" meanings that poetry is peculiarly equipped to express. But Brooks's problem is not that of establishing a unique language or system of meanings expressible only by poetry. For within such a poetic system of meanings there could well be synonyms and thus paraphrases. On such "special-meaning" accounts of how poems mean, two sonnets could say exactly the same thing, so that one was an exact paraphrase of the other. Hence, appeal to a special domain of poetic meaning cannot explain why paraphrase is inadequate.

Brooks cannot be interpreted as just another "poetic-meaning" theorist who proposes complex poetic intentional objects, for such objects would undermine Brooks's doctrine of the unparaphrasable poem. Brooks's thesis in "The Heresy of Paraphrase" is that there is no meaning-preserving replacement for the precise words of the poem. The simplest construal of this is that the account of meaning must cite the words themselves, not some mysterious magical surrogate. A satisfying explanation of why a poem cannot be paraphrased must make words themselves the elementary meaningful items, unassisted by anything like Fregean senses or other forms of *logoi*.

The poem means something that cannot be meant by any other sequence of words. But then we have a meaning for each such sequence of words, a meaning that could not exist without those words. The notion of the meaning of the poem as something distinct from the language, which the language would signify, is thus redundant.

Brooks's thesis, then, drops concepts or meanings in favor of words. But words and concepts, construed as Fregean senses, differ in important ways. Words, as concrete and material, have indefinitely many features, and lack the magical property of being by their very nature such as to select a particular referent. That is, the replacement of concepts with mere words endows the basis of meaning with all the features by which words "go beyond" concepts. All that pertains to words that is not "part of the meaning" or "part of the cognitive content" is imported into the basis of meaning. So, for instance, the obvious basis for distinguishing the rhetorical from the logical connections among words is lacking,[21] if poems cannot be paraphrased.

Given an account of meaning that thus denies the existence of magical meaning-tokens behind words, the failure of paraphrase follows from the nonidentity of distinct sequences of words. Poems have unique meaning because they are unique sequences of words, and words (construed as cultural objects with histories, involvements in power relations, and so forth) *are* their meanings.

Tropes and the Loosening of Reference

Brooks's thesis requires some substantial revisions in received notions about figuration. If what the poem says is unparaphrasable and the poem *is* its language, then what the poem says is inseparable from its figures of speech, and the figuration of the text is essential to its meaning. Suppose it is no accident that the poem cannot be paraphrased. Suppose it does not just happen that there is no literal term for the figurative use of "blind mouths." Then we could have no extra language that would express literally the meaning of the poem.

According to theories with extralinguistic, uninterpretable meanings, any meaning can be paired with some term, so anything can be said literally if it can be said at all, including the most beautiful thoughts. On such theories, poems have exact translations and exact paraphrases. That might work as follows: Whenever an unparaphrasable metaphor is produced, the Poetry Committee coins a word or a phrase that will mean exactly the same thing literally. For instance, the committee might stipulate that "orthwen rosents" is to mean literally what "blind mouths" conveys metaphorically. Thus the committee would legislate an accurate, literal way to say what Milton meant. If poetic meanings were conveyed by but not identical with poetic passages, terms could be stipulated to express those Fregean senses the poets were trying to convey with the inadequate resources of English. Something is wrong with such a proposal, as every sensitive reader of poetry knows.

Since Brooks's theory denies paraphrasability, some other account of what figure is and how it works is necessary. If the poem expressed concepts, those concepts could be literally expressed. If figuration cannot be replaced by a literal stipulated coinage, something different from the traditional must be the case about "literal" and "figural."

A further consequence of the words replacing the concept is this: All of the metaphorical, allegorical, and figural meanings of the poem are equally part of the meaning of the poem, since they are equally part of the sequence of concrete words. The "cognitive" part of the word, then, is not obviously separated from the accidents that lend themselves to wordplay, figuration, and allegory, so there is no clear basis for awarding special status to the literal meaning. Because "literal meaning" is what is fixed by the unadulterated conceptual content of a word, the replacement of concepts by words removes the accepted understanding of the "literal." "Literal" will have to be defined in terms of what persons say and in what situations they say it, unless something like "normal" situations can be defined. Such a specification of "normal," though, will be vague and contextual.

With nothing better to work with than words, truth-definition still gives the meaning of figurative and literal language perfectly well. Both sides of a truth-definition consequence have multiple rhetorical readings. The meaning of, for instance, "blind mouths" is given by the formula: "blind mouths" is true of a collective x if and only if x are blind mouths. Brooks's thesis, following Davidson, allows no difference in *meaning* between literal and figurative uses of language, since there is no more finely grained meaning than that of language itself. Still another way to see this is as follows: If a text possessed the alleged distinct literal and figurative "meanings," then beneath that text would be further "texts" (in the language of thought or concepts) that gave explicit literal renderings of the literal and figurative meanings.

This view of the meaning of a text loosens the reference of a text so that the text can be about itself as well as about mouths and blindness. The mechanism for this loosening is the "turning" that still seems to constitute the essence of tropes. Metaphor and troping generally can still be construed as a displacement, even without the ontology of meanings. A text with its figural ways of being understood or meant is displaced, and therefore is already also about something else. The next section discusses how turnings can turn without an external proper meaning to turn from.

Groundless Troping

Multiple meanings are nothing new. Dante, Philo, and virtually the whole history of interpretation agree that a text can be read on several levels. On traditional theories, though, the "level" metaphor is taken seriously. The displacements of "levels" of meaning are displacements from a privileged and unproblematic origin. This origin has two aspects, as follows.

The first requirement of the traditional theory was concepts behind words. The fundamental meaning of the text was the literal meaning, which was the base upon which other levels of meaning were built. This base was held to be the transparent, literal meaning of the text.

The second requirement was a realm of given prelinguistic objects, with their natural resemblances, that were the literal referents of the terms. The pattern of relationships that were already there in the world provided constraints and a basis for metaphor and figuration. The levels of meaning beyond the literal, for instance, analogical and allegorical meanings, build on this base by using relationships obtaining among the referents at the base level.

Given this origin, then, the turnings of the tropes and the patterns of significance in the allegories are based on firm relationships of sense at the literal level and in the natural analogies that obtain among the referents of the literal. What is said by the other levels of meaning could be said literally, albeit perhaps only in more perfect languages.

The alternative account denies both literal sense and the bare objects with their prelinguistic resemblances and analogies. Most importantly, in place of the multiplication of meaning, which implies an unfolding of a determinate number of further senses, this account posits a sort of "drift," which is captured by Derrida's term "dissemination."[22] This "dissemination" picture of metaphor depends on denying the foundations of the traditional account. Dissemination is what is left after both concepts behind words and the preconfigured world of natural objects are abandoned.

First, in this two-phased abandonment, consider the effect of the denial of the magic concept behind the word: With ungrounded turnings and no original straight meaning, the meanings of a text are not arranged in a hierarchy of more and less remote from some real meaning. Without magic concepts behind words, we cannot get the "strict conceptual content" out of the concrete word. Note that Brooks's thesis does not mean that there is nothing behind words. The denial of magic concepts means that anything behind words is also concrete, material, and thus wordlike. To be wordlike or languagelike is to have materiality, contingencies beyond just "bare message." Any nonmagic token can be misunderstood; it is not essentially just a reference determiner.

Second, consider the effect of the denial of language-independent similarity and connection. Suppose that the resemblances and analogies that make metaphors plausible are in part constituted by the application of metaphors; suppose, that is, that language (in part) creates analogies rather than reflects analogies that are given in nature. Or again, suppose that Goodman is roughly right.[23] Then the connection of a term to a nonlinguistic causal world impinging on thought is always mediated and mixed with language or the languagelike. Thus the pattern of what is extended to apply to what is not fixed by nature. The patterns of what is seen as like what can then be contradictory, both across and within languages. For instance, nothing intrinsic to pigs prevents "Arthur is a pig" from being a compliment on his cleverness rather than a remark about his greed. The conventional use of "pig" is actually less apt than the complimentary one, as anyone who has dealt with pigs knows.

If no unvarnished objects exist independently of the language-dependent metaphorical analogies, then no bare objects with their intrinsic properties and resemblances exist to serve as the referents founding and controlling metaphorical extension. Thus, without objects whose natures, connections, and resemblances are independent of language, that is, without a "theory-independent" given, there is no natural limit on what can come to be analogous to what. Dissemination is not the tracing-out of a pregiven realm of poetical meanings in the concept or of subtleties that were lying in the object waiting to be brought out.

The concept of the figural we are left with is one that lacks both absolute "literal" sense, the sense that just picks out the object, and "literal referents," objects given prior to conceptualization that provide the basis for analogy and metaphorical extension. We are left, then, with a relative notion of figure. We can say that a reading is figural in relation to another reading, but not absolutely, since literal and figural are different readings of texts, defined in relation to one another. But this is displacement not defined by distance from an absolute nonmetaphorical purely literal discourse.

Whatever we can say about meaning and words comes down to patterns of what people say in what circumstances. Those circumstances, though, are partly constituted by what they say, given that the world is shaped by how it is conceptualized. Any changes or oddities about how a word is applied must therefore come down to changes in practices, or violations of practices, or distortions of practices in what is said and when it is said.

Consequently, rather than suppose the existence of a well-defined set of distinct Platonic Forms that a word can express, so that figuration is a kind of creative homonymy, we should think of the application of words to the world as subject to drift, relative to the applications of other words. Such drift would correspond to a slow change of view, roughly. But departure from pattern can also be more abrupt.

Metaphor and other turns of speech rest on the history of such discontinuity and the possibility of future discontinuity. When a word is suddenly applied in an unusual way, we may speak of "turning." Turning differs from mere error, but in the way sarcasm differs, not in the way homonymy does. Suppose someone applies a term in a case that is not "normal," that is, not "forced" by the circumstances. (Circumstances are defined in the very terms at issue, so that one is forced to call something red when it is clearly red.) Roughly, if we are not inclined to think the person is just mistaken or is simply misusing the term, and if we are inclined to *assent* to the new application, then we have a case of a "turning," a trope.

When "hot" was first applied to desire, connections with light, kindling, and hearths were not entirely disrupted, since we came to speak of "kindling" desire, and so forth. What correspond to the familiar "metaphorical senses" of terms are the various discontinuities in practice that have already occurred. Notice that "metaphorical" extensions are carried to associated terms, in just the way that they would be if we had discovered a new kind of heat. So we have burning, fueling, and warmth of desire. As I argue elsewhere, the metaphorical extension, the discontinuity, does not differ in kind from the extension of a predicate to a new case.[24] In both situations we have proposals to accept the new application. But in the case of routine predication, the acceptance is a foregone conclusion.

What can "turning" mean, though, without senses or concepts to turn to or from? Without the notion of meaning, the nonlinguistic concept behind the word, the metaphors by which we understand tropes, in particular "trope" and "metaphor," will have to be changed. The following is a sketch of the sort of theory to which Brooks should be forced.

Our other resource for meaning something else, besides a reservoir of Fregean senses, is other rhetorical forces for words. I can mean different things by "He's a fine fellow," by being sincere or sarcastic. But saying something sarcastically is not saying something else sincerely. Notice that sarcasm goes equally well into truth-definition clauses. "He's a fine fellow" is true if and only if he's a fine fellow, however that is meant.

Without senses behind words, the various "turnings" can be understood only rhetorically, as Davidson and de Man point out.[25] Thus a metaphorical application of a term is like a sarcastic application of a term. Nothing further is meant, no "meaning" lurks behind the term, but the term is meant differently. This "meaning differently" cannot be understood as something else being meant, the hidden message, because that message, in virtue of being in material tokens, could be used sarcastically, ironically, jokingly, metaphorically, and so forth. This regress means that rhetorical force cannot be indicated by any conventional notation.

Figures of speech, then, on a theory without concepts behind words, are a kind of shift of rhetorical force. Just as with a stage use of "It is about to rain" certain expectations are suspended, such that the sentence is "turned" from the use in weather talk, so expectations are suspended with metaphor, for example with "warm" in "Arthur was a warm person." What we think follows from "He's a fine fellow" depends on a "reading" of rhetorical force. This does not mean that what follows could be neatly listed, or that rhetorical forces are nothing but adjustments of expectation. Most significantly, as Davidson has pointed out, the occurrence of a particular rhetorical force cannot be indicated by "conventions," since any such conventional indicator can be used ironically, in a stage production, and so on.[26]

Also, terms can mean in an indefinite number of ways. "Meaning something otherwise" is always an option, whatever the history of a word, whatever has already been meant with the word. As soon as a turn is familiar, uses can turn from *it*. For a new use to be understood as a trope, rather than just a mistake, it has to have connections with familiar turns—the familiar is always that from which tropes are turned.

The view of figure and allegory as rhetorical rather than semantic makes the various "turnings" equally original, ontologically. Temporally, the terms of the figure have prior extensions, what was originally called "hot," for example. Thus "hot passion" may be later, but not logically posterior, unless we are to allow that calculation can literally be done only with stones and that fornication takes place only under arches. In sum, temporal, etymological priority has little to do with the philosophical concept of the literal.

Are new metaphorical applications of terms true? Well, "Wilbur's passion is hot" is true if and only if Wilbur's passion is hot. But what we need to know in order to know whether Wilbur's passion is indeed hot is who Wilbur is and what hotness is. But those things are determined by whatever it is that fixes what terms apply to. Now, what fixes the meanings of terms are the social practices of those speaking the language—what people choose to call "hot," to put it crudely. But "social practice" imagines a unity and coherence that we do not really ever find. When a term is being applied, but no practice with it is unanimous, the application is up for grabs. "Practice" is a more or less loose notion constructed negatively from auditors' and readers' being surprised, taken aback, delighted, offended, and so forth, by a use that deviates from practice.

Truth in the usual philosophical understanding is a notion built for meanings: if the meaning fits the world, the sentence is true. Without meanings, there are only practices, a messy agglomeration of what people do with and to each other which yields some clear-cut cases of literality ("Nureyev is not a hamster") and some not so clear-cut cases ("Diseases do not attack people"). The usual philosophical sense of "true" requires approximations of ideal speech communities. But the speakers of English are no such speech community. If "meaning one thing" typically does not quite happen, then systematizable answers to the question "True or false?" are not forthcoming from any basis of reduction to patterns of behavior. The formal languages, in which truth "strictly" applies on the basis of relations of reference among components of sentences, are fantasy ideals, more or less illuminating about real languages. So "True or false?" in the reducible sense may be the wrong question to ask when practices are being shaped.

Another way to put the general point is this: On the traditional philosophical account of truth, which requires that the world and referential relations make sentences true, if one accepts magical relations and a realm of given objects, then one can have a concept of absolute truth. (Without magical relations and a given, one must treat truth as irreducible and concede that very many truths are unknowable in order to retain the notion of absolute truth.)[27] Apart from such magical relations, one cannot ask whether a sentence is "true" *tout court*; rather, one can ask whether, for a given "L" whether the sentence is true in L. But the status of the claim about this relation to L involves the same questions of interpretation. So even "relative truth" turns out not to be a stable notion for someone denying the magic language and a given array of objects. (The "given" has to be given up, if one denies a magic language, if there are no meaning conveyers better than words. The "given" cannot be something that supports correspondence, except in the sense that "There are frogs" is true if and only if there are frogs.)

For theorists taking magic-free language as a starting point, the language, being a function of the status of struggles over what is to be said, is up for grabs, since speakers differ in dispositions to assent to applications of terms. Hence, for deconstructionists and, perhaps surprisingly, Cleanth Brooks, the "True or false?" question is inappropriate. As long as one denies the magic language and the correlative notion of a given, no notion of truth that regards truth as analyzable in terms of reference, behavior, or anything else is available.[28]

If tropes, and therefore allegory, are matters of rhetoric rather than formal semantics, then literary texts are particularly illuminating about the workings of language. We seem more willing to read different rhetorical force in literature than in some other kinds of writing. In fact, such willingness may be what labels writing "literature." So literature hides the ubiquity of groundlessness less than do other kinds of discourse.

Fit and Self-Reference in Literature

Groundless figuration disseminates meaning and reference, and removes the illusion of a privileged basis of "literal sense" that could ground privileged reference. Therefore, briefly, literary language is in roughly the same referential situation as mathematical language. Any causal constraints on reference are weakened by the remoteness of the topics of conversation from objects with plausible essences by nature. Also, the "contamination" of the objects by the language discussed in the next section means that the objects cannot function as independent sources to fix references, at least not for literary works.

A poem fits whatever is a model of it, if we understand "fit" and "model" to be cashed out in terms of reception by fellow speakers. If an urn satisfies predicates $k1, \ldots, kn$, and a poem satisfies predicates $l1, \ldots, ln$ such that ki is analogous to li, then the urn can be read as the poem, and the poem about the urn is also a poem about the poem. But such isomorphisms are set by the phenomena only relative to ways of thinking about those phenomena. That is, whether pigs fit a predicate depends on how we already think about pigs, and that is in part a matter of what predicates we already apply. Our objects are constructs, not givens, so the parameters of what terms can fit what objects, or what objects can be grouped together as the same, is not fixed by an independent world of things.

Since figuration loosens the application of predicates, and the ground of these shifts is not tied to uncontaminated resemblances in nature, the notion of "fit" will not select a single subject matter. Whatever a text is figural for is a proper subject matter for the text, since the privilege of a "straight" understanding has been removed by the reflections on language above. Thus, textual readings according to which the text is really about itself are possible and plausible. Such self-referential readings are standard for the New Critics and their successors.

On Brooks's view, such self-referential readings come about because the topic of poetry is always the unity underlying diverse elements. As Brooks says, "In the unified poem, the poet has 'come to terms' with his experience. The poem does not merely eventuate in a logical conclusion. The conclusion of the poem is the working out of the various tensions—set up by whatever means—by propositions, metaphors, symbols. The unity . . . represents an equilibrium of forces."[29]

What can such a poem fit? Since the poem is about unity and, if unified appropriately, has exemplified the unity it explains, the poem has to be about itself. That is, in a well-wrought poem, the poem itself is both a case of what it discusses—namely, unification—and a discussion of it. It exemplifies as well as states.

That the self-referential reading is possible shows yet more completely how the poem unifies diverse materials into a whole. The poem itself is an instance of what it does, namely unify diverse elements. In his clearest remarks, discussing Donne's "The Canonization," Brooks claims that the poem is a case of the unification it is talking about. Citing Shakespeare's "The Phoenix and the Turtle," Brooks says, "The urn to which we are summoned, the urn which holds the ashes of the phoenix, is like the well-wrought urn of Donne's 'Canonization' which holds the phoenix-lovers' ashes: it is the poem itself."[30]

This folding of the poem back on itself is a consequence of the poem's succeeding in its function of bringing about and expressing unity in diversity. Given that the meaning of the poem is the poem itself ("the poem says what the poem says"),[31] the unification it brings about is best displayed in the poem itself. Just as a picture is necessarily a good picture of itself (given the "fitting" theory of reference), so a good poem is about itself since it fits itself.

A good poem is thus autological, just by the fact that it must be a unity of diverse verbal elements to be a poem and must portray diverse phenomena as unities to be a work of art. For New Critics such as Brooks, self-referentiality is, so to speak, an enclosing of the work on itself, enhancing unity. Deconstructive critics, using a related kind of reading of the text as figure for itself, reach exactly the opposite conclusion.

Self-Reference, Groundlessness, and Lack of System

General Considerations

For Paul de Man, the necessity of self-reference is a symptom of the failure of the tropological devices of a text to be closed, to constitute a unitary system at all. This section will explain the phrase "allegory of its own unreadability" and outline the disruption of unity that self-reference reveals in literature.

The argument of this section may be sketched as follows: If words replace concepts, the dissemination of meaning is constrained neither by the ideal structure of concepts nor by the exigencies of the prelinguistic analogies in the world. Hence, there is no basis for privileging one reading as the base, the one tied to the real order, either of concepts or of objects.

Just as the conceptual order and the natural world of objects cannot constrain the vagaries of figuration, neither can those orders, both of which are presumably total and coherent systems, force completeness and coherence on the "tropological system" in a text, mind, or culture. The "system of meaning" that structuralists sought, the unity that Brooks searches for in a text, is not guaranteed by anything outside the words themselves and their interrelations.

So the pattern of interrelationship among terms, which constitutes the patterns of metaphor and figuration that appears in a text or a culture, is determined internally. Thus a text or language, if it forms a system, must do so internally, constituting by its rules a closed network in which items are given stable and determinate places. But the unavoidability of self-reference, given the incompleteness results, reveals that even in the best circumstances no closure or completeness is possible.

So texts cannot arrive at determinate meanings, or even determinate single sets of relations of piece to piece, since the sequence of relations is unstable. In the strict sense, then, natural languages and texts formulated within them do not constitute systems.

To fill out the above sketch: First, if all further representations behind language are also languagelike phenomena (e.g., neural states, the representations that define the content of intentions), then the account of a term is always given by relation to other items that are mixed with language. The mark of the languagelike, discussed above, is the accidental and contingent. Without magic meanings behind words, there is no basis for separating out the ideality from the materiality of terms, for example, the meaning from the spellings, or the logical from the rhetorical connections among terms. Language is tied, not to a realm of forms or Fregean senses, but to other languages or languagelike phenomena, which are subject to interpretation since they do not mean one thing by their very nature.

The relational, dialectical nature of reference can then be described in radicalized Quinean terms as the interanimation of sentences or the web of belief, generalized to include kinds of sentence-to-sentence connections other than just inferential ones. That is, since we are dealing with words qua words, the web of belief must become a web that incorporates connections of rhyming, association by literary co-occurrence, spelling similarity, and euphony. The web of connection and strength of authority will include the power relations, prestige, and other valorizations that make us continue to accept sentences. "Strength of authority" is intended to be a grab-bag category that includes everything other than the "rational" and the "literary."

The account (including a truth-definition clause) of a given word is abstracted from the place of the various sentences in which the word occurs in this network, that is, their use for the individual and culture in question. The place of a sentence depends on its connections with other sentences in the language and on the changes in those connections brought about by changes in the world.

The world that affects the network of sentences is itself in part the effect of those patterns of sentences. A kind of object *F* exists for a culture if some sentences attributing "*F*" to some object are true, that is, if *F*'s must be values of variables. As Davidson has often pointed out, truth and meaning are both functions of what is said in what circumstances.[32] Since there are no translinguistic meanings or given objects, the circumstances in which "There are pigs here" is true, which circumstances constitute the extension of "pig," can be specified only as the circumstance of there being pigs around. The supposition that a culture could be usually wrong about pigs is incoherent, since a situation's containing pigs is constructed out of the culture's application of that term. We thus cannot take "the world" to be something standing outside of language and fixing its patterns of truth and falsity.[33] The world for us is always "mixed with the linguistic," in the sense that there is no coherent notion of the world apart from our language.

So the objects that exist, as well as the "senses" of terms used to discuss those objects, are relational and contextual. Neither the structure of sense nor the structure of the external world have sufficient independence to induce coherence in the interconnections. If the connections among terms are consistent and complete, the completeness must be internal. So is the result of the working out of relationships in this web stable and uniform or not? Does it determine a single set of relations among elements?

One might hold that the connections in the relational structure will be mutually reinforcing and supporting. If term *A* is determined by its relations to terms *B1*, . . . ,*Bn*, and each of *B1*, . . . ,*Bn* is determined by its relations to *A* and the other *Bi*'s, and all of these terms adjust to changes from outside, then perhaps the entire structure gives single determinations of relations among terms.

De Man's Procedure

The alternative position is that such relational determinations produce no final result but continue to modify each of the items in the array. Different starting points for tracing out relations yield different values and relationships for items. De Man's term for this lack of coherence in the reading of a particular word is "undecidability." A narrative (or segment of discourse readable as a narrative) infected by analogous difficulties is said to be "unreadable."

A long quotation from de Man will show the kinds of conclusions he supports.

The rhetorical mode of such structures can no longer be summarized by the single term of metaphor or of any other substitutive trope or figure in general, although the deconstruction of metaphorical figures remains a necessary moment in their production. They take into account the fact that the resulting narratives can be folded back on themselves and become self-referential. . . . The paradigm of all texts consists of a figure (or a system of figures) and its deconstruction. But since this model cannot be closed off by a final reading, it engenders, in its turn, a supplementary figural superposition which narrates the unreadability of the prior narration. As distinguished from primary deconstructive narratives centered on figures and ultimately always on metaphor, we can call such narratives to the second (or third) degree allegories. Allegorical narratives tell the story of the failure to read while tropological narratives . . . tell the story of the failure to denominate. The difference is only a matter of degree and the allegory does not erase the figure. Allegories are always allegories of metaphor and, as such, they are always allegories of the impossibility of reading—a sentence in which the genitive "of" has itself to be read as a metaphor.[34]

De Man tries to establish that the ungroundedness of language, the impossibility of arriving at a pure Other that fixes reference, destroys the possibility of total systematicity for the tropological patterns of a text.[35] In support of de Man's conclusion that natural languages do not form systems, his arguments always consist of examples illustrating how patterns of figuration break down and become unintelligible, if pressed in the direction of being a system. Without the idea that there are systems of thought and language in which general proofs are possible, such a demonstration is the best approximation to rigorous argument.

That language is not grounded in either idealities or nature does not *rule out* the possibility that a system exists but only removes the reasons for supposing it must exist. Some further argument is needed to show that the pattern of tropes *cannot* form a system directly, by internal coherence.

De Man's arguments against this possibility consist in examples of breakdown of system in particular texts. Given self-referential readings, these breakdowns are themselves read as saying that there is no system, so that a text becomes an "allegory of its own unreadability." De Man characterizes this incoherence of apparent system as "unreadability." To demonstrate that a text is "unreadable" is to demonstrate that the pattern of interrelations among parts is incoherent. A demonstration of unreadability is a deconstruction. But these arguments show only that system is lacking in the particular texts being addressed, not everywhere. The texts he has deconstructed, that is, might just have been defective.

On my reading of de Man, he has no general argument that a system could not exist, since such an argument is ruled out by the lack of coherence and system in his own discourse, according to his account. The position seems to be that, once the necessity of system is denied, the only reason for insisting on system is obsession with order.

De Man's arguments can be put in another way. Figuration without a ground-level literal meaning tied to ideal senses or ground-level referents tied to nature's connections removes any reason to think that a system exists. If no system exists, then a given term can have inconsistent roles, relative to different lines of connection. When a word thus functions in two ways, this shows up as a failure of sense in a system of tropes. The key word in the alleged system has to fill incompatible roles. The meaning of that word in the "tropological system," then, is revealed to be a kind of blank. What appeared to make systematic sense is revealed to make sense only so long as the connections are not inspected as carefully as a system would permit. De Man finds such places in numerous writings, places where the "system" reveals itself not to be a system.

The Application of the Metatheorems

Let us review the argument of the "deconstructive" part of this chapter. The essential consideration for the conclusion that interpretation is radically indeterminate is the incomplete groundedness of meaning and consequent incomplete groundedness of figuration. What is lost is the connection between the presumably completely coherent system of relations that constitutes the real world (or the world of ideal Fregean senses) and the connections of language. If language were sufficiently anchored to portions of the real or the ideal, then it would borrow the coherence of the real or the ideal and could be expected to form a system.

Without such anchors, we have no reason to suppose that language forms a system ordered beyond the needs of practical life. The supposition that the pattern of metaphorical relations embodies a system is part of the false theory embedded in the metaphor of "metaphor." The argument that

language is grounded neither in uncontaminated pure referents nor in idealities was a demonstration that there need not be a total and coherent system. Arguments from self-reference, though, show that there *cannot* be a
total system, at least not in substantial texts composed in any language adequate for talking about human experience. (This does not mean that individual utterances cannot be understood—just that "understanding" is
Wittgensteinian rather than Platonic.)

To fill out the metamathematical allegory, we can say that what corresponds to a "mathematical theory" in literature would be a text or a body
of work construed as a single text. What corresponds to a "proof" in literature would be a trail through the network of relationships between parts
of a text that would fix references. Thus a character, figure, or word would
be placed in relation to others by something like a proof, a literary argument. "Incompleteness" or "undecidability" is a matter of incompatible
placements of characters, terms, and narrative lines, or no placements at
all. "Undecidable" applies to a figure or a term; "unreadable" to a narrative.
The "system" of the text, the theory, does not yield an answer. Just as in
mathematical logic, "undecidability in literature is lack of proof, but now
for a thesis about a character's or term's relation to others rather than for a
sentence. Corresponding to the incompleteness theorem is the thesis that
no text is ever complete, that a text always includes parts for which incompatible accounts can be given equally well. Corresponding to the
Tarski result is the "provability," the justifiability on literary grounds, of inconsistent readings.

Given that self-reference is real, and given that self-referential readings
are made ubiquitous by the dissemination of meaning in nonhierarchical
groundless troping, a more powerful argument against the formalisms that
demand system in literature would be forthcoming if languages and texts
that refer to themselves were genuinely defective (as systems).

The paradoxes and limitations demonstrated in the idealized languages of mathematical logic reveal, when the issue is made quite precise,
that there really is something amiss in natural languages. Tarski showed
that languages that contain their own metalanguage, such as everyone's
language, cannot avoid inconsistency. Gödel showed that every language
capable of dealing with arithmetic has the resources to be ironic and to formulate doubts about the provability of its own sentences, including the
ones in which the doubt is formulated. Most significantly, then, any lan-

guage adequate for arithmetic is unavoidably self-referential. Self-reference cannot be restricted by fiat, that is, by a declaration that the language will not discuss its own sentences. Thus inconsistency is unavoidable in natural languages, discourses, and texts. Given the disseminative workings of figuration, we cannot dictate where those self-referential spots will or will not occur. For example, we can always use a sentence with a certain feature as an example of that feature, so that the sentence is about itself. That rhetorical possibility cannot be ruled out by legislation about what texts and utterances are to mean.

Now, just as Gödel showed that, for languages of a certain richness, paradoxical self-referentiality is unavoidable, so de Man has demonstrated that natural-language texts can be read as being about themselves. Since the texts and languages dealt with by de Man are always subject to interpretations according to which the text is about itself, those self-referential interpretations show language to be fundamentally fundamentless. The demonstrations of de Man are to be read as (perforce) less formal demonstrations that the relational circles of figuration and interpretation do not yield completeness and total systematicity. No natural-language text is completely understandable, if "understandable" requires having settled and coherent relations to other texts, to other portions of a given text, or to the world.

The loosening of reference by considerations about tropes and allegories creates self-reference and unreadability, if "readable" is understood as "understandable as a unified totality." So there is something fundamentally problematic about natural languages, a situation especially revealed by their literary texts. Texts that contain the metalanguage within the object language, that is, all texts in natural languages, are incomplete, inconsistent, and undecidable. They are also, among other things, about that very fact.

The above sketch of an argument sets out some consequences of what I have characterized as *the* literary insight, that the literary work is not paraphrasable. To untie language from any structuring idealities is to untie language from much of the traditional philosophical apparatus for talking about meaning and the world. Since those concepts are exactly the ones that seemed to protect natural language from falling victim to the self-referential paradoxes and the incompleteness results, the intuitions that literary writers have expressed with such metaphors as "the abyss" gain plausibility as intimations of the ungroundedness signaled by self-reference.

9

A Deconstructive Wittgenstein

ON HENRY STATEN'S *Wittgenstein and Derrida*

Unlike many other writers on deconstruction, Henry Staten often writes with great clarity and illumination. He is usually most lucid and explicit when the material is the most difficult. From his work I have learned a lot about things I had thought I understood completely. Staten deals primarily with texts by Derrida that are relatively accessible and that connect clearly with the concerns of analytic philosophers. These are early texts on Husserl[1] and the texts that deal with J. L. Austin and John Searle.[2] The early Derrida texts were written before the consequences of his deconstructive arguments for philosophical methodology itself had affected his own practice; hence Derrida's discourse in these works still observed traditional standards of argument and exposition. His examinations of Austin and Searle provide the natural entrée for an analytic philosopher trying to see what is at issue in Derrida's work. Staten's work is among the best on the issues discussed by Derrida and Searle.[3]

Staten's consideration of Wittgenstein is likewise quite accessible to analytic philosophers, because Wittgenstein is one of us. Staten's reading adapts (with acknowledgment) O. K. Bouwsma's antitheoretical/antifoundational account of the later Wittgenstein. As one might guess from the title, *Wittgenstein and Derrida*, one of the theses of the book is that Wittgenstein's practice is a kind of deconstruction—that it has a great deal in common with the practice of Derrida. Staten's reading of Wittgenstein is very fruitful, and handles the rhetorical oddities of the texts much better than do interpretations that take Wittgenstein to be proposing a new theory of language and cognition. If Wittgenstein is a deconstructor rather than a constructor of theories, the weird "remarks" format of the *Philosophical Investigations* is not an irrelevant quirk, for instance.

One of the best features of Staten's book is the attempt to give serious content to dark phrases current in much secondary material on deconstruction about "Western Metaphysics." Staten relates the detailed discussions of Wittgenstein, Derrida, and Husserl to the history of philosophy, especially to Aristotle.

I think some of Staten's broad claims about the history and character of philosophy are partly wrong, but his book exhibits none of the gross oversimplifications and stupidities about philosophy that deface many expositions of deconstruction and that so acutely embarrass philosophers who take deconstruction seriously. I disagree frequently with the connections Staten draws and the particular claims he makes about what is connected to what and about the unity of "Western Metaphysics." At some points, Staten succumbs to the characteristic weakness of deconstructionist expositors for metaphors and abstractions that, at least for me, are not grounded in anything articulable.

Deconstruction and Philosophy

In the following remarks, I examine one major issue that runs throughout the book, on which Staten is interestingly wrong. To keep the discussion focused, I ignore a number of arguable details, especially in the interpretation of particular Derridean arguments.

My disagreements with Staten start with his contrast between deconstruction and philosophy, which are conceived, it seems, as addressing the same subject matter. The two disciplines take opposite approaches to that subject matter, however: the essence of deconstruction, according to Staten, is a kind of antitheoretical, antitotalizing attitude opposed to philosophy, which is totalizing, theory-constructing, and foundational. Deconstruction consists in various ways of removing the charm of philosophy.

On this preliminary topic, I disagree with Staten at several points. First, I doubt that there is a subject matter or anything else that makes philosophy a distinctive field of inquiry (or pseudo-inquiry). Second, I think that deconstruction is not an alternative to philosophy but rather a recently self-conscious part of philosophy with a long tradition. Third and most important, I take deconstruction to have demonstrated something restricted to language and to essentially intentional phenomena, while Staten takes deconstruction to have much broader consequences.

Let me say briefly what "deconstructs" means with regard to the two figures examined by Staten. Derrida deconstructs by showing that central contrasts (which are always related to a value hierarchy and to the ideal of Form) cannot be accounted for in a principled way within a given text. That is, Derrida takes philosophical texts and shows that the contrasts on which their theories are built are undermined within the texts themselves. Derrida usually resists the temptation to construct an alternative theory, although, in a work like *Of Grammatology*, the mystic powers of language seem poised to receive our adoration.

Wittgenstein deconstructs by showing that various theories that instantiate the formal, foundationalist, totalizing dream have little to recommend them. Wittgenstein demonstrates that such theories do not fit what we say, that they do not solve the problems they were designed to solve, that those problems were engendered by the desire for a totalizing theory, and so forth. Basically, Wittgenstein tries to deconstruct not a single text at a time but the whole field of philosophy.[4] Wittgenstein, by a variety of techniques that Staten makes clear, manages to criticize and dismantle philosophical theories without proposing another theory.

Staten's accounts of these matters are excellent. Derrida's practice is treated as well as I have seen it treated, and Wittgenstein's discussion of rules is assessed in a very illuminating and helpful way. This is surely one central part of Wittgenstein's thought that Derridean interpretation displays for us in a fruitful light.

Does Wittgenstein's practice properly constitute deconstruction, though? This question presupposes that Derrida's deconstructive arguments (or Wittgenstein's "family resemblance" arguments) have failed. It suffices to say that much of Wittgenstein's handling of philosophical questions is enough like Derrida's work to make them both cases of a practice that *could* be called "deconstruction."

Furthermore, a pair of absolutely central philosophical agreements link Derrida and Wittgenstein. As I will argue, Staten runs these two agreements together, even though, as I will discuss, they are independent. The two agreements are as follows:

First, both Derrida and Wittgenstein deny the possibility of the perfectly transparent, magic words of thought so widely credited by philosophers. These "magic words" are the alleged meanings that underlie the words of natural languages and that, unlike the words of natural languages, cannot be misinterpreted. The correct interpretation of such meanings is supposed to be built into their very nature. The incoherence of the notion that there are such magic words of thought is the core realization that drives the deconstructions of Derrida and Wittgenstein, as well as those of W. V. O. Quine, Nelson Goodman, and Donald Davidson, among others.

Second, Derrida and Wittgenstein both deny the existence of a given that the terms of the magic language could designate. Such a given could be the senses of the terms of the magic language, or a realm of entities designated by terms, magic or not. In principle, one could deny the magic language and yet believe in an ontological given. That is the majority view of contemporary analytic metaphysics, discussed below.

The impossibility of self-interpreting meanings follows from the denial of essentialism, given the assumption that essence and thus necessity require certainty, and thus self-evidence, and thus self-interpreting meanings. That is, if essence requires necessity, and what is necessary is certain, and what is certain is self-evident, and self-evidence requires self-interpreting meanings, then the denial of essence is the denial of the self-interpreting meanings by which essences, in their self-evident certainty, can be known. Previous antiessentialists had betrayed their antiessentialism by lapsing into essentialism about ideas or word meanings. Wittgenstein, Derrida, Davidson, and Quine are more or less pure antiessentialists: they work out some of the consequences, for mental or linguistic entities, of rejecting essentialism. Relative to certain assumptions about meaning and reference discussed below, the denial of essentially self-presenting words of the spirit or brain has the consequences Derrida and Wittgenstein see.

Staten thinks that this view of language—that giving the meaning of words always involves, at best, a "regress to a background language"[5]—is a special case of the rejection of a more general philosophical foible, the idea of Form. The idea of Form is the idea of a pure, foundation-supplying, totalizing entity that is alleged to underlie philosophy's attitude toward meaning, among other things.

The idea of Form, according to Staten, is the source of the idea that there can be a total, context-independent, practice-independent account of anything. Forms are natures of things, the paradigms that stand apart from the vagaries of word use and constrain that use in explanations.

Staten's notion of Form thus includes both the idea of an entity whose essence is meaning and presence to the self and the idea of an entity that essentially determines objective reality and the determinacy of anything at all. This combination of features seems to me to be a Kantian and post-Kantian distortion of what were independent features for Aristotle. Deconstruction ruins the first, "meaning"-oriented idea of Form but leaves the basic Aristotelian notion untouched. Let me first sketch my views on these topics and then discuss Staten's remarks about Aristotle.

Form and Indeterminacy

In brief, I think that while Derrida and Staten are right about meaning and language, their conclusions about the indeterminacy of the world do not immediately follow, and they lead to implausible positions. I am persuaded that there is no such thing as pure presence and no such thing as a kind of representation that is self-interpreting. No thought item or "meaning" reveals what it is about just by virtue of what it is or makes this revelation by its very nature to the consciousness that entertains it. But this fact about thought and consciousness does not yet show that there are no absolute truths about the world. Prima facie, things might be self-identical and have determinate natures even though our concepts and terms do not determine self-identities and are not determinate in content.

To get from the view that there is no magic language and no given to the idea that there are no objective truths, two further theses must be accepted: that reference is a function of sense and that truth is a function of reference. At least one of these theses is part of almost every modern view of language and reality.

With regard to "true of," Derrida and Staten accept the claim that "true of," for concepts or thought-words, would be a matter of fit between concept and object. Having shown that no such fit is ultimately possible in a way that conforms to the Form model of fixity and nonrelativity, they conclude that no such thing as absolute, objective determinacy and fixedness is true of anything. But nothing about electrons, for instance, obviously follows from the fact that our terms' senses are functions of their relations to one another, their possibilities of use, and so on, which phenomena are themselves grounded in nothing else than further words, *unless reference is a function of sense.* That is, the impossibility of self-interpreting words only threatens electrons if determinate objects depend on fitting such determinate, self-interpreting words.

With regard to truth itself, Derrida and Staten accept the traditional notion of adequation: a sentence is true if and only if the meaning expressed by the sentence corresponds to the content of the world. Thus, given truths, the world fits our meanings. Derrida and Staten also accept the traditional notion that truth requires truth-makers, components of the world by virtue of which sentences that correspond to them are true. But on the basis of Derrida's and Davidson's demonstrations that no such matching is possible, Derrida and Staten deny the concept of truth.

Further deconstructing is in order to establish that this allegation of the dependence of the real on the conceptual itself rests on the acceptance of a dubious dichotomy. Above all, the thinkers accept one of the primary misconceptions in the history of philosophy since Aristotle. That is, they make the Kantian move from features of our concepts to features of the world, by arguing that the notion of "the world apart from our concepts" is nonsense since anything about the world can only be asserted in concepts.

A striking instance of this move occurs in Staten's book in the discussion of the self and self-identity.[6] The notion of the self as something that can be present is undermined by Schlegelian irony and Quinean regress to a background language. What is there and present to "inspection" is only inner words, subject to interpretation at yet another "metalevel," not some self-elucidating tokens that need no comment, as Staten correctly observes. But from the claim that there is no self-present self, it does not follow that there is no self, in the ordinary sense of "self."

Once it transpires that even mental terms and thoughts reveal nothing necessarily, either about their own nature or about their reference, the theory of meaning is cast off from the foundations that had made Kantian and post-Kantian theories down to that of Rudolf Carnap seem secure. Even though the Kantian paradigm dispensed with culture-independent objects, it still held to meanings that could connect sensations with beliefs, for instance. But this foundation fell to ruin once Davidson, Wittgenstein, Derrida, and Quine unmasked "meanings" as essentially essentialist.

The theory thereby abandoned had made the world a construct out of "meanings," in the sense that what objects there were depended on what language one spoke. Language specified the conditions for the identity, existence, and nonexistence of objects. But given that these conditions are supposed to be essential, and thus necessary, the theory that necessity must be analytic makes objects conceptual, intentional, or linguistic. In effect, both the linguistic turn in analytic philosophy and the Husserlian account of objects rendered essentialism an epistemological question, yielding "language-relative" and "intention-relative" essentialisms, respectively. So the end of essentialistic meanings meant the end of objective realities in the world.

To see how the opposition to meaning-essentialism is extended to essentialism generally, and why this has bad consequences, we need to examine how Derrida and Wittgenstein address philosophy. In the work of these two figures, the attack on philosophy is an attack on a theory-building, foundationalist move in philosophy.

One difficulty with the generalized form of antitheoretical argument advanced by Derrida and Wittgenstein is that its force cannot be corralled within philosophy. No strict line divides philosophy from nonphilosophy unless philosophy has an essence. But, clearly, if deconstruction or language-game theory is right, then there is no such essence, and Quine is right to view philosophy as continuous with science and other human inquiries. So if deconstruction works to show that philosophical concepts are misguided, the same should hold for other dichotomizing.

But rejecting all theory-building and mathematical accounts as inadequate to the slippery and ungrounded nature of language neglects the clear truth that in many areas, theory building is simply right. As Staten portrays Derrida's views—and I think his account of Derrida is accurate—nothing prevents them from being extended to physics and mathematics.[7] These fields should be subject to the same lack of connection with an objective world to which philosophy is subject.

Saving Science and Our World

The dilemma for modern philosophy has been to define itself in relation to science. The notion that ideas have an essence we can penetrate and that the transcendental or linguistic *a priori* is philosophy's special area have functioned chiefly to provide philosophy with an identity and an activity that would not compete with the obviously succeeding sciences.

The generalized deconstruction envisioned by Staten would prove that theories are inappropriate in mathematics and mechanics. Now, Staten makes some dark remarks about "the texts of science,"[8] and Heideggerians and phenomenologists will quickly point out that scientific theory building gives us objects that are still meaning-laden and so still human, if they exist for us at all. Nonetheless, my word-processor works. The eclipse occurs. The Pythagorean theorem is absolutely right. If the deconstructive arguments show that theory building and the seeking for Form are always misguided, there must be something wrong with the deconstructive arguments.

Many smart people besides Staten accept these antirealist or perhaps transrealist consequences, because they seem to flow from the disappearance of the magic language and a given domain to apply it to. But something is screwy about a view that cannot say that contemporary physics portrays the solar system better than Ptolemy did. How can one forgo a given and a magic language without abandoning the idea that at least some of our sentences are true, and that an airplane whose safety presupposes the reliability of physics inspires more confidence than would a Freudliner? Three routes out of this dilemma suggest themselves.

First, one might adopt the view that, while no terms are absolutely uncontaminated by indeterminacy of translation (or the driftings of Derridean differance), nevertheless, in the case of fundamental, asocial objects, the world applies sufficient pressure to forestall slippage of connections between language and asocial objects. But when the terms and objects are essentially layers of intentionally defined concepts, the indeterminacy of translation loosens any "rigorous" connection with a referent. The objects, institutions, roles, and so forth, of ordinary social and political life are such layered entities, constituted by intentions about intentions. Hence, although they bear a relation to the unslipping real world of microparticles, they are not reducible and so not appropriately theorizable or mathematizable. The difficulty with this view is that the metaphor of "pressure" is hard to paraphrase in helpfully scientific terms. Truths about atoms do indeed seem to differ from truths about love, but a metaphor does not help.

The initial Kantian stratagem is to put the "real" world off limits so that we will stop worrying about it: objects "independent of my concepts" are made inaccessible by my scheme of representations. This response is defective, however. The argument that, since my conception of objects is shaped by concepts, the "object itself" can never be known depends on the notion that reference is a function of sense, that is, that terms must "fit" or resemble what they are properly about.[9] The argument depends on the notion that a referring entity must designate an object by resembling the object ("resemblance" has been variously reinterpreted throughout the history of this topic). Without such resemblance, the object has not been made accessible to us, because what is "inside" is different from the object. If the criterion of "aboutness"—that is, the criterion for a term's being about something—is resemblance, this "dilemma" means that all a culture can do is adjust vocabulary to make it useful, since getting anything right is out of the question, short of importing the thing itself or its sensible or noetic Form into the soul. If truth is the adequation of concepts to objects, and concepts are no better than words, and there are no given objects, then there can be no truth.

Kantian talk about the "senselessness" of appeals to reality or the way the world is supposes that the real, to be known in itself, would have to be thought in terms with no intrinsic properties and in no particular way. That is, the denial of the possibility of discourse about things in themselves presupposes an overly stringent criterion of aboutness. The fact that we always know objects in one way or another does not mean that we never know the object in itself. Unless we suppose that a term cannot refer to an object without matching it, the necessary failure of matching due to the necessary contribution and shaping by our culture (or our categories, conceptual scheme, vocabulary, or whatever) does not affect the possibility of reference to "things in themselves." Without a theory of reference by which the referent of a term is determined by what it resembles, Kantianism and its descendants have little to recommend them.[10]

The core stratagem of the neo-Kantians or neopragmatists starts from the unexceptionable premise that all thoughts about the world have features that are not due just to the way the world is. Any representation owes something to its form. Furthermore, the contribution of the world cannot be separated from the contribution of the scheme. Such separation would require a representation with no intrinsic features and no organization qua representation. But the move from "All thoughts are partially determined by the scheme, culture, vocabulary, and so on" to "All thoughts are *nothing but* determinations by the scheme, culture, vocabulary, and so on" proceeds via the principle that what cannot be separated out as a pure component uncontaminated by anything other is not a legitimate item of ontology.

One of the tasks of deconstruction, as practiced by Wittgenstein, is to eliminate exactly this kind of demand for "pure cases" as the condition for the usability of dichotomy. Wittgenstein could try to allow science and practical knowledge to differ from more intentionally involved fields.

Thus the demand that everything ontologically respectable be a pure case, so that contamination does not admit of degrees, expresses a dichotomy that should be overcome. Although there may be no thoughts that owe their truth solely to the way the world is, that is, that are in no way "made" truths, still there are degrees of contamination. Different kinds of things are cultural constructions to different degrees, even though nothing we believe about what exists lacks a contribution by the culture that enables us to think it. These differences of degree determine how much an object's reality is made and how much is found. A copper atom, for instance, is less contaminated by cultural confection than the Renaissance, and less an artifact.

The difference might be ascribed to the degree of contamination by culture. This "contamination," the extent to which truths about a subject matter are made rather than discovered, would largely depend on how deeply layered intentionality is in that part of language. A "layer of intentionality" exists when a term applies in part because of intentional states. If those intentional states have other intentional states as content, another "layer" exists. The point is that such layers are interpreted according to their sense, and thus are subject to indeterminacy of translation, or the driftings of differance. Roughly, "justice" will be different from "electron," because justice itself is determined by the application of concepts requiring ascriptions of intentions, whose contents themselves are determined in terms requiring ascriptions of intentions, and so forth. Since the interpretation of intentions is essentially the assignment of content to a linguistic item, indeterminacy of translation is not curable by appeal to any natural, biological phenomena.

Could this be the way Wittgenstein would avoid the bizarre conclusion that atomic physics is a construction like a culture's notion of the "unclean"? The basic difficulty with the above way of expressing the view, however, is that the notion of a "given" is smuggled in as the contrast to the contribution of the culture. If there is no given, it cannot mix with the cultural. I would hesitate to ascribe this sleight of hand to Wittgenstein.

A second way to avoid the post-Kantian disappearance of the real world would be to follow Saul Kripke and cut the link between essentialism about meanings, thought-terms, or ideas, and essentialism about things. This strategy amounts to accepting an ontological "given" while denying an epistemological given. Kripke has shown that modern philosophy's attempt to make reference a function of sense, and thus to make ontological necessity and epistemological certainty the same, is unjustified.[11] That identification is contradicted by the way we use "necessity" and "certainty," and thus conflicts with the very criterion that reference is fit between concept and object. In the same way, our dispositions to apply the terms "name," "about," and "refers to" are not what the reference-as-fit theory of reference would predict.

A post-Kripkean realist theory of reference would bestow upon terms a natural significance attaching them to items in the world. What would correspond to senses of terms might be historical features that could not be read off of the term and that would not be introspectively available to the thinker or speaker.

Kripke himself makes various "causal" suggestions as to how terms could refer while having contents grossly inadequate to the subject matter. These suggestions, as Kripke explicitly says, do not constitute a theory of reference. But if one turned Kripke's remarks into a realistic causal theory of reference, a series of difficulties would emerge: The relation of reference would become central and would presuppose a natural relation between persons and the things they could talk about. But to make that notion of reference nonmagical, one would need to make reference a natural, law-governed phenomenon. But it is difficult to see how such laws would be tight enough to sustain the detailed reference relations required and still correspond to the ordinary extension of "refer." That is, from the required natural lawlike basis, most of the kinds of thing we talk about would really be disjunctive predicates without a natural principle of coherence. Examples of these sorts of difficulties appear in the recent work of David Armstrong,[12] for instance, where almost every ordinary truth turns out to be a "second-class" truth because of its loose relation to the ultimately real.

On a causal *theory* of reference, therefore, the vast majority of the things we say, since they are not related in a lawlike way to the objects described by the best laws, would be "true" only in a secondary and extended sense. "Contemporary analytic metaphysics" struggles with this problem.

This second, Kripkean route to real truth without a magic language was Aristotle's path as well. Aristotle thought very deeply about when theory is appropriate to a subject matter and when it is not. The discussion of Aristotle's thoughts with respect both to Form and to theory building is a main topic of Staten's. I will inflict upon the reader only a little of the great deal I have to say about Staten's version of Aristotle.

Aristotle is in fact an excellent example of what a successful "realism" would have to be. Aristotle's basic objects are medium-sized physical objects. The parts of objects are only potentially entities, secondary to the objects themselves, since the fundamental laws are laws about medium-sized objects themselves, the substances.

The major difficulty for an Aristotelian today is that Aristotle's science is wrong. For Aristotle, a microparticle that passed into and out of the economy of an organism would cease to be what it was on entering the organism. Whereas it had previously been a low-level substance, it becomes a part of the organism on entry. Being a part of an organism is the essence of the microparticle. When the organism ceases to be, the microparticle ceases to be as well, since it is part of something that ceases to be. The organism, as it were, accounts for the being of the entire region it constitutes.

Aristotle's treatment of the part–whole relation is required by his demand that the world consist of substances. For a substance, undergoing a change while remaining the same individual is objectively different from ceasing to exist. So if the microparticle was a part of an organism and also had its own conditions of extinction, then the microparticles would cease to exist and also continue to exist, if both being a part of an organism and being a microparticle were substance determiners.

Aristotle cannot keep both microparticles and medium-sized objects as primary beings since, if the microparticles were primary, there would be no point to regarding organisms as primary beings as well. Nothing about organisms would require that organisms have an essence, since any necessities about organisms would be derivative from necessities about their microparticle parts. Thus, if essences are interpreted as laws about objects, there would be no laws about organisms as such. Whatever substances there are exclude any overlapping substances. The case of Aristotle illustrates the central cost of being a realist who accepts an objective given that selects the objects of reference: If we accommodate the entities described by the best laws, we are in danger of losing objective truths about the medium-sized objects among which we live. Predicates of persons, tallness, and tables will be disjunctive and indistinguishable from various Goodmanoid disjunctive predicates.

Staten misunderstands the extent to which Aristotle differs from the tradition that followed him. Staten takes Aristotle to be the prime example of the metaphysician wedded to the idea of Form. "Form" for Staten, is the core constitutive notion of philosophy that has been deconstructed by Wittgenstein and Derrida. My disagreement with Staten can be formulated as a disagreement about how to read Aristotle and the subsequent history of philosophy.

Staten's account actually applies to the Plato of the middle dialogues. Plato takes mathematics to be the model of knowledge, and supposes that every topic, if it is knowable at all, is knowable by the kind of mathematical insight and total vision that knowledge of a theorem involves. For Plato, the natural, the social, the intentional, and the moral are equally parts of the structure of the universe, since the structure of laws that really is the universe is organized by the Good. The soul is a mirror of the structure of the universe, if we thus understand the "affinity" indicated by the recollection arguments.

Given the role of the Good, human concerns and categories will be subject to the same kind of rigorous, theoretical treatment that physical and mathematical laws are. Of course, the way instances *reflect* laws rather than instantiate them will mean that the sensible world qua sensible is not genuinely knowable, but anything that is graspable is so in virtue of the kind of insight that grasps a proof in geometry.

Staten takes Aristotle to be very much a Platonist in identifying the Forms that allow scientific knowledge with those that constitute the essences of objects. It is true that, for Aristotle, our knowledge of objects consists in having Forms of those objects in mind (literally) without their matter. But this can be viewed, not as essential to those Forms, as in the case of Plato, but merely as a kind of happy accident. Aristotle is such a thoroughgoing naturalist, and so clear about the inappropriateness of expecting mathematical, exact, Form-like accounts of many subject matters (for instance, ethics) that it is unreasonable to read him as obsessed with rigor.

Furthermore, the "magic words," the present-to-consciousness, self-presenting meanings that set the problem of language and the world for post-Kantians, are not prominent in Aristotle. The Forms exist in the mind but they are not to be identified by the kind of visual inspection that reveals their essence, as in Plato. In fact, nothing about the Forms or our consciousness explains how a person knows which Form is in his head, since the tokens are sensible Forms, Lockean ideas of particulars.

The grasp of essence, for Aristotle, is not present to consciousness in any introspectable way but comes out as a disposition to sort objects into their real kinds. That is, Aristotle requires that knowledge have a natural, preintrospective basis in unmediated connections. Our fundamental way of knowing, for Aristotle, is due to our being the sort of organism that knows, that is naturally disposed to get things right. This "natural disposition" is a matter of mechanisms and physical structures. Replace his teleology with the Darwinized teleology of Ruth Millikan,[13] and we have essentially the same naturalistic theory of how terms are connected to objects.

Aristotle still appeals to magic, since the mysterious *nous* is supposed somehow to drag essence out of images. But the issues of Form and meaning are clearly separable for Aristotle. Later philosophy runs these notions together, by something like the following series of steps: first, since Aristotle in fact makes certainty accompany the deliverances of *nous*, certainty becomes a mark of necessity. By the time of Descartes, certainty is the *criterion* of necessity. But with Descartes especially, the "magic meaning" problem becomes the crucial and elemental one: what is needed is an internal criterion of certainty. But any image is just an image; and any intentional state, likewise, is just that. Any connection to an outside that can be absolutely relied on is dubious. But if it is dubious, then it is not necessary. Only an idea's internal constitution and relations to other ideas can be the object of certainty.

But now, a sequence of deconstructors *cum* replacement theorizers point out that ideas themselves, if they are treated as regular entities, would not reveal their inner natures. They must either be magic, intentional, necessarily self-revealing things (e.g., for Husserl) or be replaced by words and their meanings (e.g., for analytic philosophy).

But the whole idea that certainty and necessity go together was a mistake, a Platonic extrapolation from mathematics. A naturalism that does not suppose that what goes on in knowledge is present to consciousness can still have Form without having meanings.

The third way to avoid the Derridean difficulty—the post-Kantian disappearance of the real world—is to deny that truth requires the fit of sentences with anything. In effect, this reverses the Derridean move from the failure of the traditional conception of truth to the inapplicability of "true." One can, with Davidson, concede the lack of a given and of meaning bearers more staunch than language and conclude that truth cannot consist in the adequation of sentences by the world. Derrida's response to the failure of correspondence is to deny that sentences are true because the necessary match cannot obtain. The indeterminacy and drift that the lack of a given and of a magic language entail undermines the only notion of truth, that of adequation, because that notion presupposes mistaken philosophical notions. The alternative that I ascribe to Davidson takes truth to be primary and irreducible to reference or to adequation, except in the trivial sense that "Fred is a frog" is true if and only if Fred is a frog.

The difficulty with the Davidsonian account, at least prima facie, is that the independence of truth means that indeterminacy of interpretation is epistemological, not in the sense that some truths are not known but in the sense that some truths are sheerly unknowable. If truth is irreducible, then whether a specific sentence is true will in some cases be independent of every other truth about anything whatsoever. That is, for some sentences, their truth-values are absolutely independent of all possible evidence, even though they have the truth-values they have.

Hence, Davidson, unlike Quine, argues that an interpretive situation in which no evidence could adjudicate between two alternative hypotheses will be one in which the sentence being interpreted has a definite truth-value, as well as definite truth conditions. (These are independent considerations. The vague utterance "Fred is a tall man" can be said to have the determinate truth condition that "'Fred is a tall man' is true if and only if Fred is a tall man.") Hence, while Davidson holds that there is no fact of the matter about whether a given interpretive hypothesis is true, he does so only because there are no facts making sentences true in general.

Thus Davidson can be a realist insofar as he believes that there are objective, culture-independent truths, while still denying a magic language and a given, whether epistemological or ontological. With these views, Davidson can countenance both medium-sized objects and microparticles without being a reductionist. All the truths about the microparticles making up entities can be known in microparticle terms, and the question of whether those entities are organisms or not, or whether they are a particular species of organism, can be indeterminate relative to all of those truths. However, such an entity either is or is not an organism and is or is not a squirrel.

The analogous Davidsonian move for the necessity of natural laws would be to deny the premise, common to Derrida, Quine, and most other thinkers about modality, that necessity and possibility must be reduced to truth. Derrida and Quine, holding that no such reduction is possible, conclude that necessity is an illegitimate notion. Modal theorists invoke either various ontological givens, magic languages, or a combination to construct theories of modality. Davidson, holding as he does that truths need not be made true since truth is primitive, is in a position to be a primitivist about modality.

That is, Davidson can deny that abandoning the given and the magic language means abandoning a world governed by necessities. Natural laws, mathematical laws, and other necessities can be treated as primitive. The possibility of taking necessity as primitive is just a consequence of taking truth as primitive. Modal primitivism is a claim about reducibility: The fact that no analysis of necessity is available in terms of truths of nonmodal kinds is a special case of the fact that truths generally are irreducible to other truths. We know a lot about necessities and possibilities, but that does not mean that our knowledge of modality can be reduced to knowledge of anything else, or that modality itself can be so reduced.

Thus there is an alternative to the conclusion that since the requirements of the magic language and a given world cannot be met, nothing about reality can be known. The Davidsonian route is to deny that truth depends on a given and on a matching between a representation-system and that given. The cost of the alternative is quite high: one has to hold that a vast number of sentences have truth-values that are essentially undetectable. But the alternative, that there is no such thing as truth, renders the world in which we function so well, boarding airplanes with confidence and going about our lives in more or less effective ways, incoherent. The idea that we can think at all or understand anything presupposes that some things are true, and that we know some truths.

Wittgenstein as Deconstructor

On my understanding of Wittgenstein as a deconstructor, he is a conservative deconstructor in something like Davidson's fashion. That is, the fact that truth, necessity, meaning, and the like have no foundation of the traditional kinds shows that foundationalism is defective, not that truth, necessity, and meaning are nonexistent. Philosophy will leave everything intact, for Wittgenstein. The agreement between Derrida and Wittgenstein on the lack of a given and a magic language is in itself a compelling reason to think that those philosophical inventions must be unnecessary to truth and meaning, not grounds for denying truth and meaning.

10

Wittgenstein as Conservative Deconstructor

Deconstructive literary theory has been an important part of literary thinking for some time. Belatedly, some analytic philosophers are coming to realize that deconstruction has common ground with "analytic" philosophy both in presuppositions and in strategies.[1] This realization typically starts with reading Derrida but leads to an interest in literary theory generally.

Literary thinkers have led some philosophers to read philosophy in the light (or shade) of different questions. Some analytic philosophers have thus come to appreciate the possibility of rhetorical readings of philosophical texts and the relevance of such readings for philosophy. More kinds of reading than "getting the argument" are beginning to seem interesting. More directly, there are some parts of the philosophy of language on which literary thinking is vastly more subtle and sophisticated than is analytic philosophy. On a topic such as metaphor, learning from literary theorists and critics can banish the underpracticed, self-confident naiveté with which philosophers have dealt with figuration.[2]

Among the connections between literary theory and philosophy are very strong affinities between deconstructive thought and the thought of the later Wittgenstein. The single most striking difference is that Wittgenstein does not take his deconstructions to have dramatic consequences outside philosophy. Wittgenstein's diagnoses of incoherence in philosophical theories seem to leave the application of the deconstructed concepts untouched. I call this Wittgensteinian reaction to the dissolution of a dualism "conservative deconstruction."

This chapter will discuss deconstructive arguments, focusing on the question of what follows from a demonstration that a dualism is incoherent. In particular, I show that Wittgenstein's thinking has important consequences for those who practice various sorts of "reading for contradiction." In particular, I want to show that some political critiques using deconstructive arguments can, by adapting Wittgenstein's conservative deconstructive thinking, avoid the apparently crushing rebuke that their political position uses dichotomies that themselves are subject to deconstruction.

Dichotomy in Philosophy

The history of philosophy has numerous examples of the following move: A pair of contrasted terms in ordinary language is extended and adapted to provide an account of a certain kind of phenomenon. The dichotomy represents the actual phenomena as a mixture of the two elements in the dichotomy. The sides of the dichotomy are thus, by a systematizing ontological move, projected into a pure case and a generally amorphous "Other." Since the concrete phenomenon is supposed to be really a mixture, each side of the dichotomy must be thinkable as conceptually, if not actually, uncontaminated by the other. Examples of such dualisms are the literal versus the metaphorical, logical consequence versus rhetorical connection, cognitive meaning versus "other" meaning, analytic truth versus synthetic truth, reasoning versus feeling, and conceptual scheme versus the material organized by the scheme.

These distinctions can be understood as descendants of the basic Platonic dichotomy in the middle dialogues that distinguished between the character itself, which is in no way other than its own nature, and an amorphous Other, variously described. Physical things that have a given character have other features and randomnesses besides, owing to mixture with the amorphous Otherness. Such physical cases of the character are thus imperfectly and indeterminately of that character. The Forms in the middle dialogues are the pure, uncontaminated cases of which the material instances are more or less corrupt copies. The negative, completely unstructured side of the dichotomy is some type of Otherness, whose characterization turns out to be a problem.

The dichotomy of Forms and stuff supported and was supported by an epistemological dichotomy. For Plato, knowledge of something is a relation that can only be total.[3] If knowledge is to be total, every feature of an object must be known if the object is known. Thus the only objects that can be known are either very simple ones or objects whose features can be grasped in a mathematical way. Since Forms, if they are numbers or ratios, have an infinity of distinct properties, they can be known in the way that the number series is known, by a rational grasp of an infinite totality. But clearly nothing with contingent properties or indeterminacies can be known. The conception of knowledge as a total grasp of the entire object requires that what is known have a deductive, single-focus structure.[4] Knowledge is thus domination of utterly perfect entities, while belief and lower forms of awareness are uncompleted graspings toward incomplete failures to be. Total mastery requires that both the knowing and what is known be organized deductively around one principle. Such a deductive structure both masters and allows mastery.

Both knowledge and being are conceived in terms of a mathematical structure that can be grasped as a whole even when it is infinitely complex. Greek mathematics was geometrical, and the model is that of a visualizable totality. Such a foundational model does not allow the kind of folding-in on itself that is characteristic of the results of deconstruction discussed below. The self-referential, involuted structures deconstruction points out cannot be visualized, since their unlimitedness is different from the masterable infinity of a mathematical progression.

A language that grasped forms would denote *logoi*. The relations traced among *logoi* would be logical and would follow the true account of the natures of their signifieds, rather than mere rhetorical and poetical connections of word to word and sentence to sentence. Someone persuaded by logic would be persuaded by the real connections revealed to reason, not by the accidental and irrational connections that obtain at the level of mere physical words.

The distinction between the logical and the rhetorical appears in a pair of distinctions in analytic philosophy that continue the Platonic pattern of deductive mastery and purity versus mixture. These distinctions are, first, that between cognitive meaning and other aspects of language that we are tempted to call "meaning," and, second, that distinction's supplement, the analytic/synthetic distinction. The analytic/synthetic distinction is driven by the demand that, since truth is determined by both the world and convention, it ought to be possible to separate out the contribution of the world so as to be left with the pure contribution of the language. The logical relationships would then be the relationships among the meanings and could be given a complete account.

The distinction between the cognitive meaning of an expression and the emotive, connotative, or "other" meaning of a term is a precondition of the analytic/synthetic distinction. That is, both sides of the analytic/synthetic distinction are themselves components of cognitive, truth-value-determining meaning. That the cognitive can be distilled out of concrete language use is yet another instance of the dichotomous, two-factor, theory-building scheme.

The dualisms above have three major features I want to examine.

First, they are foundational. "Foundational" must be explained in terms of the intentions of theory constructors. A foundational dualism is a pair of contraries designed to be the unproblematic components out of which an explanatory scheme is built. These contrary component terms are derived from a descriptive contrast that already exists in the conceptual equipment of the system builder. A descriptive term and its contrary are extended and generalized. By the characteristic dichotomous move, these expanded terms are taken to divide the phenomenon absolutely and exhaustively into components.

Second, the dichotomies harbor a value hierarchy. The left side of each dichotomy is the positive side and the right side the corrupting or negative side. The pure case of the left side of the dichotomy is typically the state from which the other is taken to have fallen, or relative to which the other is defective. Whether this is of any significance for their real character depends on whether the dichotomy of cognitive meaning versus other meaning resists deconstruction. If it does not, then the hierarchical aspects of a pattern of thought are as relevant to its evaluation as thought as are its "cognitive," factual parts.

Third, since some of the dichotomies are concerned with the question of what constitutes good grounds for conclusions, the very discussions are reflexive. This format of theory building, which systems built on these dichotomies seek essentially and exclusively, endorses the "Platonic-Formal" kind of connection among beliefs and a corresponding conception of the systematic. Thus the very demand for a certain type of completeness is itself one side of the dichotomy format that is at issue. A serious attack on the distinction between logical and rhetorical connection, for instance, will (according to its lights) change the criteria for when an attack has succeeded. Both sides of the discussion have this self-referential, question-begging aspect, since the very rules of discourse are among the points at issue.

The central dichotomy for purposes of understanding both deconstruction and this reflexive structure of the debate between theory and deconstructivist argument is the distinction between cognitive meaning versus "other" meaning. "Other" here includes virtually all aspects of words, including emotive, rhetorical, metaphorical, historical, phonic, etymological, and so forth. The related distinction between cognitive connection and other connections among words and sentences is correspondingly diverse on the "other" side. Whether this distinction remains erect after deconstructive attempts to undermine it basically determines what argument and reason-giving are.

Strategies of Deconstruction

Deconstruction is a currently appropriate term for the practice in the history of philosophy of arguing that neither pure case of a dichotomy makes sense. The condition for a dichotomy to function foundationally is that the pure cases of the sides be coherently describable. A deconstructive argument shows that each of the pure cases in fact presupposes the other half of the dichotomy. Ontologically speaking, the allegedly pure case of one side must in fact contain the reference to the other side. So both sides of the dichotomy are in fact impure, and the foundational project cannot succeed.

We can provisionally distinguish two phases of deconstruction as practiced in and upon contemporary philosophy. In the first phase, the deconstructor attacks a standard while holding his argument to that same standard. The standard under attack is the standard of cognitive meaning current at that point, that is, the standard that informs the dichotomy of cognitive meaning versus "other" meaning. The deconstructive argument at this phase reveals the dichotomy to be logically incoherent. Derrida's early writing and some of Quine's and Davidson's work correspond to this model.[5] The second phase of deconstruction begins when the cognitive-meaning/other-meaning distinction has been abandoned. Now the deconstructor need no longer abide by the pre-deconstructive standards of argument and of what counts as incoherence. Once the notion of the "incoherent" is expanded to cover more than "logically incoherent," the work of deconstruction will be likewise expanded to include the exposure of this more broadly conceived incoherence. Thus after an initial success in phase one, deconstruction becomes in phase two as much a rhetorical practice as a logical one, because it now no longer recognizes the rhetorical/logical distinction.[6]

Such two-phased deconstructive arguments can proceed in four basic ways. First, the philosopher can attempt to show systematically that no dichotomy drawn as a given dichotomy is drawn will work. Such an argument establishes that a certain kind of dichotomy is in principle defective because a theory employing one side of the dichotomy must presuppose the other side of the dichotomy. Any account of one ineliminably mentions the other, so that the phenomenon being theorized about cannot coherently be imagined to consist of a mixture of the two components. The difficulty with this strategy, historically, is that the point of view from which one establishes such a conclusion is itself a theory, a foundational, totalizing, conceptual edifice that is itself subject to the same kind of criticism. That is, to demonstrate that a particular sort of result is *in principle* impossible, one needs principles strong enough to determine what kinds of conceptual configurations can exist.[7]

Second, a philosopher can try to undercut the dichotomy by arguing that what the theory incorporating it takes to be a natural division is in fact a product of other factors entirely. This argument reveals that a position is ideological, not scientific—that, for instance, economic interests, gender practices, diseased spirits, Freudian phallicism, or other extralogical concerns actually motivate a dichotomy. When such an argument exposes a "contradiction" (in either a phase-one or a phase-two sense) in this ideology, it counts as deconstruction.[8] Thinkers arguing in this way often succumb to a temptation to be essentialists and theory builders about their own preferred dichotomies. For instance, to claim that something is ideology and not science supposes that true science would be uncontaminated by the interests and motives that constitute an ideology. It is difficult to use a dichotomy to attack another dichotomy without supposing that one's own set of contrasting terms can provide a foundational theory.

Third, the most characteristic strategy of deconstruction as practiced by Derrida is to discuss a particular text and show how that text undermines itself by implicitly denying the division it is explicitly promoting.

(The use of "implicitly denying" is rhetorically complex here, since it must employ criteria for being implicit which are themselves under discussion.) Such deconstruction does not presume that there is a well-defined single "type of view" underlying a whole culture or literature. Such an underlying view would presuppose the division between real meaning (or the essence of a view) and the mere words that convey it. By attacking only texts, one avoids proposing a theory, dividing rhetoric from logic, and positing the thesis behind the text. The most accessible example of this strategy in Derrida is his treatment of Husserl's notion of the expressive sign.[9] There he examines how the account of pure presence in fact presupposes what amount to positings into the past and future—that is, nonpresence. What makes Derrida's argument accessible is that he uses no modes of persuasion that are not already part of standard philosophical practice. What makes later deconstructions so bizarre is that they operate via new notions of consequence.

Fourth, deconstruction attempts to end dichotomous foundational theorizing by demonstrating that the dichotomy has no basis in what we say. This strategy shows not that the dichotomy misrepresents the "facts" about the language but that the theory generates no logical compulsion to restructure what we say. In the purest case, Wittgensteinian deconstruction, the argument basically takes the form of observing *what* is actually said *when.* This strategy transfers the burden of proof to the dichotomizer by denying that the conceptual scheme we have is dichotomous at all. This strategy would deny that extrapolation of "pure cases" is required by anything other than the illegitimate impulse to theorize. Thus, a given "incoherent" dichotomy is argued to be incoherent only because of an illegitimate oversimplification of an unproblematic practice. The practice itself only appears to have the problems the theory was designed to solve, because the theory insists on extending concepts past the points where they continue to make sense. The dichotomy itself, as theoretically understood, is an illegitimate projection. Thus, for such a deconstructor, what is deconstructed is not the equipment of thought but a certain philosophical disease of theorizing. The dichotomy is shown to be incoherent only as extended, not in the form in which it exists in its original habitat.

This is the basic idea of Wittgensteinian deconstruction, the paradigm of the "conservative deconstruction" discussed in the next section. Wittgenstein is not committed to any theory at all, or to any views about the perfection of ordinary language. An "ordinary language" attack on dichotomies that did not itself presuppose foundational, dichotomous accounts of language would concentrate on dichotomies in the philosophy of language and on understanding the workings of language in a way that avoids theorizing.[10]

Consequences of Deconstruction: Revolutionary and Conservative

What if a dichotomy has no pure cases, so that no theory built on the dichotomy can have the simplicity, completeness, and visualizable totality that is hoped for? What follows from a "proof" that the extended and completed dichotomy is incoherent? Deconstructors take two characteristic positions, one revolutionary and the other conservative.

For the revolutionary deconstructor, a deconstructed dichotomy should be completely discarded and replaced by a way of speaking that does not depend on this dichotomy. The incoherence disqualifies the distinction as an acceptable piece of linguistic equipment. (A conscientious deconstructor would ironize the "equipment" metaphor, since it both implies choice and implies the independence of tool and user.) The difficulties of "reform," of communication during reform, and of coherence while a reform is being argued are some of the most interesting topics in deconstructive thought.

The revolutionary position is not that dichotomies can just be abandoned. The apparently radical view that the concepts surrounding a defective dichotomy can be summarily jettisoned presupposes the dichotomies that deconstruction overturns, and is inconsistent with the notions of concepts and persons and cultures that "deconstructive" nondichotomous thought implies. The notion of jettisoning a conceptual scheme supposes that the linguistic is separable from the factual, that there is a way of changing the words yet keeping information constant. As Davidson has argued, the very notion of a conceptual scheme into which we can put our factual beliefs about social justice or the correct relations among the sexes is incoherent.[11] Barring a Platonic conception of meaning as something that stands outside languages and links them across times and cultures, the division into scheme and material organized must be rejected. But rejecting this and recognizing that we are partly constituted by and not just users of a language, renders the rejection of an important part of language paradoxical.

The revolutionary thus has a characteristic difficulty: To dismantle one dichotomy, one must use a language that employs other dichotomies that are similarly defective. To attack a dichotomy by using "Platonic" philosophical terms and Platonic standards is to presuppose other dichotomies. Furthermore, these presupposed dichotomies are interconnected, and more or less invade our entire apparatus for thinking about theoretical issues. Thus, in a general project of excising incoherent dichotomies, the target dichotomies cannot be attacked one by one, because they presuppose one another. To get beyond a dichotomy and think apart from it is to think apart from all dichotomies that cannot be sustained without it, and this would seem to mean thinking in entirely new ways. But to abstain from using all such dichotomies at once is to drop out of the conversation by abandoning the links of understanding that make communication possible.

To eschew "dichotomous" concepts and argument forms is to abandon the formats of argument that are recognized as serious discourse. Strategies such as using terms "under erasure" acknowledge this problem without solving it. The actual result of an acute consciousness of such problems is a kind of ironic philosophy in which the writer distances himself from the conclusions and expressions of the text, hoping to keep at bay the implications of all the terms being used. Such consequences seem to some thinkers to disqualify deconstruction as a tool for those who would change our ways of thinking. The accusation "You're presupposing the same kind of totality" seems an effective way to force deconstructive arguers into quietistic irony.

Conservative deconstruction finds a way out of such binds. The conservative tactic avoids self-referential incoherence by rejecting the theorizing extension of a dichotomy. Unless a dichotomy is forced to pure cases, uncontaminated by their opposites, incoherencies do not appear. But unless we adopt Platonic premises, we have no grounds for supposing that those incoherencies are already implicit in ordinary language, waiting, as it were. Unless the logical demand that a dichotomy be purified, extended, and turned into theory is already there in the true nature of our concepts, the fact that deconstruction exposes the incoherence of theorized dichotomies says nothing about the nontheorized concepts. But, of course, concepts possess no "true nature" beyond what our discussions in their terms construct. So the theorizing impulse is the villain, not the dichotomy. This is the idea behind Wittgenstein's deconstructions.

I call this "conservative" deconstruction because it attempts to preserve the patterns of what is said and when it is said. That is, it attempts to preserve the language without which we do not exist. Since dichotomies are a very important organizing part of this language, the dichotomies (or something like them) must be preserved as well. Conservative deconstruction claims that the theory can be removed while the dichotomy is still in place. That is, the supposition is that the theory is inessential to the dichotomy, which can be used in its normal ways without the hyperbole that constitutes philosophical theorizing. According to conservative deconstruction, there is nothing wrong with the dichotomy itself. Rather, the difficulty is with the theorist who insists on pushing the dichotomy past the point where it makes sense. Its failure to make sense is basically the same type of "presupposition of the opposite" that other deconstructors point out.

For a conservative deconstructor, for instance, the failure to make coherent a principled distinction between the metaphorical and the literal just means that *principled* distinctions are not required. One need not find a principled distinction between the metaphorical and the literal in order for there to be a difference between more and less literal speech. A principled distinction would derive from a statement of necessary and sufficient conditions embedded in an appropriate complete theory, defining the pure cases from which real-world mixtures are derived. Conservative deconstruction tries to preserve the useful dichotomies ("ordinary language is in order") by eschewing the drive to theorize. The theorized and overextended dichotomy is the target of deconstruction, not the dichotomy itself. The obsessive Platonistic demand for total vision is something to be cured.

Wittgenstein as Conservative Deconstructor

In this section I sketch some important views and attitudes about language that the later Wittgenstein shares with Derrida, Quine, and Davidson. I then argue that Wittgenstein's descriptions of language, remarks on what must be and what need not be, and proscriptions against theorizing constitute a kind of deconstruction. Specifically, I claim that Wittgensteinian deconstruction is conservative deconstruction.

Wittgenstein's thought can be organized around one important attitude: his suspicion of the notion of meaning as something behind language. Derrida, Davidson, and Quine share this suspicion. Wittgenstein denies the existence of a Form that various languages express or approximate. For Wittgenstein, language is an aggregate of what people say in specific situations. Such aggregates of events, or practices, are not separable into a component that is the meaning and a component that is the instantiating phonetic or inscriptional stuff.

He abandons that fundamental dichotomy. For Wittgenstein, there are no such pure cases, any more than there is such a thing as the expression of a piece of music which can be played without the music. There is no basis for believing that actual concrete practices are divisible into rules and behavior shaped by rules, or into meanings and the words that carry them.

The Wittgensteinian slogan "The meaning of a word is its use" is not a theory but a remark about what role "meaning" plays in our language. "For a *large* class of cases—though not for all—in which we employ the term 'meaning' it can be clarified thus: the meaning of a word is its use in the language."[12] We have no reason to suppose that Wittgenstein thought this clarification could be systematized into a theory. The whole thrust of the discussion of language games and forms of life is that the language is not capable of being peeled off from the practices in which it occurs. As I will argue below, such practices are not constrained by anything like codes of deductive laws. Practices are the bottom level of explanation, because there is no representation prior to practice-constituted languages; there are no meanings separate from concrete language.

Wittgenstein denies the kind of isolation into pure cases that would permit a theory of meaning, a theory of the forms into which natural-language words fit. The discussion of language games illustrates the inseparability of language, meaning, and practice by denying a level of signification behind, beneath, or prior to the concrete language being used.

Wittgenstein calls language games "games" for complex and intertwined reasons. What counts as a "game," he says, is not to be determined by a common property that links all cases of games. This does not mean that we acquire a mysterious faculty that can extend this predicate to new cases. It means, rather, that there need be no criterion for being a game *in other terms*. Such "other terms" require language to have a foundation that essentially transcends concrete practice.

Wittgenstein's critique, then, should be understood as a deconstruction of the thesis that "game" must have nontrivial, necessary, and sufficient conditions in order to be a coherent term. The demand for common properties, if a common property must be some other property than that of being a game, presupposes views that Derrida, Quine, and Davidson, as well as Wittgenstein, would deny.

I can think of three grounds for holding that such "illuminating" definitions are required. These grounds all demand that accounts of terms be theory engendering. First, the requirement for such illuminating definitions may spring from the belief in a language ontologically more basic than the one we speak. "Game" must have an account in this basic natural language. Second, the requirement may issue from a belief in natural properties that are prior to any language. (Such properties might be natural kinds of sense data, or properties constructed from such.) "Game" must be explained in terms of these properties. Third, the requirement for common properties and illuminating definitions may derive from the view that a language has a hierarchical, interlocked structure that would allow all of its terms to be explained in terms of a proper subset of its terms. Wittgenstein's argument rejects the above views. The inseparability of language and forms of life that Wittgenstein talks about really means that there need be no standards *prior to* practice or language to which practice and language conform.

A consequence of the independence of "game" from outside constraint is that "language game" will itself be a term whose application need not have definition in other terms. Without meanings as translinguistic forms that natural languages instantiate, languages are left embedded in and inseparable from practices, from forms of life. Wittgenstein's conception leaves languages without any pure, uncontaminated external controls. But only on the view that such controls are essential to the workings of practices is this a defect.

Wittgenstein's discussion of rules of language and mathematics confirms the above reading of his discussion of language games. Rules would be the sort of thing that would naturally restrict language if anything could. Wittgenstein argues that rules themselves can be nothing but practices. No external constraints determine the application of a rule. Rules themselves rest on and are practices and have the kind of justification practices have.

The point about rules can be made by noticing that there is a regress in supposing that we follow rules in order to use language. If rules have se-

mantic content, then rules themselves need to be understood. If the interpretation by which they are understood is determined by following rules
that are themselves to be understood, then we have a regress. As Wittgenstein insists, rules followed as *instructions* require interpretation. So if we
speak of rules of language, they are not instructions but *what we do*. Eventually, we have to acquiesce in a practice, to accept a practice without appealing to yet deeper rules that themselves need to be understood by still
deeper rules.

All of this is really a consequence of Wittgenstein's view that all
meaning bearers are languagelike. Nothing semantic determines its own interpretation. The appeal to rules, then, must stop somewhere, given that
rules guide by virtue of carrying meaning. Where such appeals stop, the
rules cease to be prescriptions that are obeyed and become regularities instead. Only when we resign ourselves to "This is what we do" do we have
an end to interpretation. But, realizing that interpretation always ends in a
raw appeal to practice, we deconstruct the necessity that practices be guided
by rules. Practices cannot stand in need of guidance by rules generally, because the understanding of rules rests on practices.

All of the above remarks about the independence of practices from
rules apply only to rules that guide by virtue of the meaning they carry.
Wittgenstein need not deny that language practices are thoroughly governed and constrained by natural necessities at some level. But such "rules"
do not constrain by virtue of semantic content, and they are not obeyed by
being understood. Wittgenstein's views about language are completely
compatible with naturalism and physicalism.[13]

Wittgenstein does not deny the possibility of natural necessities, as
long as it is not supposed that we have supernatural access to them. Likewise, nothing in Wittgenstein prohibits the mathematization of physics or
number theory. He attacks only the notion that there is a type of certainty
that transcends physics; that there are rules whose binding force differs in
kind from the binding force that gravity exerts. Mere regularities are the
strongest rules we have. Only in contrast to *a priori* rules did regularities
seem "mere."[14]

But if there are physical necessities, and physics can be legitimately
theorized about, why can there not be a philosophical theory of language
and mind? I think Wittgenstein basically shares Davidson's position in
"Mental Events" that there is no reason to expect a physical reduction of

the workings of language and the intentional, even though there is nothing over and above the workings of natural law.

One reaction to Wittgenstein's antisystematic thought has been the claim that he holds the extension of "game" to new cases to be *random*. Such a reading of Wittgenstein's remarks assumes that only a criterion of "game" that is somehow not embedded in a language or set of practices can properly decide what is what. Similar comments can be made about the application of a rule to a new case. To accuse Wittgenstein of believing that because we apply such rules without principles, we apply them "in an unprincipled way" assumes that only a pure rule that stands apart from the language in which it is stated can be an effective rational control. But this is exactly what is at issue in the discussion of what language is and what it must be in order for language to function. If no properties or ontological constraints are isolable from language, if we cannot separate *logoi* from *rhemata*, then there is nothing "mere" about a practice and nothing "mere" about the restriction imposed by a rule enforced "only" because "that's what we do." The fascination of Platonism—what Wittgenstein thinks of his writing as therapy for—is precisely this feeling that only an absolute external form can be an alternative to chaos.

The extended discussions of rules in Wittgenstein's works show the reader that the demand for Platonic absolute rules is unsatisfiable. Nothing could satisfy the demands for an absolute imperative rule that determined what one should do next in a number series or, say, next in an inference. Wittgenstein, in numerous passages in *Philosophical Investigations* and throughout *Remarks on the Foundations of Mathematics*, undermines the notion that inference is constrained by rules external to and uncontaminated by concrete social practice. That is, if there is an inference procedure that is determined purely by the nature of logic and not by mere practice, which is constrained only by the exigencies of socializations, following mathematical rules would surely be it. Wittgenstein's strategy here is to try to reveal that the demand for such constraints is senseless. What, after all, could this absolute constraint be? Saying it is a compulsion just redescribes how we feel and does not provide this link to a noumenal demand.

Wittgenstein here adopts his characteristic strategy of showing that the theory he opposes is mistaken even in the case in which it is most plausible. This is the very same tactic he uses in discussing the possibility that the extensions of predicates could be determined by the natural characteristics of the subject matter, in isolation from social agreements. In that discussion, the famous "private-language argument," he takes sense impressions and sensations as alleged objects that could plausibly be said to be identifiable by virtue of their own nature, if anything could be.[15] He demonstrates that, even in this case, the notion of a rule determined by the subject matter itself is senseless. Thus, by refuting the strongest case, he shows that "natural" rules for the extension of any kind of predicate are illusory. The "idea" idea is the notion that contents of consciousness are objects whose nature is transparent to consciousness, so that the language of thought, by having tokens designating sensations, could in principle be a language that we create in isolation. The "private-language argument" proves this to be an illusion.

Wittgenstein does not hold such views as that "reality is a social construct," that the world is created or shaped by language, that language is nothing but social practices, or that meaning is nothing but *what* people say and *when* they say it. To the extent that he draws a conclusion, his conclusion seems to be that none of these items is conceivable in isolation from the others. Thus language is always "contaminated" by practice, practice is always contaminated by language, the world is always contaminated by language, and so forth. Wittgenstein denies that there are pure cases of any sort here. Language use is a thoroughly embedded feature of forms of life, and can no more be separated from these forms of life than the expressiveness with which a piece of music is played can be separated from the act of playing the music.

Wittgensteinian deconstruction does not try to show that the application of a dichotomy misrepresents some facts or leads to a contradiction. Wittgenstein just argues that there is nothing to be said in favor of the dichotomous theory, that the dichotomy is embraced out of a sort of pathological phallic urge, not out of obedience to the facts.

Is this strategy of quelling the impulse to theorize sufficiently similar to the tactic of displaying inconsistencies that it can be called "deconstruction"? Wittgenstein's discussion is very uncharacteristic of the rhetoric of philosophy and does not argue a thesis and is not anything like a treatise. When we combine these features with Wittgenstein's strong anti–theory-building tenor and his renunciation of the *logoi*, the answer seems to be "yes," given the family-resemblance nature of the term "deconstruction." In fact, given that Wittgenstein's goal is to dissolve philosophical problems, it is clear that the antitreatise is a method, like using concepts under erasure, of destroying a theory without replacing it with another. Whereas Derrida in the early works writes treatises asserting the impossibility of treatises, Wittgenstein has found another way.[16]

Wittgenstein's conservative approach to dichotomies, then, is to accept their usability. A dichotomy is incoherent only in *theory*. There is nothing wrong with a dichotomy qua dichotomy, as long as the mad rage to theorize does not extend it past the point where it makes sense, where it has a home in practice. Wittgenstein, then, is the paradigm of the conservative deconstructor.

Is Conservative Deconstruction Conservative?

Less conservative deconstructors could pose several objections to the characterization of Wittgenstein as a "conservative deconstructor." I am convinced that Wittgenstein's text is completely compatible with some of the positions urged in the objections. I am not so sure what Wittgenstein should reply to others. Wittgenstein's conservative deconstruction need not be a "quietist" position about change in our forms of life.

The first objection is that the conservative approach to bad dichotomies seems to suppose that the dichotomy can be separated from the history of theory building that surrounds it, at least in our culture. Is the effect of philosophy on terms like "logical" something that we can remove? It would seem not. Once a pair of terms has a literary history from its treatment in philosophical theories, we cannot very well excise the "philosophical part" of the pair while leaving the "ordinary language" core intact. Much depends here on just how central philosophy is to our forms of life, how much the tradition from Plato on has transformed things. This *may* be the central difference in spirit between Wittgenstein and Rorty, on the one hand, and Derrida and Heidegger, on the other. For Rorty, apparently following Wittgenstein, philosophy is quite marginal in its effects, corrupting certain susceptible individuals, but not really corrupting the culture. For Derrida, following Heidegger, philosophical contamination has deeply affected the whole culture, bringing the attitudes implicit in the extended dichotomies into the forms of life of the culture as a whole. Wittgenstein, I think, has mixed opinions on how pervasive philosophy is, for reasons outlined below.

The second objection offers one consideration why the "theorizing impulse" may be more than a marginal philosophical disease: according to a deconstructor of whatever ilk, the values and other "noncognitive" elements "attached" to the sides of the dichotomies are as much a part of their nature as their logical structure. Without the support of the dichotomy of cognitive meaning versus other meaning or logical versus rhetorical connection, there is no such thing as a pure, rhetoric-free, truth-conditional language. Wittgenstein, with his "forms of life" conception of what it is to have a language, would surely agree. But this raises problems for the restraint of dichotomies, for the values attached to the left sides of the dichotomies are precisely valuings of the foundational, decisive, complete, phallic, pure, and direct. Thus the "theoretical impulse" to extend the dichotomies beyond the point where they make sense is no mere accident but is part of the very structure of those pairs of concepts. A form of life that thinks in terms of these dichotomous concepts is a phallic, linear, theory-mad one. So the disease is not just that of philosophy but part of the forms of life in which these concepts are embedded.

Dichotomies can therefore be harmless only if the terms of a dualism can be separated and isolated from the valuings that go with them. But if deconstructions succeed, there is no basis for calling a value attachment or value connection "mere." Then retaining "the same dichotomy" without the value attachments is impossible. But this conclusion is precisely Wittgenstein's concept of "form of life" and of language as a way of constituting a culture and as something lived. One expects Wittgenstein especially to agree with a conception of language that treats all aspects of words as inseparable parts of one whole social practice. So a "quietist" conservative conclusion from the conservative deconstructive strategy—that deconstructed dualities are still legitimate because ultimate incoherence is not a defect—is inconsistent with Wittgenstein's whole corpus.

A dichotomy is a totality of the interrelations of words with each other and with the life of the culture. To suppose that one has the same array of pairs of concepts, even when important parts of their connections with our lives are removed, is to suppose that the deconstructions have failed. As an example of what is really implicit in Wittgenstein's views, one might imagine that sexual figures of speech and metaphors of domination in academic life could be "cleansed," so that, for instance, a seminal paper, a penetrating question, an overpowering point, and a knock-down argument were all understood on a purely intellectual level.[17] This imagined insulation requires that language work in segregated ways that deconstructive arguments of all sorts have attacked.

Since neither the deconstructor nor the theorist can avoid starting from within some system of presuppositions, the model of how anyone has a change of mind or heart has to be different from that of such a "cleansing." It cannot be that change occurs by a powerful analytical argument starting from absolutely firm premises and begging no questions. The quietist conservative would claim that any change of mind is actually due to a change of heart, and is illegitimate because not rational. A conceptual revolution cannot be like one of the Vienna Circle's designs for a perfect representational system constructed from the outside.[18]

The third objection, then, is this: Conservative deconstruction seems to suppose that it's okay to leave ordinary language alone. Students of Wittgenstein seem to have drawn this conclusion from Wittgenstein's reluctance to theorize and engage in systematic reform of the "ideal language" sort. However, Wittgenstein need be committed to this quietist conclusion only if all intentional changes in a form of life must be falsifying systematizations. But that model of how one would change one's mind depends on deconstructed dualities. Deconstructive thinkers deny that intentional changes in forms of life must be accompanied by organized, totally visualizable blueprints.

In my view, then, Wittgenstein is committed to no "politically" or conceptually conservative conclusions. Wittgenstein's antitheorism need not be taken to claim that ordinary language is unflawed, just that it is in order. Its defects are not defects of orderliness.

So conservative deconstruction can suppose that, to a degree, systems of words are malleable and flexible. Wittgenstein can certainly recognize that forms of life have social consequences. Wittgenstein's antitheoretical remarks are compatible with these realizations. His apparent willingness to accept ordinary-language practices as they appear in their natural environments could be read as just pointing out that those practices are secure *from philosophical attack.* Whatever is wrong with them is not failure to conform to conditions for being a proper language.

On this reading of Wittgenstein, what becomes of conservative deconstruction? The fundamental insight of this position, it seems to me, is this: The fact that a dichotomy becomes incoherent when it is extended too far tells nothing about that dichotomy's worthiness or lack thereof. Contradictions that arise when one follows out a chain of connection do not prove that there is anything wrong with the dichotomy in discourse. To suppose so is to value systematization and totality, rather than particular local working. (Only in mathematics do hidden contradictions mean that everything is a theorem.) Wittgenstein's conception of the workings of language is more or less Maoist, rather than centralized.

The attack on dichotomies, from this point of view, would show that an argument for a dichotomy—namely, that it systematized some phenomena and made them coherent—would not work. That does not destroy the dichotomy; it just renders it unsuitable as the locus of a kind of privilege. The thought system founded on that dichotomy does not have the justification of corresponding to the real ways of nature. So the effect of deconstruction is to democratize dichotomous ideologies. A dichotomy must then be criticized on the same basis as anything else—that it does harm.

In summary, these reflections on Wittgenstein argue that his "conservative" interpretation of deconstruction has a particular type of negative role: to show that a certain kind of privilege is absent from a dichotomy, so that we can abandon and replace that dichotomy if need be. A successful deconstruction does not show that distinctions *must* be abandoned or that a particular dichotomy is defective.

Thus, the demonstration that a certain phallocentric discourse is ultimately incoherent does not discredit it but only allows for the possibility of its abandonment. Any discrediting must be accomplished by showing that the dichotomy does harm. By the same token, the *tu quoque* accusation that, say, a deconstructive feminist critique is itself subject to deconstruction and can itself be exposed as ultimately incoherent does not discredit the critique or the position from which it is made. All such questions are decided by the considerations that we have always taken to be relevant—considerations of good and harm.

Deconstructed Distinctions Are OK

This paper examines some alleged consequences of deconstruction for some traditional distinctions. First we need to say what "deconstruction" is. In the loose and popular sense, "deconstruction" points out inconsistency or incoherence in a distinction, text, or discourse.[1] In this sense, most philosophical critiques are "deconstructions." A main burden of this paper is to characterize "deconstructive" so that Derrida's early work[2] is "deconstructive," for the most part, while most other philosophical work is not.

What Is Deconstruction, Anyway?

Derrida's discussions differ from other philosophical critiques in a number of ways. These differences stem from the consequences Derrida has worked out from a central insight about language and reality, an insight he shares with Quine and Davidson. I will first briefly describe in Quinean-Davidsonian and Derridean terms this premise about language and the world, sketch some of its apparent consequences, and then discuss some differences such a conception of language forces in the notion of "critique" and the notion of "incoherent."

In the course of this characterization of "deconstruction," I will show that deconstruction deconstructs the very terms in which "deconstruction" is understood. A consequence of this self-dismantling will be that many of the supposed "postmodern" consequences of deconstructive critique do not follow. I will then sketch some distinctions that have been hastily attacked, leaving detailed defenses as exercises for the reader.

There Is No Magic Language

"Magic language" is my gloss on a core part of the notion "logocentric." A magic language is a system of representation such that the senses and referents of that language's terms are determined by the intrinsic[3] nature of those terms. Candidates for the terms of a magic language are Plato's Forms, the various forms of Ideas, and especially the various intentional entities and states posited by Husserl.

The notion of a magic language is the notion of a system of thoughts or meanings that stand behind "natural" human language as the meanings expressed by the terms of the natural language. Such items are interpretation-stoppers: items about whose meanings there can be no question, which wear their meanings on their sleeves. For instance, there can be no question of what I mean by my thoughts. The question of what sense I am expressing has a determinate answer, if there is a magic language.[4]

Deconstruction can be understood as the working out of the consequences of denying that such a magic language exists. Briefly, with no magic language, regular language is the best vehicle of meaning available, so all its alleged "defects"—that it is other than its meaning, that it cannot portray the real adequately, and so on—apply to any explicating language as well. A first example of a standard motif of deconstruction, then, is this: since the notion of "sign," as used in the language games that give it a home, presupposes a meaning that grounds interpretation, the term "sign" is no longer quite appropriate once the magic language is denied. So we use "sign" "under erasure." Derrida's critique of Husserl is a critique of the most sophisticated account of the magic language. "Logocentric" is a characterization of accounts and explications that essentially rest on *logoi*, the set of terms of the magic language. As I have argued elsewhere in this volume, the denial of the magic language is the crucial premise of both Quine's thesis of the indeterminacy of translation and Davidson's denials of the dogmas of empiricism.

The basic thought common to Davidson, Derrida, and Quine is that any language consisting of any kind of marks, whether marks on paper or marks in the soul, is no better than words. The marks that constitute intentions, for example, are also material, and thus are present to us as something other than their essence. The same would be true of any proposed meaning-bearing items posited behind the intentions as the source of the intentions' meaning. This "nonpresence" of the "essence," the true meaning, goes all the way down. There is nothing better than Quine's "regress to a background language." Every mark is subject to interpretation. If we think and intend using marks that are just like words, then the material of the word cannot be distinguished in a principled way from its form. Even marks in the soul lack a separable essence, since any mark must have a materiality, that is, accidental features that guarantee the possibility of being misunderstood. Hence the logical connections and features of language are inseparable from the rhetorical connections and features. That is, you cannot get to "meanings" that have only essential connections, that are related only to the things to which they are supposed to be logically related.

To deny the magic language is to be nonessentialist even about language and intention, since the magic language is a language that has only the essence of representation, outwardly expressed in accidental embodiments. Terms of the magic language are thus concepts or transparent representations of concepts. "Transparent" here means that nothing about the expression of the concept adds anything to the concept. Thus in intellectual apprehension of the sense expressed, for instance, there are no accidents of the medium, no rose-tinting or disfigurement from the particular representation to affect the item before the mind.

Giving up the magic language, then, is the last of a series of renunciations in modern philosophy's attempt to renounce essentialism, the idea that there are objective necessities to be apprehended by the mind. This series can be seen as a sequence of attempts to renounce Aristotle's idea that we have a natural access to the kinds of thing there really are, that is, to the objective necessities. When philosophers lost confidence in intuitions of the essence of external objects, essences or *logoi* became restricted to entities that philosophers thought we could intuit, such as thoughts and, eventually, meanings or the rules of language. While they were trying to be nonessentialist, the philosophers managed to retain in one form or another the essentialism implicit in supposing that the nature of anything could be directly intuited.

Thus the British empiricists supposed that Ideas were the tokens of thought that were directly present. An Idea of Red could not be mistaken for an Idea of Yellow. Ideas wore their senses and references on their sleeves. An Idea's reference was fixed by "fitting" its referent—a notion whose difficulties were solved variously by Berkeley and Kant. In phenomenology, the Ideas yielded to intentional objects as the only self-revealing essences. In the logical-empiricist tradition from which Davidson and Quine free themselves, Ideas yielded to meanings of words as the only self-revealing essences. Meanings of words were construed as magically represented stipulations of sets of self-revealing experiences.

Thus, to abandon the magic language is finally to see what it is to be post-Aristotelian. If there is no "magic language," then, roughly speaking, there is nothing better than words, and nothing behind words that is not itself wordlike. The end of the magic language has deep consequences, some of which have been recognized by Quine, some by Davidson, some by Derrida, and some by all three.

Let me spell out a few of these consequences. If there is nothing better than words, nothing whose interpretation is transparent, then features of the words of natural languages that are "merely part of the linguistic formulation" are ineliminable. One cannot analyze a meaningful mark into the two factors of meaning and material features that bear meaning.

Further oppositions resting on such magic "pure thoughts" will also be insupportable. The magical notion of "cognitive meaning" presupposes a kind of representation without contamination by emotive feel or other particularity of the word used to convey the meaning. If we have no alternative to the wordlike, then the analysis of the difference between "John is illegitimate" and "John is a bastard" cannot be that a valuation is "loaded" on a neutral, purely cognitive meaning. More generally, if no principled distinction obtains between the pure meaning and the miscellaneous accidents of a sentence, then no principled distinction can be made between logical consequence and rhetorical connection among statements. (In fact, without this distinction, talk about "sentences" as items reidentifiable in a principled way becomes dubious.) Finally, without the magic language, traditional accounts of metaphor must collapse, since there are no words that can be taken only literally.

Derrida puts these points into an analysis of "binary oppositions" that connects his discussion of philosophical analysis with structuralism and complements Quine's and Davidson's discussions of dogmas of empiricism. A binary opposition is a pair such as form/matter, nature/culture, analytic/synthetic, logic/rhetoric, and so forth. As used in philosophical analyses, binary oppositions typically portray a phenomenon as a mix of the two parts of the opposition. Thus the truth of a sentence is a mixture of facts about language and facts about the world. A dog is a mixture of form and matter. An analysis could work only if the phenomena were conceptually or actually separable, so that the phenomenon being explained could be the mix of those two factors.

Binary oppositions are crucial to a grasp of what Derrida's deconstruction is about. Let me begin with some observations on distinctions in general. A distinction could be theoretically acceptable in two ways. First, the distinction may correspond to what is the case, so that one side of that opposition, at least, refers to a component of the world, for instance a property or natural kind. Second, the distinction, though arbitrary in relation to the phenomena, may be scientifically right if it is pragmatically useful and if the theory associated with the distinction is coherent, both internally and in relation to other parts of what we believe.

The first justification might make a distinction usable and correct even though the contents of the concepts of the distinction are confused and incoherent. The concepts of male and female may be like this. Aristotle was dead wrong about what the difference is, but his distinction still reflected an objective divide, founded on chromosomes, unbeknownst to him. For the first kind of justification to be acceptable, one would have to accept that a distinction in a theory could refer to an objective distinction in nature even though nothing in nature fit the theory. Derrida would find the notion of such a distinction incoherent, since he is wedded to the idea of truth as adequation, and the view that adequation must be understood in terms of fit.[5]

For Derrida, the second kind of justification is the only justification for a distinction. A good distinction must at least be coherent and, roughly speaking, the sort of distinction that could describe a real world. Whatever else truth is, a true theory cannot contain principles about a distinction that are contradictory or circular. A true theory with a genuine distinction characterizing its elements would say what the positive side was in a way that did not make reference to its lack. So, for instance, the even integers can be characterized as natural numbers divisible by two, and not just as the numbers that are not odd.

Deconstructing a binary opposition is showing it to be incoherently circular, in its theory. That is, neither side of the distinction is, by the very theory, able to be independently specified. Thus the distinction cannot give a theory that would, roughly, correspond to a world part of which had a property that the other part lacked.

Derrida's arguments assume that the user of a distinction "knows what he means," in some sense to be explained. For someone who "knows what he means" and uses a distinction, the distinction can be read off from the theory implicit in the distinction. The traditional idea of knowing what we mean, Derrida argues, appeals to meanings as *logoi*. Derrida has argued that such "pure presence," in which a mind has the object transparently before it, is impossible. His demonstration starts from the best phenomenological analysis of consciousness and from conceptual truths about the essential repeatability of the property as well as any alleged magic term for that property.

The fundamental binary opposition that is deconstructed, then, is the opposition between the *logos* and the material clothing it wears in words. Among the distinctions that abandoning the *logos*/clothing distinction undermines are the use/mention distinction and the token/type distinction.

If there are no given real natures and there is no magic language, then what gives the meaning of a term? And what would give the extension of the term? Without a given, relations to other terms are crucial to the meaning of any particular term. (Saussure's and Quine's arguments are important here.) The meaning of any particular term is always mixed inextricably with the other terms of the language. For a binary opposition, the crucial relation for the favored term is to the other term—the not-logical, the not-male, and so on. This is its definitive "other." For a genuine, theoretically acceptable distinction, other relations to other terms would have to be able to supply independent determination of one side of the distinction. In that case, the relation to the "other" would be like the relation of even to odd. While it is essential that even numbers are not odd, the concept of "even" has independent grounding.

A deconstruction of a binary opposition is a demonstration that a distinction is essentially a relation in which neither item of the relation has an independent footing. A deconstruction shows how the favored term of the opposition really depends on its other, and how the opposition itself thus does not give a genuine "two-factor" analysis of what is the case. Thus Quine, for instance, shows that there is no independent sense of "true in virtue of meaning" that will separate the analytic from the synthetic. Deconstructing the binary opposition that founds a distinction does not mean erasing differences. So deconstructing the analytic/synthetic distinction does not make "Bachelors are unmarried" just the same as "Guinea pigs are sometimes cute." It does mean that the difference cannot be analyzed as a mixture of the purely verbal and the purely factual.

That a binary opposition is not founded on a direct reflection of an opposition in the nature of things does not automatically imply that the dichotomy is suspect but rather raises the possibility of incoherence of various kinds. The firmest ground for deeming a system of concepts to be coherent is that it is tied at various points to reality, whose coherence will induce an overall coherence on the system. If essentialism were true and the meanings of terms could be presented transparently, then the coherence and order of nature would induce its stability and order in a system of concepts about nature. But if essentialism is false and no magic language exists, then any stability would need to be founded on human interactions. Such stability is much different from that envisaged by a Platonic system. While we will continue to use and must use systematic connections and must have "theories" of each others' speech, such connections are constantly in flux and are always subject to multiple nonequivalent, incomplete systematizations. When we describe and understand a discourse, we must use the truth-definition format that provides systematic truth-conditions for an infinity of sentences, and thus provides a matrix for descriptions of what people are doing in speaking. But as Davidson has argued,[6] such theories are not unique but are instead indeterminate. (A complication here is that Davidson's and Quine's "indeterminacy" corresponds to Derrida's and de Man's "undecidability." Davidson would not want to use "undecidable" because of its connection with completeness proofs; Derrida does not want to use "indeterminate" because it implies fuzziness.) Without a magic language, those systematizations are not distinguished by matching an underlying conceptual order, but can be understood only as making sense of a causal order. As Quine has observed, once we abandon the magic language, there is just no fact of the matter about what someone means, as opposed to what someone is interpreted as meaning, any more than there is a fact of the matter about which real number corresponds to the current temperature. The assumption behind Quine's example of temperature is that there is a given that stays the same behind such alternatives. Without such a given, denying that there is a fact of the matter can mean either that truth-values and truth conditions are irrelevant, as Derrida concludes, or that there are unknowable truths independent of every other truth, as Davidson seems to hold.

But notice that "making sense of" is an intentional and therefore teleological and conceptual notion. So the question of the relation of the intentional to the causal is complicated by the interpreter's being an intention-possessing entity and a self-interpreter. Thus we have a systematization of our own intentional states, and try sometimes to make the phenomena fit. Such reflexive feedback is one reason that "systems" are not just abstractions but influence what they systematize. For Davidson and Derrida, the rejection of the magic language cannot result in epiphenomenalism, the idea that the conceptual is only an interpretation of the causal, which is all that is really going on.

Why would we expect unfounded, interrelated arrays of concepts to be incoherent? (Put off for a moment the question of what "incoherent" means.) Two answers are available here. First, such incoherence seems likely in view of the purely formal difficulty that a natural language falls under the scope of its own truth predicate. Second, since terms are applied in new ways and under the vagaries of "political" and other "nonlogical" concerns, the chance that a language forms a system in the usual sense is rather small.

"The usual sense" of system means a structure that naturally separates form from contents, that naturally distinguishes the force with which something is said from the truth conditions of what is said, and that has the deductive structure of the familiar formal systems. That is, the difference between a "system in the usual sense" and a system such as we actually find in discourse is that the form/content distinction in the latter is not given in the nature of things and does not fit the phenomena completely or in a unique way. Of course a discourse can be made to fit a system by appropriate interpretation, because there is no limit to the auxiliary hypotheses that can be imported to save a theory in the face of recalcitrant data. But such interpretation is bad theory building.

Just from the limited and idealized standpoint of cognitive theory-formation, a network of beliefs will be inconsistent at any particular time. With a magic language, the inconsistencies can be explained as deviations from a "basic underlying system": there is a pattern of *logoi*, the world of forms, the "meaning of the theory," or "the theory itself," which may be imperfectly embodied at any time in the actual discourse. Without a magic language, the inconsistencies cannot be explained as deviations from such an underlying system, for no such system exists. There is only the discourse itself, a pattern of utterances in situations. That our network of beliefs does not constitute a complete theory, in the mathematical sense, could be demonstrated in two ways. First, one could construct a proof that no such theory is possible. Here we need not use notions of "proof" and "possible" that transcend any particular theory, and so we need not suppose a magic language in which to formulate such proofs and their principles. Second, one could attempt a case-by-case demonstration that no theory is actual. This kind of "proof" would use standards and a metatheory that would themselves be subject to deconstruction. Derrida engages in both kinds of activities. The "proof" that no theory is possible does indeed use a theory that is incomplete, but it is not for that reason unusable.

Deconstruction and Critique

Given these consequences of denying a magic language, Derrida's critiques of dichotomies will proceed differently from standard philosophical discussions. Part of Derrida's distinctive contribution is his conscious adaptation of his own practice in light of the consequences of undoing founding dichotomies. Here I will sketch three important differences in approach.

First and most obviously, what a deconstructive critique criticizes and shows to be at odds with itself cannot be a "theory" in the sense of a set of statements with given cognitive meanings, since such an object presupposes a magic language. If no principled distinctions separate facts from meaning, facts from values, rhetoric from logic, or sentences from other meaningful items (that is, if these are not natural dichotomies), a critique must be a critique of a discourse or a concrete text. And in view of these different objects of critique, considerations that would be "irrelevant to the argument" in a standard philosophical discussion may well be relevant to showing a discourse incoherent. If other connections besides meaning connections are the "binders" of a discourse, then Freudian considerations, aesthetic coherencies, "literary" connections and resonances, and so on, may all be part of the "coherence" of a discourse.

Once we ask what a "theory" or its replacement can be without the magic language and the oppositions it allows, we are driven[7] immediately

to the next differentiating characteristic of any deconstruction of an organizing opposition.[8] This second major difference is that the very idea of incoherence is called into question.[9] Let us start with the most extreme inco-
herency, inconsistency.

Inconsistency is the strongest kind of incoherence. If the notion of
"inconsistency" is absolute, that is, not relative to an interpretation, an
understanding of it requires the essence of statements, the cognitive content alone. (Unless we withdraw to the syntactic level, which has its own
problems.)[10] For a discourse to be strictly inconsistent, there must be formulations among the assertions of the theory whose meanings conflict. So
according to the denial of the magic language, there can be no absolute inconsistency, in the logocentric sense.

Without the magic language, inconsistency is a localized phenomenon,
based on an interpretation. In positing an inconsistency, an interpretation is
at maximum stress, as it were, since an inconsistency is the best evidence that
an interpretation is mistaken. Thus no such inconsistency can be unambiguously established.[11] So if the denial of the magic language is correct, we
have no hope of a strict proof that there cannot be a magic language.[12]

So, without the magic language, the conception of the "architecture"
of a natural-language system is a much richer extension of a Quinean ide-
alization. The kinds of connections to be discussed and the way binary oppositions organize a discourse are more than a set of sentences and their
logical and evidential relations. For example, without a magic language, the
cognitive is not isolable from the evaluative. Thus the evaluative is part of
every term's meaning. Thus, important valuations will permeate a system
of terms in much the way that a central belief will, according to Quine and
Davidson. The web of belief[13] must really be a web of desire and belief,
both conscious and unconscious.

Connections among parts of a discourse are in some ways weaker and
in other ways stronger than logocentric accounts allow. Some connections
are weaker, because the absolute connections of analytic containment that
the magic language supplied are now lacking. Other connections are
stronger, though, because they are not "merely linguistic." That is, various
resonances and connotations now count as genuine connections, even
though they are nonlogical.

"Incoherence," then, must be a much broader notion, a notion including "inconsistencies" of evaluation, action, and other kinds of lack of
fit. In addition to "inconsistencies" in some analogous sense, "incoherence"

has to cover lack of connection. But by definition, no operating discourse lacks of connection. In fact, we would suppose that for Quine and Derrida, connections tie in more numerous ways than the positivists recognized. Without the magic language, though, what is the status of connection itself, and how does such connection have effects?

Another way of putting this is as follows: Without the magic language, "systems," in the sense of theories or conceptual underpinnings, are not sharply separate from "systems" in the "merely causal" sense. A culture discoursing in the world is a system of causal and biological relations. How is it also a "conceptual system," and how does a "conceptual system" fit with the causal and material system?[14]

There are three basic answers to how a conceptual system fits with a causal system. First, Plato's idea is that the causal and conceptual are the same.[15] Second, the post-Cartesian idea is that the conceptual is a special mental realm of the terms of the magic language. Third, what? The rejection of the magic language rejects the notion of a conceptual system as a real underlying structure that exists independently, and the rejection of magic-language essentialism rejects the coincidence of conceptual and causal systems. But we cannot think of ourselves as speakers and thinkers and actors in the world without thinking of ourselves as concept users, and we cannot think of concepts and intentionality apart from systems.

As Quine and Davidson have effectively argued, there is no single best way of mapping systems of the conceptual, "intentional" sort onto such causal systems. A deconstruction shows that any such matching will have alternatives and will be "incomplete" by Platonic, mathematical standards of a "conceptual scheme." If there is no magic language, no basis separating a natural linguistic system from the causal system, and a real language has no "underlying semantic structure" that is precisely separable from causal connections, then how are we to think of systems and the distinctions on which they are built?

Understanding a language or a text is having an interpretation or a truth-definition. Such interpretation sorts the events and their mass of interconnections into words with meanings and intentions, and sorts the connections into "logical," "rhetorical," and so on. Hence, texts and natural languages are systems, in that every effective way of treating them as spoken by persons systematizes, that is, finds truth-definitions. But those truth-definitions are not exactly discoveries of a structure in the magic language and they are not exactly "impositions," either. That is, given that we exist and that, as persons, we are essentially intentional, we cannot think that intentionality is just epiphenomenal. For Derrida (and Davidson) intentionality and semantic systematization (truth-definition) are not epiphenomenal "interpretations" of a causal "hard reality." Such hard reality supposes that it is possible to make the very separations that deconstruction would deny. Without a "given," there is no "organizing" of a given.[16]

Such truth-definitions take place in a metalanguage, which brings up the third distinguishing characteristic of deconstruction: Deconstruction realizes that the metalanguage is part of the account being deconstructed. That is, if we are deconstructing a notion that is central to our system, we are deconstructing from within the discourse. The system both provides the equipment to mount a deconstruction and is itself being shown, by its own "principles," to be incoherent and deficient with respect to those principles.

If in fact philosophically interesting notions pervade entire discourses, then the philosophical deconstructor can take no position outside the theory from which to find standards to evaluate it and show it to be "incoherent." Rather, a proof of incoherence is a proof that works within the discourse itself, employing the very standards endorsed by the theory to show that the theory fails to meet them. (Even for a deconstructor who stood completely outside the discourse, the critique would be conducted from a position and by means of principles which themselves would be deconstructible.)

In a deconstruction of any philosophical interest, the critic operates within the very discourse he is criticizing, and so criticizes in accordance with those very precepts he is showing to be incoherent. Deconstruction is constantly aware of the self-referential consequences of a deconstruction. So a deconstruction cannot have the consequence that a system has no systematicity and no principles, since any argument must function according to something.

So What If It's Deconstructed?

What do deconstructions show? Roughly, a deconstruction establishes that a given theory or discourse is in the same situation that, on general principles, we would expect every theory or discourse to be in: it is not a perfect theory; it is not a coherent conceptual unit, in some mathematical sense of "coherent."[17] But such imperfection does not distinguish that discourse from any other. So there are two things deconstruction does not show.

First, that a discourse has been deconstructed does not immediately show that it is defective, except relative to discourses that are perfectly coherent. But there is good reason to believe that, failing a magic language, every discourse that contains its own metalanguage must be defective. Thus, it is not a prima facie embarrassment that a discourse is incoherent.

Second, that a discourse has been deconstructed does not show that it is unusable as a practical device for running a culture or for directing spaceships or computer hardware. It may not even be unusable as intellectual or theoretical equipment. We have numerous demonstrations from Derrida that incoherent theories can have standards of argument that permit us to argue very effectively, since every deconstruction "from within" is such a demonstration.

An important issue is at stake here: Many of those reacting to deconstruction's theses, including some who regard themselves as convinced by deconstruction, take a deconstruction to show a fatal inadequacy in the distinction or discourse. But such an evaluation presupposes the very standards that the deconstruction has shown to be unreasonable, because unfulfillable. That is, to suppose that a discourse that is not governed by a magic language is unusable is to accept an important part of the logocentric picture. Once the overall ideals that rest on presence and the magic language are shown to be impossible of fulfillment, it is only our retention of essentialist views about conceptual connection that allows us to continue to think that the theory or discourse is unusable.

This plausible response to the naive deconstructionist, though, is not quite adequate. A distinction or discourse often cannot be resurrected without its magic-language-associated theorizing.

First, there is a difficulty about using the same distinction without its connection to magic-language theorizing. Since the deconstruction has taken place within a theory or discourse that "accepts" such standards, the reaction that the distinction has been ruined makes sense within the theory. And deconstructions typically take place from within. A deconstruction is an analysis by someone who uses the distinctions and discourse that is being deconstructed. If such meta-axioms are pervasive parts of the deconstructed discourse, then the distinction resurrected after the deconstruction must be in a new discourse, one without the illusions that require the magic language. That is, to the extent that a distinction is part of a theory and the theory is part of a distinction, that theory cannot be simply excised from the distinction. For instance, we cannot just say "Look, by 'analytic' I don't mean anything about meaning containment. I just mean obviously true." Only with a magic language can we, by an act of stipulation or willed excision, remove a connection from a term. One of the really interesting lessons of deconstruction is that, since there is nothing deeper than words in which to think, we think in the words we have, with the connections there indeed are.

On the other hand, if the discourse is incoherent in the ways demonstrated, then no rigorous demonstration that the discourse "as a whole" "accepted" the unfulfillable standards will be forthcoming. That is, maybe in many areas, we can use "essentially" without appeal to essences. I think this is right. It is part of the illusion of the magic language that associated with each term is a list of axioms or rules of use that apply in all circumstances.

Second, there is a difficulty about how distinctions can be used at all if they cannot be made precise. How can a distinction formulated within a deconstructed theory still function as any distinction at all? Take the analytic/synthetic distinction again. We want to say that "Guinea pigs are sometimes affectionate" is more empirical than "Triangles are three-sided figures," which is more conceptual. A routine answer is "It's a matter of degree, not a metaphysical distinction." But the construction of this as "a matter of degree" is fraught with difficulties: The talk of "degrees" seems to imply that the distinction has a zero point and an upper bound; in short, a metric. But that is only possible if pure cases exist. So how do we apply distinctions when we do not have an algorithm or pure cases or a genuine metric?

Derrida says the following: "What theoretician ever renounced this axiom: in the order of concepts (for we are speaking of concepts and not the colors of clouds or the taste of certain chewing gums), when a distinction cannot be rigorous or precise, it is no distinction at all."[18] Is this true of all distinctions? If it is, then there is no distinction between bald and nonbald men, or between persons and nonpersons. Every contrast between a term for a medium-sized object and that term's negation is imprecise, and cannot be made precise. This indeed shows that we cannot explain baldness as the possession of a natural property. But that does not mean that no one is bald, or that there is no difference in terms of baldness between Eisenhower and Cher. Derrida has to be mistaken on this occasion.

Here is a way out: Distinctions of ordinary life are not distinctions "in the order of concepts," and so need not be precise. Precise distinctions are important in philosophical analyses and scientific explanations. There, we seek two-factor analyses, explanations that will give understanding beyond description. Of course the distinction between the order of concepts and ordinary life is itself a binary opposition, ripe for deconstruction. So, although we cannot we isolate the philosophical from the ordinary precisely, we can in a rough and ready way. So, even though philosophy and Platonism pervade ordinary speech, they are still distinguishable (but not precisely) from the ordinary.

I conclude with the following four examples of contexts in which this way of dealing with distinctions can rescue common sense from theoretical paradox. The common theme of each of these exercises is that a contrast may be useful and important even though there is no two-factor analysis of a binary opposition. First, even though no principled line divides the aesthetic from the moral and political, still they can be contrasted in valuable and illuminating ways.[19] Second, even though no principled line divides the analytic from the synthetic, this does not mean that there are not "more conceptual" and "more empirical" statements. In fact, Quine has given us an alternative understanding of the ways in which statements differ on this dimension. Third, even though no principled line divides the rhetorical from the logical, nonetheless a good argument differs from a fallacious one that merely appeals to passions. Finally, even though no principled line divides interpretation from fact, because each always contaminates the other, we can still distinguish between what is hard fact and what is looser talk.

Can ordinary distinctions be saved from the fate of deconstructed philosophical ones? I do not know. Derrida and Heidegger differ from Quine, Wittgenstein, and Davidson on this point. Whereas Quine and Wittgenstein seem to think that philosophical difficulties are marginal, Heidegger and Derrida think they are pervasive. While Wittgenstein proposes therapy, Heidegger talks about "The West" and how a Greek temple changed everyone's thought. My opinion is that Quine, Wittgenstein, and Davidson are right. There is a clear if unprincipled contrast between engineering and speculation that even humanities professors accept in practice. We do not get on airplanes whose principles of construction and operation are only as firm for us as psychoanalysis or our philosophical theories.

12

Derrida's Differance and Plato's Different

This essay examines the ways in which Derrida's discussion of "differance" is remarkably parallel to Plato's discussion of Difference in the *Sophist* and the *Parmenides*.[1] As I argue below, the metaphysical problems that motivate these accounts are also similar. Very roughly, Derrida's differance is a phenomenological version of Plato's Different Itself. Plato's presentation of "Parmenides'" discourse on the generation of the physical world from a One that Is is an early version of the preconceptual spacing that Derrida finds implicit in Husserl's "phenomena." Derrida has never made the Platonic parallels and common grounds explicit, so this essay takes the exposition of these connections as its first task. I argue for and discuss the parallels between Difference and differance, assuming with only the slightest arguments some rather controversial interpretations of Plato.[2] I will show how Derrida's obvious reference to Plato both implicitly interprets Plato and explains many of the prima facie obscure features of Derrida's "differance." I then argue that Derrida's paradoxical remarks about differance are almost exactly what Plato implies about Difference, in his discussions in the *Parmenides*.

Roughly and briefly, the idea brought into question by Plato in the *Parmenides* and scouted by Derrida is that we cannot coherently describe the construction of the world as we know it by, for instance, starting with our scientific theories and describing how we as organisms derive the world as we know it, because our scientific theories presuppose the very concepts that are being explained. So Derrida's notion of differance addresses the puzzle of how, if all "sameness of kind" presupposes "falling under the same concept," and all concepts are constructed, not given, sameness and difference get a purchase on the world, as it were. The model of concepts dividing up the world seems to presuppose a contradictory set of priorities: Concepts are required to construct the objects in a plurality of objects, but concepts cannot differentiate unless there is already a plurality of objects. Plato's version of the same problem is a notational variant of Derrida's Husserlian dilemma.

Throughout, I suggest that Plato and Derrida can be construed as questioning the very idea that there are isolable simple entities that can found meaning and being. Plato and Derrida question this by showing that the best such foundational system they know does not quite work. Plato differs from Derrida in continuing to suppose that there is a foundation for necessity, namely mereology, whose transparency guarantees its truth. Davidson, as opposed to both Plato and Derrida, tries to show directly that the project is incoherent.

Why Does Plato Need Difference Itself?

The following interpretation of Plato's thought in the middle and late dialogues is not unusual. It owes much to J. N. Findlay and other thinkers who take Aristotle's comments about Plato seriously. In any case, the exegetical point about Derrida holds if Derrida understands Plato in this way, whether or not Plato himself thought this way.

On my understanding of Plato, the Different comes to have a central place in Plato's account of the world. We first need to see why Plato is committed to the existence of such an entity. Here, as is often the case with Plato, it helps to look for Parmenidean theses that Plato accommodates. Three such Parmenidean considerations can be discerned:

The first consideration leading Plato to find that Difference Itself is an entity is the Parmenidean principle "Is or Is Not." I interpret this as the plausible thesis that anything required to give an account of what is the case must be a being, something real. That is, reality has no "components" that are halfway between being things and being nothing.[3] That is, being an entity is an all-or-nothing matter.

Hence, if difference is required in order to account for what is the case, then difference is something, and we can speak of Difference Itself, that Being that is this factor in what is the case. If the world is a plurality, Difference Itself must exist, since a plurality requires that each of the items in it be different from the others.

The second consideration to which Plato responds is a powerful Parmenidean argument for the unity of Being. Plato's responses to this challenge will establish the antecedent of the conditional "*If* difference is required in order to account for what is the case, then difference is something, an entity." It is not obvious whether Difference Itself is in fact required for such an account.

Someone could claim that being different is a merely verbal property, that cases of Difference in fact have nothing in common between them. Thus, no entity need be posited as the element common to the states of affairs "A is distinct from B" and "C is distinct from D." Perhaps all such facts of difference reduce to facts about what other properties things have, so that no further property of being distinct needs to be postulated.

However, there are powerful reasons for explaining difference by reference to an entity, Difference Itself, which will turn out to be logically and metaphysically prior to Forms. The reasons emerge from an argument attributable to Parmenides. Suppose that Plato understood Parmenides to argue as follows for the conclusion that there is exactly one Being: Suppose there were two Beings, A and B. Then, by the principle "is or is not," something would have to make them distinct; that is, some being would have to be to account for this part of the way things are. A candidate entity might be a property that A had but B lacked. But such a property would itself be a Being, and, to do its job of distinguishing A from B, would have to be already distinct from the two things it distinguishes. Thus we cannot explain distinctness by appealing to properties that distinguish, since such properties presuppose the very fact of distinctness that is being explained.

An argument that this consideration is behind Difference Itself comes from Aristotle's version of Parmenides' argument. In *Metaphysics* B, 1001a30–b1, Aristotle says: "If Unity itself and Being itself are beings, there is a difficulty how there can be something else beside these, that is, how things can be more than one. For what is different from being does not exist, so the word of Parmenides must follow, that all things are one and this is Being." This argument can be understood as resting on the following considerations: Suppose that there are two entities, A and B, and that Being a Being is a property. Then consider the possibility of some other property, say c, which entity A has but entity B lacks. Insofar as c is real, it is an entity and is in that respect like the things A and B that it is supposed to distinguish. The differentiating part of the differentiating feature c must be something other than the property Being a Being. But then, what could there be to it other than Being? Anything we could arrive at would also be a Being. If we subtract the Being component from c, we once again have something that must Be, and so must have Being. If we subtract that Being component, we are left with a residue that must still have Being. And so on. If we try to isolate something a thing has other than being, that component itself must be and so must have being. So, as it were, Being drives out every other property. But then Being is the only property, if it is a property at all.

Aristotle presents this as a familiar consequence, so we can suppose that this argument was familiar to Plato as well, whether or not it was what Parmenides had in mind. Plato may or may not wish to have "Being" be a property. My view is that these and other problems (which we see explored in the *Sophist*) lead Plato away from the idea that Being is a property at all. But the underlying difficulty would remain if "One" replaced "Being." Isolating individual components as themselves is a general difficulty that is independent of whether Being is a feature.

So if we formulate Parmenides' challenge as "What can make two beings distinct beings?," answers that appeal to such beings as properties or distinct spatial locations fail to answer the challenge. Such entities already must be distinct beings in order to separate being from being. Thus, it would appear that nothing can separate Being from Being, for Being always cleaves to being, as Parmenides says.

The beginning of an answer to Parmenides must be a regress-ender: Plato needs an entity that will distinguish itself without requiring a further object to make it distinct from the things it distinguishes. The only possible object of this sort would be Difference Itself. If there were an entity, Difference Itself, which explained all difference, then that entity would explain its own difference from all others. Since Difference Itself is that in virtue of which things are different from each other, Difference Itself can be different from Being while still being a being. It is different from the things it distinguishes in virtue of itself. (Many will be reminded of some famous arguments for the existence of God.)[4] Sameness is another such entity; it makes things be the same, and likewise makes itself the same as cases of sameness. So the participation regress disappears.

The third consideration from which Plato argues that Difference Itself is an entity is Parmenidean in the sense that the character Parmenides in the *Parmenides* develops it: If natures were self-sufficient, independent entities, then Difference would take its place among them, perhaps having especially wide and interesting scope.

The "Third Man" argument[5] shows that we cannot think of Forms as being anything other than the natures they explain. If the Form "Man" were anything other than the nature it explained, that is, if it were the nature Manhood in a kind of ideal substratum, then the nature itself would be something other than (i.e., in addition to) the Form. So Forms must be nothing other than the natures they are. As soon as a Form has more than one component, those components become objects of inquiry. In particular, the component that is the nature itself becomes yet another Form. Hence, Forms must be simple objects, entities that *are* the natures they explain. This seems to be the import of the first section of the *Parmenides*.

This result, however, turns out to be impossible. There can be no simple objects. The arguments in the second part of the *Parmenides* prove that such single items are not possible: Suppose that there is a single being. Its singleness is distinct from its being. So, given the Parmenidean principle above, a single being is immediately two. Furthermore, given that the singleness and the being of the entity are different, there is a third thing, the difference between them.

But now these three entities are each single beings different from each other. And each of them is thus plural, and so on. Entities are never just one thing. Even the very natures that Forms are supposed to be must become indefinitely complex, as soon as we try to isolate the character just by itself. Difference makes impossible any character's being just itself. The play of difference divides every nature from itself. According to the argument of the *Parmenides*, we cannot have a nature just by itself present before the mind. As soon as we put such a nature before our minds, we see that the nature also has other components, at least being and difference from others. But the effort to pare such accretions away and get to the pure nature itself is always frustrated, since any such core must itself exist and be different from other things.

By the arguments of the *Parmenides*, every entity is both the same and different from itself. Each nature or Form is different from itself in the sense that there is something to it besides the nature itself. Each of these entities that is supposed to be *F* Itself turns out to be *F* plus something else.[6] On my interpretation, the *Parmenides* is a demonstration that there cannot be an entity that is in no way plural. So even a nature is something distinct from that nature.

One could say, reading Plato as a source for Derrida, that any Nature Itself is always deferred: it is different from any grasp we can have of it, and different from any being that could "express" or have it. We might even speak of the "materiality" of the Form, the fact that any Being that might be supposed to be a Nature Itself is always something besides that nature. The *Parmenides*, then, seems to have implicit exactly Derrida's ideas of deferral. We can never get at "Man Itself," because it is always (at least) also the distinct natures One and Being.

Each physical thing is the same and different in the sense that it is the same as itself while having distinct features is *being* different things. Furthermore, anything lasting through time is, as Plato notes, both the same and different, since it is the same thing existing at different times. Sameness and difference of a single thing *is* temporality. Furthermore, the occurrence of distinct instances of the same nature at different places or times makes the instances same and different and may be interpreted as making the nature same and different as well.

Derrida's characterizations of differance as spacing (spatial) and deferral (temporal) have almost exact parallels in Plato. Difference Itself is both the same as itself and different from itself, since Difference Itself is and Being is different from Difference Itself. If Difference Itself accounts for distinctness, Difference Itself is manifest in the Receptacle and Time, since each of these is a way of making things both the same and distinct. That is, if we think of the Receptacle as something like Space, and treat the Receptacle as a manifestation of the Different, then this aspect of Difference Itself permits natures to have multiple cases. As Aristotle describes Plato's theory,[7] the Forms are generated by the application of the One to the Great and the Small (the latter entity is identical to Difference Itself, the principle of Differentiation), and then the Forms are applied to the Great and Small again to generate the spatiotemporal particulars. Roughly, the Forms or natures are the various different ways of being one thing; and spatiotemporal particulars are spatiotemporally different cases of those different ways of being one thing. The Different is manifest in spatiality and temporality and in any differentiation. So it is the great instancizer and subdivider. Thus, following Aristotle's remarks, the One or Being becomes the many Kinds, that is, ways of being one being, each of which is then differentiated into the many spatially and temporally distinct cases of being each of the many kinds of Being.

To illuminate Derrida's notion of differance, several other important properties of Difference Itself should be emphasized: Difference Itself is not an ordinary nature, according to Plato, and according to the exigencies of the case. Difference Itself is prior to the Forms, the entities that are natures of Beings. (Parts of the Different Itself seem in the *Sophist* to be the natures of nonbeings, as noted above.) Each of the Forms must already be different from everything else in order to be an independent being that can be a nature. By the regress argument ascribed above to Parmenides, Forms must be distinct entities not in virtue of the natures they are but rather in virtue of Difference Itself. So Difference Itself distinguishes objects prior to there being Forms. That is, the various properties things have are distinguished by raw difference, that is, by Difference Itself, not by anything present in one and lacking in the other.

Derrida says similar things about differance: Differance is not exactly a thing and not exactly a concept,[8] for reasons that are analogous to Plato's.[9] Differance distinguishes prior to any imposition of concepts, and generates the manifold for concepts to organize. Conceptual systems, according to Derrida's Saussurian account, are systems of differences; thus, differance is prior to concepts. That is, things are not different because different concepts apply; rather, different concepts apply in virtue of differance.

The consideration that Difference Itself is not quite a nature means more than merely that Difference Itself is a metanature. Being and Sameness are similarly metanatures. Difference Itself is especially problematic because it is that being in virtue of which instances can exist. It is, as it were, half of the metanature Instancehood Itself. Instances of natures are different from each other and from the natures of which they are instances. If we believe Aristotle and identify the Great and Small with the Different Itself, then natures themselves, the Forms, are different instances of Oneness, that is, different ways of being one thing.

This characteristic of Difference Itself infects all entities whatsoever. Earlier dialogues such as the *Phaedo* take the feature of "being both the same and different from itself" as a characteristic of physical sensory objects that distinguished them from Forms. The *Parmenides*, as is widely recognized, shows that every entity whatsoever, including Forms and the One, has this characteristic. So Plato removes one of the distinctions between "reality" and the sensible world. In effect, his argument in the *Parmenides* is a deconstruction of his earlier position that the world is to be understood on the basis of simple entities.

Why Does Derrida Need Differance?

Suppose that Derrida has shown that there is no presence-before-the-mind in the way required to have Husserlian meanings. Derrida's argument in *Speech and Phenomena* is roughly as follows: Any meaningful object, that is, any token of speech, writing, or thought, must be repeatable. Any essentially repeatable object presents itself as having other possibilities of occurrence. But such "possibility of recurrence" is not a presentable property, not something that an entity can wear on its sleeve. Thus a meaningful item, as such, necessarily is something that cannot be there all at once. Its essence, as it were, involves absence.[10]

The obvious question at this point is, What is meant by "presence," and why can't a modal feature be "present"? Derrida's major exploration of this question occurs in "White Mythology," where he makes it clear that he thinks this prejudice has no basis beyond a persistent obsession with light and vision metaphors for the intellect, an obsession that is indeed constitutive of philosophy. That is, only a certain picture of what thinking is, namely having something before the mind in the way that we have a visual sense-impression before the mind, leads us to think that only what is visualizable is clear and available as a starting point for understanding a given topic.

This consideration is quite powerful. In particular, by this argument no particular is properly namable in virtue of a meaning. No meaningful state can occur only when a particular event is happening, for instance. This has consequences for the desire to designate the present, the self, and the moment by thought-tokens that are also meanings. In particular, consider presence: For the present to present itself *as* present is for it to present itself as directly after the immediate past and directly before the immediate future, as Husserl himself has established. But these properties that presence is "presented as" having involve necessary reference to the nonpresent. Husserl takes the "now" to be a point, so that no distance will separate the sequence of interior words of a silent monologue from the meanings they express in thought.[11]

The general point of the argument, apart from the details about Husserl's theory, is that such terms as "I" and "now" are meaningful, and so repeatable apart from the specific application they have at a moment. What can "interior meanings," the tokens of the language of thought, then name? Only repeatable, general terms. But that means that no meanings can convey a particular. In particular, no term can be true only of this very moment or this very person.[12] By their very nature, meaningful items have application elsewhere.[13] Hence, my term "I," to the extent that it means anything, is a term that can be used without me. Likewise, my term "now" can be so used. We hear on a dead man's answering machine, "I am not here now." What does this imply about presence, the place where these meanings are displayed? It implies that the "now" and the "I" are both Forms, rather than pure particulars, so that there are no "cases" of individual experience to collection into categories. At the very bottom of experience and the world, there is always already repetition and bringing under concepts.

Derrida examines the idea of explaining how a language/world/conceptual system gets under way on the basis of the environment and the biological underpinnings common to humans as organisms. After all, he says, "Differences do not fall out of the sky."[14] To call what we start with "the world" or "experience" would be to have already applied some predicates that would imply a given. But there is no experience and no world as an array of objects with properties prior to conceptualization. So "differance" and "instituted traces" could be imagined to start the process in some way. On the one hand, we cannot really talk about a "conceptual scheme," "uncategorized world," or "unconceptualized experience" for precisely the reasons Davidson outlined in "On the Very Idea of a Conceptual Scheme."[15]

But according to Derrida, we have to recognize that something goes on before a person begins to talk and think. While "the world" does not come divided up into entities and categories, it is not homogeneous either. Both "divided up" and "homogeneous" presuppose a world as an entity already there divided up into one or more objects. Something about what happens must allow concepts to get started, by providing some "texture" to make distinctions. Or so it seems. Derrida and Davidson would agree that if we cannot say how this happens, we cannot whistle it either.

Of course, Derrida here uses modal notions that have not been constructed out of clear and distinct ideas. "Allow" would not be allowed at this point in a foundational, systematic construction of the world. If we held Derrida to a Husserlian project or took his enterprise to be something like David Lewis's in *A Plurality of Worlds*, then of course such use would be illegitimate. But apart from such projects, we have something like Quine's "Epistemology Naturalized," an account that describes the world but does not construct it.

This "texture" that would give differentiation a starting point cannot consist in distinctions between spatiotemporal regions such that one region has a feature that another region lacks, because features require differentiation (and the construction of subjects to have them), and differentiation requires features. Rather, the preproperty, preconceptual, predifferentiation texture is "differance." Why can't we just notice how things are different? Derrida, along with Davidson, Quine, and Goodman, holds that no sameness is "given" in nature.[16] So how does differance work? For Derrida, as for Plato, the possibility of repetition requires a mix of sameness and difference. Two occurrences of the term "frog" or of real frogs, for instance, are the same and different. They are two occurrences of the same mark, and they are distinct occurrences of that mark. Derrida takes this to be true both of signs and of things, since two occurrences of either must be identified as of a kind in order to be the same thing or sign repeated (as the Same) on distinct occasions in distinct spots. We are making the sign or thing be the same sign or thing by taking distinct events to be occurrences of the Same. Such takings are not random, but they are not dictated by anything either. In the sense of "arbitrary" as "arbitrated, judged, thoughtfully decided," they could be said to be arbitrary. Judgments of sameness are not determined, but that does not mean that anything goes. How does this accommodate the fact that, even if sameness is not entirely present in nature, there clearly are innate dispositions to respond in the same way, on some construction of "same way"? I discuss this below.

The sign relation has the place in Derrida's thought that instantiation does in Plato's. And the differences between the sign relation and the relation of a Form to its instances bring about the important differences between Derrida and Plato. The basic issue is that of presence. Plato's Forms were supposed to stand before the mind as entities that mean themselves. His paradigm of the grasp of a mathematical proof from a diagram compelled him to take the mind to be something that just does grasp Forms as they are, until the logical and Parmenidean considerations occurred to him. Plato does not conceive of knowing as grasping interior tokens that mean their referents. Rather, thought grasps the Form Itself, as Plato discusses in dialogues such as the *Phaedo*. The difficulty, which leads to the self-deconstructions of the *Parmenides*, is that such natures cannot be grasped as just what they are, since they cannot be isolated from their necessary accompaniments. Plato thus addresses his version of the "materiality of the signifier" but does not question the necessity that is grasped in the Form.[17] Plato comes to realize in the *Parmenides* that the mereology does not start with atomic elements but rather has parts and wholes all the way down. Thus Plato questions not the apprehension of necessity, as Derrida does, but rather the apprehension of fundamental elements.

For Derrida, following Sellars,[18] the difficulty with Forms is that they would have to be present as essentially repeatable, as being the sort of thing that necessarily could have instances. Derrida argues that such features cannot be present. So he replaces the natural Form/instance relation with the arbitrary sign/referent relation.

The representation of a sign does not differ from its reality. A photograph of a letter "A" is itself also a letter "A," as are the names of "A" in quotation marks. A sign is not quite an "instance" that fits a Form, since its being an entity cannot be specified apart from the Form of which it is an instance. Thus, the occurrence of another case of a sign does not fit the "type/token" distinction, because that would suppose that we could identify cases of the sign and then group them into types. But the type is essential to the sign. It is part of the essence of being a sign at all that it be repeatable as a case of this Form. The sign is a sign at all by virtue of being repeatable. So the meaningfulness of a sign, what makes it be a sign, is iterability, having the possibility of distinct recurrences. Therefore, the sign cannot be present as what it is, since it must present itself as necessarily iterable, necessarily something that can have or could have had other occurrences. Thus it is not quite a token, since what it presents itself as, having other occurrences, is not present. It is also not quite a type, since it is located in space and time.

To put this another way, since we are, by denying the given and denying that there is a magic language, making concepts into signs, the concepts under which signs fall in order to be the signs they are involve us in a regress. Signs become, as it were, the foundation of Forms, so the constraint imposed upon them by the Forms under which they fall cannot be a genuine constraint.

To deny "presence" is to deny a "given." To deny a given is to say that sameness always partly depends on contingencies about what we take to be the same. And that makes undetermined, arbitrary judgments of sameness, of falling under the same sign, primary.

Derrida and Plato, Differance and Difference

What about Plato's Different and Derrida's differance? Plato's construction of nature is like Derrida's construction of the world-and-experience, with an important difference, namely, that between Difference Itself and differance. Plato's Different divides things up according to what is best, and does so for eternity. Thus, the major difference between Plato and Derrida is that Plato's generation of the world is necessitated and therefore permanent, whereas Derrida's is contingent and fluid. Plato still invokes a transcendental, the Good. As I have argued elsewhere,[19] the Good is a modal notion. Thus Plato, unlike Derrida, seeks a construction of what must be from what is.

In almost every other way, Plato and Derrida agree. The following are the four major points of agreement between these figures.

First, remember how, for Plato, Triangle is different from Square in virtue of Difference, not in virtue of the natures Triangle and Square. It is Difference that makes those natures distinct, not anything "given" about the natures themselves. Otherwise, a regress would result: If we appealed to the natures' own natures to explain how the two natures are different, then those two natures of natures would already have to be different in order to make the entities of which they are natures different from each other.

Second, Plato's Difference divides things in space and time, if we understand the *Timaeus* and the logic of the situation and accept Aristotle's characterization of the Great and Small as a function of Difference. So Plato's Different is the source of both distinctness in space and deferral in time, just as Derrida's differance is.

Third, an apparent difference between Difference and differance is merely apparent. One might think of Plato's account as ontological and Derrida's account as conceptual. But for both thinkers, this distinction is suspect. Without presence, there is no world *as opposed to* the conceptual scheme that organizes it. Thus, Derrida's account is an account of the world as much as an account of "conceptualization." For Plato, the soul's affinity with the structure of reality likewise makes the distinction between a conceptual account and an ontological account suspect. Plato's generation of the world is logical, that is, based on the *logos* and its requirements. Hence, the conceptual and the ontological are not really distinct for Plato.

Fourth, both differance and Difference are quite peculiar natures or entities, since they both are prior to any "conceptual scheme" or universe of entities with features. In the *Sophist*, Plato says that parts of the Different are natures of "what is not F."[20] But such negative Beings are very different from entities that instantiate positive natures. Differance likewise, if construed as real at all, has to be construed as some kind of phenomenon prior to the beings of the world. On my reading of Derrida, differance is a mythical phenomenon, a fiction describing what would be required to construct the world from a foundation. That is, Derrida may be taken as thinking not that differance is indeed a phenomenon in the world but rather that the project of construction of the world from foundational entities requires this very weird quasi-phenomenon, differance. This I construe as an argument not for the existence of such a strange pseudo-phenomenon but against the project itself. Derrida therefore agrees with Davidson that the very idea of a conceptual scheme is impossible.

Thus, Derrida's concept of differance conceals an attack on metaphysics. He shows that seeking an understanding both different from natural science and nontrivial leads to mysterious quasi-entities that should lead us to question the motives for the entire project. The principle that reflects the demand for such a science is the principle of noncircular conceptual construction: No explanation of B by A is possible if the understanding of A requires that B exist. Briefly, this is the requirement that a kind of understanding be available that orders the world intellectually, according to the demands of reason.

Let me state this Davidsonian interpretation in more detail. Davidson, in "The Very Idea of a Conceptual Scheme," argues that it makes no sense to suppose either that "the world" is homogeneous *or* that it is textured independently of what we say about it. This does not mean that

Davidson thinks that the world we describe pops up out of nowhere, or that we make everything up. Rather, Davidson's position is anticonstructionist, antifoundationalist, and deeply antimetaphysical. On Davidson's simple exposition of what is the case and what we say, there is no room for the science of metaphysics to exist beside real science.

Davidson says that the question of whether the world is already divided up (metaphysical realism) or instead divided up by us (idealism and some construals of deconstruction)[21] is a bad question, a question needing to be deconstructed, that is, shown to presuppose precisely what it is trying to explain away. According to Davidson, we say how the world is with our terms, in our language. What it takes for "There are frogs" to be true is that there are frogs. No explanation of that phenomenon is any better except the (metaphysically unhelpful) exposition of the conditions required on a given planet for frogs to come into existence. No "analysis" in terms of properties and the subjects they inhabit gets anywhere. English sentences provide as good an exposition of what is the case as sentences of any other language. The end of metaphysics is actually as simple as that.[22]

Now, there are contingencies about what we say—features of the way we talk about the world that could have been otherwise. These contingencies provide the basis for change in what we say, when we say it, and "how we conceptualize the world." If things could have been otherwise, then they can be otherwise, and such contingencies need to be stated somehow. The appeals to differance, traces, and so on, and the speculations about the origin of consciousness are Derrida's version of the phenomenological attempt to make such a statement.

Davidson and Derrida can perfectly well say how things could be different, but without supposing that the world needs to be described in some "preconceptual" terms. Davidson's suggestion would be just to use our regular terms to describe how organisms respond to the environment and how consciousness arises, even though the terms in the explanation could only have been arrived at by the very processes they explain.

Here is the phenomenological and, more generally, philosophical principle demonstrated by Derrida to lead to weird concepts like "differance": In the understanding of a phenomenon, we may not use any concepts that already presuppose the phenomenon being understood. This principle, which I take to be the operative principle of phenomenological analysis and of metaphysics universally, presupposes a foundational project that makes no sense unless there are meanings that magically connect to their referents. Apart from such meanings, it is perfectly legitimate to describe situations, including the situation in which we acquire language and understanding of the world, in the terms of our current language. As Davidson says, what else can we use?

REFERENCE MATTER

Notes

INTRODUCTION

1. See my essay "Indeterminacy of Radical Interpretation and the Causal Theory of Reference."

CHAPTER I

NOTE: This chapter has profited from the comments of John Vickers, who critiqued the essay as a whole, and from my discussions with John Searle and John Troyer about Derrida's central arguments.

1. If a sense is given by description—i.e., "the sense that Fred was discussing yesterday"—access to that sense must come via direct and unmediated access to some other senses. In this case, the other senses are those of "sense," "that," "Fred," etc.

2. See, for instance, Husserl's *Logical Investigations, Volume 1*, p. 287, where Husserl makes many of the same observations we find in Frege.

3. For instance, see ibid., Investigation I, sec. 7, pp. 276–78. The first few sections of Investigation I deal with expression, indication, and the investment of signs with meaning. Some of Derrida's arguments for the indeterminacy of interpretation consist in detailed analysis of Husserl's particular attempt to construct senses out of intentions, to make inner signs specially connected with contents, and to explain how the meaning of natural languages becomes determined (or enmeshed) in the history of these pure intentions. See Derrida, *Speech and Phenomena*.

4. Empiricist theories used sense contents as "present." These theories analyzed "senses" in terms of the sensual contents of something rather than as Platonic objects, but still in terms of something present to intuition. Chisholmian theories of knowledge, too, require some kind of entity to which we have epistemologically and therefore semantically direct access. Chisholm is brilliantly explicit about this in *Person and Object*, chap. 1 and app. C.

Empiricism of the above sort also held that the contents of certain acts are present to unmediated inspection. We know how we meant something on a given occasion, for instance. Quine and Derrida reject these ideas. The notion of "definition" required for the concept of "true by definition," as Quine pointed out in "Necessary Truth" (p. 55), seems to require that a determination about how we will speak can stay attached to a term or sentence. Quine's dismissal of the force of such a promise agrees with Derrida's insistence in "Signature, Event, Context." Derrida develops the point at great length in "Limited Inc.," an essay on the detachability of utterances from their originating contexts and intentions.

5. Saussure, *Course in General Linguistics*, chap. 4, especially p. 111.

6. See Quine and Ullian, *Web of Belief.*

7. The phrase "interanimation of sentences" is from Quine, *Word and Object*, chap. 1, sec. 3.

8. See Derrida's critique of this difficulty in his *Of Grammatology*, chap. 2.

9. These far-reaching claims are made in Derrida's "Limited Inc." and other works.

10. Derrida, "Signature, Event, Context," p. 315.

11. The "type/token" contrast is ultimately rejected by Derrida but is useful here. I wrote this discussion of iterability and its consequences in response to questioning from John Searle and John Troyer. Their comments made it clear that I had not gotten Derrida's argument straight. That may still be true.

12. Goodman's discussions of sameness, objecthood, and related topics occur throughout his works. See especially *Problems and Projects.*

13. Chisholm, *Person and Object*, p. 100.

14. Derrida, "Limited Inc.," p. 185.

15. Derrida glorifies the marginal, nonserious, etc., as part of his project of "deconstructing Western metaphysics." The point here, though, is that the marginal uses are not really deviations from an ideal but rather are paradigmatic of the basic sign-relation.

16. My source for these remarks by Davidson is his 1968 class in philosophy of language at Princeton that I attended. The parallel with Derrida shows up strikingly in this quotation from Derrida's "Limited Inc.," p. 208: "No criterion that is simply *inherent* to the manifest utterance is capable of distinguishing an utterance when it is serious from the same utterance when it is not. . . . Nothing can distinguish a serious or sincere promise from the same 'promise' that is non-serious or non-sincere except for the intention which informs and animates it."

17. Derrida argues the illusoriness of presence on many other, less rigorously formulable grounds. Perhaps the most important of these is his reading of Freud as doing away with the illusion of the transparency and unambiguity of the self.

18. Sellars rejects the "myth of the given" in his "Empiricism and the Philosophy of Mind," among other places.

19. Derrida, "Signature, Event, Context," p. 318.

20. For this argument, see Quine, *Word and Object*, p. 221.

21. Derrida, "Signature, Event, Context," p. 327. See also his "Limited Inc." Derrida also seems to argue that just the structure of iterability alone suffices to

guarantee that context cannot make meaning fully present in a sign. If meaning were present, it would not be deferred by the sign.

22. Putnam, "Realism and Reason," p. 127. Rereading this paper makes it clear that a paper called "Derrida and Putnam" could be written for a Putnam conference. What is less clear is how intuition would help. How would direct access to a Form give one anything semantic? Why couldn't a Form be misapplied?

23. Quine, "Ontological Relativity," p. 49 and passim.

24. See Derrida's essay "Differance."

25. See Derrida, "Signature, Event, Context," p. 316: "This essential drifting, due to writing as an iterative structure cut off from all absolute responsibility, from *consciousness* as the authority of the last analysis . . . "

26. One statement of Davidson's version of the indeterminacy of interpretation is in his "Belief and the Basis of Meaning."

27. Quine, *Word and Object*, chap. 2, p. 21.

28. This dualism is abandoned by Davidson as a "third dogma of empiricism," in "On the Very Idea of a Conceptual Scheme," p. 189.

29. Ibid.

30. Wilson, "Substances Without Substrata."

31. Actually, Davidson's texts are not homogeneous on this matter. In a piece written before "On the Very Idea of a Conceptual Scheme," he says: "Indeterminacy of meaning or translation does not represent a failure to capture significant distinctions. . . . If there is indeterminacy, it is because when all the evidence is in, alternative ways of stating the facts remain open" ("Belief and the Basis of Meaning," p. 154). Are facts about what is believed and meant real? This passage and "On the Very Idea of a Conceptual Scheme" should be read together with "Mental Events," where Davidson seems to claim the primacy of nonmental concepts. There, the constraints on translation seem to constitute a scheme in which the physical facts are interpreted, and the constraints on physical theory constitute another and more inclusive scheme. It is difficult to read these texts as expressions of a single position.

32. If we have an indeterminacy about what "right" means, for instance, since it is an important term in practical thought, many actions as well as sentences will be ambiguous.

33. This second point is often made by Quine in his metaphors of holism (in *Word and Object*, passim). If our web of belief connects all the sentences of our theory, and if the achievement of consistency in a region in the face of changes in occasion-sentences-held-true requires adjustment throughout the web, then at any given time, our theory will not be consistent. For interpretation of one part of our theory in terms of another part will be subject to the same indeterminacies of interpretation that obtain among theories of distinct persons. In this internal interpretation, adjustments will require changes that themselves require changes in the spots where the original adjustments were made.

A typical Quinean example of holistic adjustment is the adjustment of theory to the stresses and inconsistencies imposed by the results of the Michelson-Morley experiment (see Quine and Ullian, *Web of Belief,* p. 47). When this Quinean example is juxtaposed to the Derridean deconstruction of Rousseau in *Of Grammatology,* we have an illustration of the ways these traditions differ.

34. The most sober presentation of this thesis is in Derrida, "Signature, Event, Context."

35. Husserl, *Logical Investigations, Volume 1,* Investigation I, especially chap. 1, secs. 1–11.

36. Derrida, *Speech and Phenomena.* This seems to me the major topic of the book.

37. Quine, "Ontological Relativity," p. 46: "radical translation begins at home."

38. Derrida, "Signature, Event, Context," p. 317.

39. Added in 1999: The major difference between Davidson and Derrida in their interpretations of "indeterminacy of interpretation" is that Derrida is more of a Quinean than Davidson about what to say when all possible empirical evidence leaves a question undecided. Since Davidson takes truth to be primitive, he can regard ascriptions of truth conditions to be correct or incorrect in indeterminate situations. Derrida, on the other hand, along with Quine, holds that if all possible evidence cannot yield an answer, the question is not a question of fact. So Derrida and Quine take indeterminate situations to be ones in which there is no truth; while Davidson must take them to be situations in which there is a truth, but an unknowable one.

40. Ibid., p. 311.

CHAPTER 2

1. Derrida, *Husserl's "Origin of Geometry."*

2. Miller, "Critic as Host."

3. The phrase "The death of meaning" comes from Harman's paper, "Quine on Meaning and Existence, I," p. 124.

4. See especially Goodman, *Structure of Appearance* and *Fact, Fiction, and Forecast.*

5. Quine, "Ontological Relativity," p. 46.

6. Derrida, "Signature, Event, Context."

7. More ills are attributed to "logocentrism" by various deconstructors. This is not the place to sort out those discussions.

8. This point became clear to me thanks to a remark by Melvin Woody in conversation. It seems to be a sensible way of taking "il n'y a pas de hors-texte" ("There is no 'outside the text'").

9. The relevant texts of Aristotle are *Metaphysics* Zeta 3 and Zeta 5. Zeta 3 acknowledges that matter is not a "this," while Zeta 5 discusses the Snub. I have dis-

cussed the passage on the Snub as recognizing that there are no features that are just features, in "Aristotle on the Snub."

10. This suggestion is among many derivable from "Philosophy as a Kind of Writing: An Essay on Derrida," in Rorty, *Consequences of Pragmatism*, pp. 90–109.

11. Davidson, "What Metaphors Mean."

12. Added in 1999: Davidson can retain the literal and the figural only by supposing that the utterances have truth-values even when those truth-values are necessarily unknown. I now think that this is what he intends.

13. Nozick, *Anarchy, State, and Utopia*, p. 269.

14. De Man, "Shelley Disfigured."

CHAPTER 3

1. The most important arguments for the premises behind this rejection are found in Derrida, "Speech and Phenomena." In Derrida's lexicon, the cognitive meanings of terms are *logoi*, and philosophy that accepts *logoi* is "logocentric." Another important text on these topics is Derrida's *Of Grammatology*, especially part 1.

2. The explicit development of these lines of thought about rhetoric is most clear in Paul de Man's work, especially the chapter on Rousseau in *Allegories of Reading*.

3. Some important papers on these topics are collected in Davidson's *Inquiries*.

4. Davidson's classic papers on logical form are also collected in *Inquiries*; see the five essays in the section "Truth and Meaning."

5. See especially Davidson's essays "Moods and Performances" and "Communication and Convention."

6. I have argued this in another essay in the present collection, "Wittgenstein as Conservative Deconstructor."

7. I do not deny, of course, that it is very tricky to say how distinctions that have had their theoretical home in a logocentric discourse can be used after the suppositions of *logoi* are abandoned. The problem is widespread; for example, Derrida wants to claim in "Limited Inc." that Searle misreads him in "Reiterating the Differences," even though no principled line can exist between misreading and correct reading without a *logos* to match.

8. "Pragmatics," the formal study of the way truth-values of context-dependent sentences vary according to context of utterance, would seem to fall under "logical" properties, if pragmatics is indeed able to become formal. But to the extent that the formal theory is incomplete, pragmatics would be part of rhetoric. Or what? I think the difficulty of drawing a good line is another indication that no distinction in kind can be made out between logic and rhetoric.

9. Derrida, in *Speech and Phenomena*, deconstructs the self-presenting essences required for *logoi* to supply their own interpretation.

10. I take this to be a main result of Aristotle's *Metaphysics*, especially Book Zeta.

11. This point is different from but intricately related to those marshaled by Sellars in "Empiricism and the Philosophy of Mind." There, Sellars argues that sense data cannot both be objects and be representations that can function as premises of arguments. Roughly, the idea of a "given" foundation of knowledge is undone by the properties of the sign relation and the fact that sense data have to have truth-values to function as premises.

12. Davidson, "Moods and Performances" and "Communication and Convention." In these papers, Davidson makes many of the same points that Derrida makes in "Signature, Event, Context." A basic idea for both philosophers is that there can be no convention for the way a sentence is meant, since any such convention could be used for other, nonstandard purposes. For Davidson as well as for Derrida, these "marginal," nonstandard cases show the impossibility of a genuinely conventional account of speech acts. For Davidson as well as for Derrida, interpretation cannot be reduced to an algorithm.

13. De Man, *Allegories of Reading*, especially the chapter on Rousseau. I explore in some detail the resemblances between Davidson's and de Man's treatments of metaphor in "Metaphor According to Davidson and de Man," in the present volume. It is striking that both de Man and Davidson treat "metaphorical meaning" as a difference in force.

14. Derrida's clearest statement of this position is in the Afterword to "Limited Inc."

15. Davidson argues that there are no "truth-makers," parts of the world that make sentences true, in "True to the Facts."

16. For Davidson, modality must be primitive since it is part of truth. That is, modal truths cannot be reduced to nonmodal truths since the very notion of truth conditions rests on counterfactuals. This is a topic for a book, which I am currently trying to write.

17. The most thorough presentation of the classic account of conversational implicature is Grice's *Studies in the Way of Words*.

18. There is no telling what new terminology or practices could come up. Since no "routine" can give us ways of inventing new terms, no algorithm for theory construction can be devised. Such an algorithm would be a complete inductive logic.

19. I am ignoring accounts according to which a universal claim "presupposes" that the class in question has members. Such accounts give up too much for too little. Conversational implicature can handle the points that make presupposition have a point, and the logical theory is far more elegant.

20. Added in 1999: The argument I have presented here is that, given the lack of a magic language, there is nothing in situations, described exhaustively in physiological or physical terms, that distinguishes between rhetorical and logical connection. Thus truth and truth conditions are not derivable even from all the know-

able "facts" about an utterance. In reviewing this argument now, however, I would point out that if truth conditions must be a function of such facts about the utterance, then utterances do not have truth conditions *simpliciter* but rather truth conditions according to an interpretation. The positions of Davidson and Derrida differ in an important way. Davidson, by asserting that truth is basic and irreducible, allows the possibility that truth and falsity obtain even though nothing about any empirically determinable phenomena make them obtain. Thus Davidson can hold that utterances have truth conditions in all cases even though those truth conditions are in principle unknowable. So, for Davidson, indeterminacy of interpretation is empirical, not ontological. Derrida takes indeterminacy in the way Quine does, and takes the absence of any fact of the matter to mean that truth and falsity do not generally apply. Unlike Quine, though, and with Davidson, Derrida does not assume a given in which the "real facts" obtain, permitting genuine truth and falsity *tout court.*

21. In Derrida, *Speech and Phenomena.*

22. Davidson, "Myth of the Subjective," p. 164.

23. The primary article addressing the issue of "constructed" objects is Davidson, "On the Very Idea of a Conceptual Scheme."

24. Derrida, "Differance," p. 7.

25. See the Afterword in Derrida, "Limited Inc."

CHAPTER 4

NOTE: This essay's arguments were improved in response to a careful critique by John Troyer.

1. Knapp and Michaels, "Against Theory II," p. 49.

2. Ibid., p. 50.

3. Michaels told me that Davidson's lectures at Berkeley persuaded him of the thesis advanced in Knapp and Michaels, "Against Theory II."

4. An especially early discussion of this thesis is Davidson's "A Nice Derangement of Epitaphs." See also Bilgrami's "Norms and Meaning," where the anticonventionalist view is endorsed vigorously.

5. I will argue below that public languages differ from individual languages. Some of the differences between Davidson and Derrida arise because Davidson concentrates on interpreting individual speech and does not much consider how a public language can be regarded as a "collective" idiolect, whereas Derrida emphasizes the public language, in which indeterminacy is greater because of the diversity of interests and information.

6. Knapp and Michaels, "Against Theory II," p. 68.

7. Ibid., p. 49n, my emphasis.

8. The work of Davidson in "Theories of Meaning and Learnable Languages" is the clearest argument that an infinity of different meanings requires a truth-

definable semantic structure. Such structures, if they occur in the notation in which intentions arise, would make intentions inscriptions in the language of thought.

9. According to Knapp and Michaels, there could be items that are meaningful but that have a meaning on only one occasion of utterance. Their example of a nonlinguistic sound that tells the driver to stop ("Against Theory II," p. 65) suggests that the sound would be meaningful even if it could not possibly occur with the same meaning on another occasion.

10. See, for instance, Quine, "Two Dogmas of Empiricism," and Davidson, *Inquiries.*

11. Knapp and Michaels, "Against Theory II," p. 67.

12. Davidson, "Communication and Convention."

13. Derrida, "Signature, Event, Context," p. 327.

14. Ibid., p. 326.

15. Ibid., p. 315.

16. Knapp and Michaels, "Against Theory II," pp. 61–62.

17. Derrida, *Speech and Phenomena,* p. 50.

18. Derrida, "Signature, Event, Context," p. 318.

19. In the case discussed by Knapp and Michaels in "Against Theory II" (p. 65), the iterable items are words and sentences in the language of the soul. When a person utters a nonsense word thinking that it means "stop," and the person is understood to mean "stop," the representation in which the person thinks it means "stop" is the privileged one, which would not have this meaning unless it were possible for the same kind of item to recur.

20. Being a token of a type is constituted by the other possible items of the type, so the distinction between type and token cannot start with an unproblematic notion of "token." Since the "token" includes the type in its very identity conditions, it is not helpful to reduce the type to a set of tokens. As Derrida argues in "Limited Inc.," the classical type/token distinction presupposes essentialism, since the token would have to have the type as its nature.

21. Derrida, "Signature, Event, Context," p. 326.

22. Quine, "Ontological Relativity," especially pp. 47–50.

23. Davidson, "A Nice Derangement of Epitaphs," p. 446.

24. Ibid.

CHAPTER 5

NOTE: This essay originated as a reaction to an early version of Richard Rorty's "Unfamiliar Noises: Hesse and Davidson on Metaphor."

1. See especially Davidson's "On the Very Idea of a Conceptual Scheme."

2. When disagreement occurs within a speech community, exactly where the disagreement lies may be indeterminate. If my friend says, "Kissinger has physical

charm," I can decide that she means something unusual by "physical charm," that one of us is wrong about Kissinger, or that she is trying to annoy me, for instance. The odd remark can be taken as the utterance of a rational being by adjusting ascriptions of meaning, belief, or rhetorical force. Given further disagreements, more discussion may not resolve the question. Since there is nothing more semantically elementary than the words, there is no answer to the question of what is really meant when two systems of what is said and when it is said fail to match up in an isomorphism of roles. No "behind the scenes" facts determine where the deviation should be located. When translation or interpretation is indeterminate, there is no fact of the matter.

3. Davidson's semantics is set out in the papers in the first section of his collection *Inquiries into Truth and Interpretation*, including "Truth and Meaning," "Theories of Meaning and Learnable Languages," "True to the Facts," "Semantics for Natural Languages," and "In Defense of Convention T."

4. This Yeats example is borrowed from Rorty's "Unfamiliar Noises," p. 170.

5. Davidson, "What Metaphors Mean," p. 246.

6. The Saturnian example occurs ibid., p. 251.

7. In my articles "Reference and Vagueness" and "On That Which Is Not," both written in the 1970s, I discussed some difficulties with the determinateness of truth-values of utterances. [Added in 1999: I now realize that Davidson is willing to accept unknowable truths, and so would treat indeterminacy as epistemological.]

8. Added in 1999: "No fact of the matter" means that nothing that exists makes the utterance metaphorical or literal. There being no fact of the matter, though, is compatible with the claim that the utterance is literally true. Since Davidson takes truth to be primitive and irreducible, a sharp line can be drawn between the literal and the figurative even though nothing explains the difference.

9. De Man, *Allegories of Reading*, p. 146.

10. Rousseau, *Essay on the Origin of Languages*, pp. 246–47.

11. De Man, *Allegories of Reading*, pp. 152–53.

12. Such representation of what is strictly not is a necessary part of language. It turns out that the "purely referential," de Man's term for the literal object-language assertion, is a heuristic fiction. Note here that for de Man, who follows Austin in many ways, "true" is a predicate of speech acts, not of their contents.

13. The "decentering of the self" questions exactly the kind of access a person is supposed to have to her real intentions. The self that knows its thoughts by thinking them in the magic language could be a unitary self whose intentions would be clear to itself. Such a self requires and supports the idea of a magic language. But if the self has textlike, languagelike thoughts, then levels of self-consciousness are analogous to sequences of tests and commentaries. In that situation, "privileged access" does not supply final answers. I find the decentering arguments persuasive on Quinean-Davidsonian as well as Freudian grounds. Someone who accepts Chisholm's ideas about the self, as expressed in *Person and*

Object and *The First Person*, requires very different ideas about meaning and thought, and will be committed to denying de Manian premises needed for rhetorical indeterminacy. A self-presenting self, that is, must present itself to itself in the magic language.

14. This point is made most thoroughly in Derrida's "Signature, Event, Context" and the subsequent "Limited Inc."

15. Since de Man wants to say that slippage occurs at every level, the temporary supposition that there is a starting point—namely, an inner thought for which logocentric principles hold—allows the slippage to be described as the thought moves from the intention to the language. But this is an "as if" to be abandoned as soon as the point is made.

16. The main precursors to de Man's meditation on this kind of groundlessness are the thinkers concerned with self-reflection, including the German romantics Fichte and Hegel, who conceived irony in terms of consciousness of consciousness. From the possibility of a sequence of levels of irony, it is only a short step to the generalization that rhetorical force may be questioned at each level of self-reflection on the previous self-reflection. From de Man's rhetorical analysis of figuration and meaning, it is again only a short step to a deep indeterminacy of meaning.

Clearly, Davidson's formulation of the impossibility of markers of rhetorical force finds its precursors in Frege's attempt to have a judgment stroke as a part of an object-language notation, and Wittgenstein's commentary on that attempt in *Tractatus* 4.442. A modern version of romantic irony is Quine's "Ontological Relativity," in which Quine shows that indeterminacy of translation relative to a background language continues as far back as one wishes to push the regress of background languages. That is, as soon as one asks what one means, alternative interpretations arise. De Man's discussion can be thought of as a Quinean indeterminacy thesis applied to rhetorical force rather than, as in Quine's case, applied under the assumption that assertions can be detected unproblematically.

17. Rousseau, *Second Discourse*, in his *'Discourses' and 'Essay'*, pp. 155–57.

18. De Man, *Allegories of Reading*, p. 146.

19. De Man here follows Goodman, who has argued in *Ways of Worldmaking* and elsewhere that "resemblance" of some kind obtains between any pair of objects, so that no coherent system of groupings need follow from grouping things by resemblance. For de Man, the incoherence in a metaphorical "system" like Proust's is a case of the incoherence of predicate systems generally. See his discussion in "Reading (Proust)," in *Allegories of Reading*, especially the note on pp. 60–61.

20. Such a supposition would require the whole extension of "is a frog" to be hidden in the use of the term. Only the magic language could manage this predetermination of future and marginal frogs.

21. De Man, "Epistemology of Metaphor," p. 21.

22. Ibid., p. 28.

23. Davidson, "What Metaphors Mean," pp. 248–49.

24. This needs to be qualified in numerous ways. For instance, given our opinions about the epistemological capacities of organisms and the environment of the other person, we may not seek agreement on contents of beliefs.

25. Interpretation accurately construed maximizes agreement, as qualified in the previous note, in all propositional attitudes. The constraints on assigning intentions to speech acts, for instance, maximize agreement in desires, among other things.

26. Davidson's and Quine's denial of a magic language behind words supplies a theoretical background for the example I focus on in "Deconstruction, Cleanth Brooks, and Self-Reference" (in this volume), namely, Brooks's "Heresy of Paraphrase." The unparaphrasability of metaphor is to be expected given that every term has its own pattern of occurrence, that what is said and when it is said determine meaning, and that such accidents as literary citation, rhyme, and personal history determine how we adjust in order to understand metaphor. Relevant here is Benson Mates's demonstration that, on the most plausible criterion of synonymy, there are no synonyms; see his "Synonymy."

27. For discussions of how such relativizations might work, see, for instance, my essays "How Paintings Can Be Joyful" and "Attributives and Their Modifiers."

28. Suppose someone says of my guinea pig, Celeste, "She's an eggplant with fur and feet." This is perceptive, even illuminating, as anyone with guinea pigs knows, but not true. While it might be possible to take "eggplant" in this utterance to be true of vegetables and other things having a certain ovoid and dumpy configuration, few would interpret the utterance this way, and no one should revise their ideas about eggplants to make this a true assertion.

29. Davidson, "What Metaphors Mean," p. 249.

30. So, for instance, the metaphorical usage "all fired up," as in "The Raiders are all fired up," is far more usual than the literal application of the phrase to the steam-driven etymological source. The judgment that some utterance is a metaphor seems to be a matter both of routine connections in interpretation and of etymological opinions.

31. A relevant text here is Wittgenstein's *Remarks on the Foundations of Mathematics*, where exactly this point is made about rules in the setting most favorable to the existence of constraints beyond practice, namely, mathematics.

32. See, for instance, de Man's essay on Proust in *Allegories of Reading*.

CHAPTER 6

NOTE: Versions of this essay were read at Wesleyan and Brandeis. It was in conversation with Eli Hirsch that the necessity of treating sorites paradoxes and metaphors in the same way dawned on me. John Troyer provided helpful, if unpersuaded, commentary.

1. Sorensen's articles "The Ambiguity of Vagueness and Precision" and "Vague-

ness Within the Language of Thought" are useful starting points for understanding what Davidson's position on vagueness would have to be.

2. Nietzsche, "On Truth and Lies," p. 42.

3. See, for instance, Davidson, "Radical Interpretation."

4. See my articles "Reference and Vagueness," "On That Which Is Not," "Persons and Their Micro-Particles," and "Indeterminacy of Radical Interpretation and the Causal Theory of Reference."

5. An electron can have only this precise charge. Such kinds of objects would satisfy the condition that any item is either an electron or not. No kinds of medium-sized object satisfy the concept of object that requires any object to be of a kind and that requires nature to determine whether a given object is of that kind.

6. Notice that in a sense, "person" *does* have a well-defined extension. The class of persons is the extension of "person." The sorites rests on constitutive dimensions. Just as being tall is nothing but a question of height even though we cannot find a line between tall and not tall in terms of millimeters, so being a person is nothing but a matter of certain capacities and conditions, even though we cannot find a line between person and nonperson in terms of those capacities and conditions.

7. The contrast between the "verbal" and the "substantive" is not sustainable as a principled distinction but is rather a dimension that allows more or less. No purely factual or purely linguistic characteristic is required for some kinds of change to be more "merely verbal" than others.

8. Sorites paradoxes also bear on the possibility of magic-language terms, if the terms of the magic language of thought are supposed to fix extensions. Reference is a function of sense, and terms of the magic language have their sense in virtue of their nature. If the contents of such terms were available to introspection, then we could have no doubt about whether an arbitrary object was in the extension of a magic-language term or not. Given our assurance that decisions about borderline cases of persons and tall men are always arbitrary, persons and tall men cannot be extensions of magic-language terms.

9. Crawford Elder has shown that such "social objects" are not just what people think they are. See his "Realism, Naturalism, and Culturally Generated Kinds."

10. My use of "contingent" as a way of saying that things could have been different without supposing "alternative conceptual schemes" is borrowed from the first piece in Richard Rorty's series of articles in the *London Review of Books*, "The Contingency of Language."

11. Some of the theses in the following section were proposed in "Truth and Training," an unpublished manuscript by John Troyer and Samuel Wheeler from 1973.

12. How does "the women" come to exist as a group? Such a group is not just preculturally there, and to think that *this very group* lost out in an initial world-historical defeat would be a mistake.

13. What we resolve to say may not work out even for us. Sometimes things we

have decided upon force us to say things we would prefer not to. So, keeping both "all men are equal" and "blacks are not equal" in our collection of truisms will require that some extensions we are inclined to assign be modified.

14. Compare Kitto, *The Greeks*, p. 234: "*We* find perfectly good evidence that women went to the theatre—often to see plays which *we* would not allow *our* women to see" (my emphasis). This comment occurs in a passage pointing out that while English women are equal in every way, equality is an unreasonable standard to apply to ancient Athens.

15. Davidson, "A Nice Derangement of Epitaphs," pp. 445–46.

16. But they, as part of this culture, come to see themselves *as* outside and *as* oppressed. How can a group (constituted by the culture) have interests *as* a group that are different from the interests the oppressors would assign to the group (cooperation in their appropriate role, with all doing their bits)?

17. Alleged "hegemonies" are themselves incoherent, and thus less than totally determining of what we say. Perhaps collections of people can exist that are simple enough that no discontented underlings arise (i.e., collections in which no one disputes the dominant discussions). This collection would be like a perfectly simple being.

18. Kuhn, *Structure of Scientific Revolutions*.

19. The scripture on which this is midrash is Davidson's "True to the Facts."

20. Added in 1999: The relation between public languages, which are construed here as a negotiated intersection of individual idiolects, and those idiolects themselves is complex. A man could in principle say what he chose and mean what he chose, but his purposes would be generally defeated if he did not mean by his words what others mean. Now, eight years after the original publication of the present essay, I would recast my discussion in terms of a general theory of how idiolects interact with public languages. Power relations are still relevant, since we are susceptible to coercion and persuasion even about what we say to ourselves, but their workings are much more complex than is recognized in this chapter.

21. "Possible kind of object" is itself a mysterious construct. Are we supposed to be able now to imagine or conceive of every possible kind of object? What kind of godlike language is it that would distinguish every possible way of thinking about manna, snow, honor, or microparticles?

22. Davidson, "What Metaphors Mean."

23. In "Metaphor According to Davidson and de Man" (above in this volume), I argue that there is no "natural" basis for applying predicates to new cases.

24. I have proposed such sorites paradoxes in "Natural Property Rights as Body Rights," a paper that "justifies" property rights by a borderline-case argument moving from rights to control bodies to rights to unlimited property. In that article, I argue that pieces of property such as cars are entitled to treatment as parts of bodies because no ethically significant lines divide the continuum between "real" bodies and the "extended bodies" that consisted of cars and houses.

25. If the use of "tall" approached that of "lean," then we might have genuine disagreements that did not seem arbitrary.

26. Sometimes the dispute concerns the meta-issue of who gets to decide, rather than the issue of what particular ramifications a kind of usage has. A lot of discussions "on principle" do not matter except that they keep the determiners determining. Look how unhappy we get when "metaphysics" comes to mean the occult.

27. For instance, whether it suits someone's interests to be a "real Marxist" depends on the political and social surroundings, which are essentially connected to what else is being said and done.

CHAPTER 7

1. The anecdote, along with the judgments of Eliezer and the Rabbis, is mentioned in the Mishnah tractate Kelim, chap. 5, Mishnah 10. That would perhaps have been the logical place for the anecdote, but Kelim contains no Gemara whatsoever, and someplace had to be found for a full account of such an interesting sequence of occurrences. The incident is referred to elsewhere in the Talmud, usually citing Rabbi Yehoshuah's opinion that a bath kol is not authoritative. See Berakoth 51b–52a, Pesahim 114b, Yebamoth 14a.

I first became acquainted with this passage through Daniel Boyarin, who told me how interesting it was. I should note as well that Boyarin's oral and written discourses have thoroughly shaped my understanding of Talmud and midrash, for good or ill.

2. Commentators differ in their interpretations of the initial situation. On another interpretation than the one I offer here, the question is whether an object is subject to uncleanness, that is, whether a stove is a stove at all after being taken apart and not quite put back together. In Kelim 5, Mishnah 10, the stove is described as "clean" according to Eliezer and "unclean" according to the other Rabbis. Maimonides interprets the case in the *Code of Maimonides* (the Yale translation of the *Mishneh Torah*), book 10 (The Book of Cleanness), treatise 7 (Laws Concerning Utensils, essentially a commentary on the Mishnah tractate Kelim), chap. 16. There he discusses the following two cases among several others: (1) When a stove becomes unclean, is cut into sections, and is remade with fresh clay holding it together, it is then clean. (2) If the stove itself is constructed by having sand or gravel put between the rings into which it has been cut, but the whole is plastered over with clay, it is susceptible to uncleanness. (The issue is whether it is a single item. In another case, where there is a gap between the sections and the clay that holds everything together, the complex is not a single item at all, according to Maimonides, and so is not subject to uncleanness.) If we take Maimonides to be always agreeing with the sages, then the issue on which Eliezer was wrong was that of whether the stove is subject to uncleanness.

3. See Kelim, especially chaps. 5 and 6, for the general discussion of cleanness and uncleanness of stoves of various kinds in various circumstances. The stove in

question, the "stove of Akna'i," is discussed in Berakoth 19a as well, in the context of a discussion of "excommunication."

4. "Heavenly voice" is the Soncino Talmud's translation of "bath kol." This expression occurs at least 40 times in the Talmud, and about 30 in Midrash Rabbah. Literally, it means "daughter of a voice." The Talmud says a number of things about benoth koloth, and benoth koloth do a number of things: they sometimes quote Scripture (Hagigah 15a, quoting Jeremiah); they lecture people (Chagigah 13a, Rosh Hoshanah 21b, where the bath kol quotes Torah); and they give or withhold divine information. A bath kol will often speak of itself in the first person in ways that imply that it is God's voice. (One bath kol says, "The time of the coming of the Messiah is *my* secret.") On the other hand, benoth koloth are not the same as prophetic inspirations. In Sotah 48b, prophecy has departed from Israel, but the bath kol is still granted to the people. (See also Yoma 9b.) Benoth koloth will often render divine judgments after the Holy One has made a decision. In one instance, Kethuboth 77b, when Rabbi Joshua B. Levi tricks the Angel of Death into getting him his place in paradise early, the Holy One judges that he can stay, and the bath kol instructs the Angel of Death to give Joshua's knife back to him. The bath kol knows lots of secrets about the fatherhood of Judah, future spouses of unborn children, etc. Two other striking instances of benoth koloth and their interventions are as follows.

First, in Sanhedrin 104b, after several other miraculous interventions, a bath kol tries to talk the men of the Great Assembly into including Solomon in the list of those with a place in the world to come. The men of the Great Assembly ignore the bath kol, which then declares that Solomon will be included anyhow. An interesting fact is that the men of the Great Assembly are making adjudications in all the other instances.

Second, in an important episode that is referred to several times, a bath kol judges that the halakhah is always with beth Hillel, even though both Hillel and Shammai speak the words of God. In other passages, when a reason is given for accepting a ruling of beth Hillel's, this judgment of the bath kol is often cited as a problem. But since Rabbi Yehoshuah thinks we should not listen to a bath kol, the reason in question is still appropriate, in case we think he's right.

5. This verse from Deuteronomy, as it occurs in its context, seems to be primarily about the ability of humans to obey "this mitzvot," and not about the source of the Torah. However, it does clearly say that the mitzvot is "in your mouth and in your heart," so Yehoshuah, while he is giving a new understanding of the verse, is not thoroughly distorting the plain sense.

6. Elijah is the prophet who did not die but was taken up to heaven directly (2 Kings 2:1, "Yahweh took Elijah up to heaven in the whirlwind"). The Rabbis occasionally meet him and receive word about heavenly states of affairs; see Berakoth 23a, 29b, 58a, etc.

7. Eliezer was being punished for not going along with the majority decision.

Exactly what this punishment amounted to is debated, but it did not amount to a permanent and irrevocable removal from the religion, and did not strip the title "Rabbi" from Eliezer's name.

8. From the overall interpretive principle that the Torah is the word of God, specific principles follow, notably, in the present context, that the text contains no redundant words and no accidental features. Numerous other interpretive principles follow as well, most of which seem to me to be justified by a combination of logic and the postulate of a divine author. For example, given such an author, any passage can be read in the light of any other passage. See Boyarin's discussion in *Intertextuality*, especially chap. 2, for an account of how reading a verse in the context of other verses affects meaning.

9. In Mishnah, tractate Hullin 11a, Exodus 23:2 is cited as evidence that the correct procedure generally is to decide halakhic matters by majority rule. Interestingly, Exodus 23:2 is also taken to mean that one should, in some cases, make the judgment that is most probable. If I have a hundred birds and Jones has one bird, and an unidentifiable bird is discovered after a tornado, I get it. This principle is paired with a principle of proximity, derived from Deuteronomy 21:3, which would award the bird to you if it was found closer to your cote. (Bava Bathra 23b.) In cases of conflict between these two principles, majority rules.

10. The Torah in question here will also include "Oral Torah," instruction that was supposed to have been transmitted teacher-to-student from Moses down through the current Rabbis. Scriptural arguments that God's instructions include more than is written can be found in Exodus 12:21, where God refers to the methods "I have laid down" for the slaughter of animals, even though no such instructions appear in the Pentateuch. The term "Oral Torah" (*torah shebea'l pe*) occurs in Talmud, Shabbath 31a, in an anecdote quoting Shammai's use of the term. In addition to halakhoth that are binding but not written, Oral Torah includes principles of rational interpretation, ways of understanding what the ruling is in a given case. Much more can be said here: Parts of Torah are not on a par. Some parts come from the divine and some from rulings by the Rabbis. But such rulings are sometimes described as enacted below and endorsed above. See also Chagigah 10a.

11. Parts of Torah are themselves Torah interpretations and commentary, it would seem. See Fishbane's *Biblical Interpretation*.

12. This relative strength of connection has often been noted. For instance, Chagigah 10a speaks of three categories of halakhah: rules of dissolution of vows are said to rest on nothing; rules of Sabbath, etc., "hang as mountains on a thread"; and rules of cleanness, forbidden relations, etc., have a firm textual basis. The last category is then said to be the core of Torah. The written Torah has a kind of priority. Chagigah 10a is a Mishnah text, so it has authority. Thus this is an Oral Torah text that comments on the authority of oral Torah.

13. See Quine's famous works "Two Dogmas of Empiricism" and *Word and Object*.

14. The creation of Torah should be thought of as creating moral facts. Torah is described by the Rabbis as a gift of which the angels are jealous. Torah is a part of the "furniture of the world," in fact the most important part of the furniture. God Himself studies Torah every day in the early morning, according to 'Abodah Zarah 4b.

15. Akiba says: "There is no possible argument against the words of Him who spoke and the world came into being" (Mekilta Beshallah 7). But the Rabbis do argue, and sometimes win. This also happens in the Bible. Abraham argues with God about Sodom's fate and persuades God to change the conditions. In our very passage, a bit later, Rabbi Gamaliel reminds God of his reasons for excommunicating Rabbi Eliezer, and God quiets the storm.

One way in which the Rabbis' conception of God may differ from that of the Greco-Christians and of the later Greco-Islamic-Jewish philosophy attributable to Maimonides is that for the Rabbis, God is omniscient only about those things that are knowable. If the future is not yet real, then there is nothing of which God is ignorant. The view that the future is not yet real, so that there can be sentences whose truth-value is unknowable, is compatible with God's knowing some important things about the future, for instance that He will keep His promises.

16. Note that this claim has nothing to do with Maimonides' view that all such speech ascribed to God must be in some sense other than physical speech. The metaphysical completeness of speech acts is an entirely different issue from that of whether the words are of a distinct, unrepeatable order. (Although, given Maimonides' other views, I imagine that he would assign God a Platonic/David Lewis language.) Lewis's views are clearly expressed in *On the Plurality of Worlds*.

In the case at hand, Maimonides interprets Rabbi Eliezer as trying to add to Torah by appeal to signs. In book 1, chap. 9 of Mishneh Torah, Eliezer cites Deuteronomy 30:12 in that connection. His reading seems to be that God smiled because His sons had successfully resisted a temptation in which God had been a kind of party.

17. Without magic words, it is questionable whether there really is a set of possibilities, let alone possible worlds, already well defined. If possible worlds are constructions of words, and words are incomplete, then so are the possible worlds. The very idea of a full possible world seems to me to depend on "magicality." But this sort of magicality occurs only in Platonic words, not in real words.

18. See my "Reference and Vagueness," "Indeterminacy of Radical Interpretation and the Causal Theory of Reference," "Persons and Their Micro-Particles," "On That Which Is Not," and "Natural Property Rights as Body Rights."

CHAPTER 8

1. See, for instance, Culler's *On Deconstruction*, especially the entries under "undecidability." The literary theorists' use of this term covers rather more than

the technical use in mathematics, but usually applies to the incompleteness of systemhood revealed by self-reference.

2. Pope, *Essay on Criticism*, ll. 356–57. Hollander's *Rhyme's Reason* uses the device even more thoroughly.

3. The term "grounded" is borrowed from Kripke's "Outline of a Theory of Truth," but I use here only an intuitive notion, not Kripke's technical notion.

4. The semantic paradoxes include the liar's paradox, in ancient and modern versions; the paradox of heterological terms; and the paradox of the least number that cannot be named in fewer than 75 words. Some set-theoretic paradoxes—for instance, Burali-Forti's and Cantor's paradoxes—are paradoxical only relative to the idea that open sentences determine sets, so that, for instance, "is a set" should determine a set. Russell's paradox is clearly in part a semantic paradox of a special sort, since it explicitly refutes the notion that an arbitrary open sentence determines a set. The basic problem with naive set theory, really, was that the criterion for set existence was linguistic and so subject to essentially self-referential difficulties. Any standard reference work, such as Kneal and Kneale's *Development of Logic* or Beth's *Foundations of Mathematics*, gives accounts of these paradoxes.

5. Tarski, "Concept of Truth," pp. 164–65.

6. Such hierarchies are "set up" so that reference to objects of level n can be made only at level $n+1$ or above. Level $n+1$ contains terms referring to objects of level n. Thus, the "object language," level 0, has terms only for nonlinguistic objects. The next level, metalanguage 1, has terms for terms of level 0 as well as terms for nonlinguistic objects. Therefore, only at level 1 (or above) can the relation between terms of language level 0 and nonlinguistic objects be discussed. Likewise, the relations between language level 1 and anything else can be discussed only in a language with terms referring to terms of language level 1, i.e., a language at level 2 or above.

7. That is, if the sentence in quotation marks were at level n, it would have to refer to expressions at level n, and therefore, by the constraints on canonical languages, would have to be a language of level $n+1$. Thus, no sentence of a canonical language can be paradoxical.

8. A function is a mapping from objects (called arguments) to objects (values of the function) in which a determinate object is fixed as the value of the function for every argument. Every possible pairing is a function. Nothing is implied about one thing's bringing about another.

9. For a precise account of models and interpretation for purposes of mathematical logic, see *Computability and Logic*, by Jeffrey and Boolos.

10. See Putnam, "Models and Reality"; and Benacerraf, "What Numbers Could Not Be." Mathematical writers occasionally refer to something called the "intended interpretation" but rarely discuss what these intentions are and how one determines what mathematical objects an intention grasps. "Intended interpretation" really means no more than the regress to a background language. See also Quine's "Ontological Relativity."

11. The resources needed to prove theorems of arithmetic add axioms that can be regarded as premises in every proof. Some of the generalities required extend the logical apparatus beyond what can be given completeness proofs. The representation of the numbers in a way that allows the calculations of arithmetic to be mirrored in logical-consequence relations requires that the language have resources beyond the languages for which the Gödel completeness result can be proved.

12. Such a theory *represents* sufficient mathematical relations to prove in the theory whether any calculable relation obtains or not in a given case. A relation is "represented" if its obtaining or not in a case is mirrored by the provability or unprovability of its representative in the theory.

13. "Defined" means constructed out of clearly calculable functions in clearly calculable ways; hence whether a relation so defined obtains between a pair of numbers is a matter of routine, if lengthy, computation.

14. The numerical relations are calculated by ordinary arithmetic, formalized by the theory. The appropriate relations have been shown to obtain among expressions if and only if the corresponding arithmetical relations hold. Thus, by the criterion of mathematical reference, those numerals *do* mean those expressions.

15. Gödel identifies the notions of sentencehood, consequence, proof, and other syntactic features with mathematical features. He justifies the identification by proving that the linguistic phenomenon holds if and only if the corresponding mathematical relation holds. Gödel shows that since "is a proof" is a *syntactic* predicate and since syntactic predicates are interpretable as mathematical functions, there are mathematical functions that have a given value if and only if a given sequence of sentences constitutes a proof. Given this relationship, that mathematical function can be said to "express" the predicate "is a proof of formula X," for variable X. Building on this predicate, Gödel constructs a mathematical predicate that is true of a number just in case a sequence of sentences exists that constitutes a proof of a given sentence. The mathematical predicate is true of the number representing the sentence in question in virtue of the principles of arithmetic just in case there is no proof of the sentence in the axiom system for which the version of Gödel's theorem is being constructed.

The self-referential trick, then, is this: among the numbers to which that predicate can be applied is the number for the sentence that applies that very predicate to that very number. Such a predication is an identity sentence about natural numbers that says there is no proof of that very identity sentence. Crudely, the sentence says, "There is no proof of me." If the axiom system is consistent, that remark is true. Thus, given any axiom system for which the appropriate predicates can be constructed, and a language capable of expressing the truths of arithmetic, some truths of arithmetic cannot be proved in that axiom system. The gap between the existence of a proof of this mathematical sentence and the sentence's truth means that this proof shows the incompleteness of any formalization of arithmetic rather than the inconsistency of arithmetic.

16. A "trail" of reference arises from a sequence such as this:

Fred: "What John said is right."
John: "What Arthur said is right."
Arthur: "Fred always lies."

To know what is being talked about, we have to know the referents of a sequence of singular terms.

17. See my "Indeterminacy of Radical Interpretation and the Causal Theory of Reference."

18. Some of these arguments appear in my "Indeterminacy of French Interpretation" and "The Extension of Deconstruction," both in the present volume.

19. Brooks, "What Does Poetry Communicate," in *The Well Wrought Urn*, pp. 72–73.

20. Wordsworth, "Essays upon Epitaphs," III, line 180. Thomas de Quincey, expanding on Wordsworth, gives essentially my argument about separating out the message from the words that convey it. See his fourth essay on style, in de Quincey, *Collected Works*, pp. 229–30.

21. See my "Extension of Deconstruction," in the present volume, for an account of how the conception of words as fundamental removes this distinction.

22. The term "dissemination" occurs in many places in Derrida's writing. For a relatively clear account of dissemination, as opposed to polysemy, see Derrida, "Signature, Event, Context," pp. 307–30, especially pp. 316–20.

23. Goodman, *Ways of Worldmaking*.

24. See my "Metaphor According to Davidson and de Man," in this volume.

25. See Davidson, "What Metaphors Mean"; and de Man, "Epistemology of Metaphor" and his chapter on Rousseau in *Allegories of Reading*.

26. See Davidson's article "Communication and Convention."

27. See the introduction to this collection.

28. The only way to accommodate genuine truth would be to follow Davidson in his radical abandonment of the traditional account of truth as correspondence and as depending on a relation between the world and the language that makes true sentences true. The cost of a Davidsonian primitivism about truth would be acceptance of indefinite numbers of truths that are in principle unknowable.

29. Brooks, "The Heresy of Paraphrase," in *The Well Wrought Urn*, p. 207. One way to see how de Man's aesthetic differs from Brooks's is to speculate on what de Man would say about this unity. For de Man, what is most interesting about a work are the stressful disunities that result from incoherencies in theory and attempts to mask those disunities under an appearance of total cohesiveness.

30. Brooks, "The Language of Paradox," in *The Well Wrought Urn*, p. 20.

31. Brooks, "What Does Poetry Communicate," in *The Well Wrought Urn*, p. 73.

32. See, for instance, Davidson, "Truth and Meaning."

33. As Davidson has pointed out in "On the Very Idea of a Conceptual Scheme," there is no "manifold" that is apportioned into objects.

34. De Man, *Allegories of Reading*, p. 205.

35. The essays in de Man's *Allegories of Reading* are good examples of this kind of argument.

CHAPTER 9

1. Derrida, *Husserl's "Origin of Geometry."*
2. Derrida, "Signature, Event, Context."
3. Another excellent discussion is Fish's "With the Compliments of the Author."
4. Implicit here is that Wittgenstein takes there to be a field, subject matter, or province that turns out to be the pseudo-province of grammatical illusion and overweening theory.
5. The phrase is Quine's, from "Ontological Relativity."
6. See Staten, *Wittgenstein and Derrida*, p. 131.
7. Analogous remarks could be made about Wittgenstein. As noted above, Wittgenstein seems to presuppose a special region that is the province of philosophy and that is demarcated from the real stuff. But this seems to require an essentialist view of subject matters or problems, or at least a notion of the merely linguistic and grammatical, which would certainly be incompatible with, say, Quine's deconstruction of the analytic/synthetic distinction. Thus Wittgenstein has no real basis for limiting his antitheoretical moves so that only philosophy will be deconstructed.
8. "Chomsky's project is not privileged merely through his claim to be scientific, but because his text has been minutely and rigorously tied to the text of scientific investigation." Staten, *Wittgenstein and Derrida*, p. 178.
9. That a "thing in itself" is beyond sensation even though it is the object of sensation seems remotely plausible only if Kant is right that space and time are mental artifacts.
10. This is not to say that for no terms are their objects determined by fit. For objects that are essentially cultural, that is, for objects that are defined by intentions and intentions about intentions, the resemblance theory of reference may be true. The confusion of such objects with the objects of science may well be due to the idea that reality is God's language.
11. Kripke, *Naming and Necessity*.
12. Armstrong, *A World of States of Affairs*.
13. Millikan, *Language, Thought, and Other Biological Categories*.

CHAPTER 10

1. See Staten, *Wittgenstein and Derrida*; and my essays in the present volume.
2. This is not to say that philosophers can contribute nothing to the work of

literary theorists. The kind of thinking at which analytic philosophy excels indeed has a role in theorizing about literature and language. But analytic philosophy's interest lies primarily in learning from literary theory, not in straightening out the muddled thinking of benighted literary types. Such straightening, however, would sometimes be a good thing.

3. This is argued in my "Conclusion of the *Theaetetus*."

4. If the world is a mixture of Form and the formless, and knowledge is total if it is truly knowledge, then Forms make real knowledge possible. And if the real is knowable, then the determinacy entailed by knowledge's being a relation requires that only what is determinate is real. So awareness is only truly awareness if it is a grasping of Form. A knowledge of the forms of things is a systematic and total grasp of reality. Awareness that takes in the particular instances achieves nothing permanent or constant but only the evanescent surfaces of things.

5. For discussions of Davidson and Quine as engaged in essentially the same project of deconstruction as Derrida, see my "Indeterminacy of French interpretation" and "The Extension of Deconstruction," both in the present volume.

6. Forms of discourse that do not assume the dichotomies from the outset are bound to seem and to be alien. A "phase one" deconstructive argument can then get us to see that some absolutely wacko "argument" is actually worth following, when that discussion would have been so beyond the pale of our standards that we could not take it seriously.

7. For instance, Aristotle's demolition of the theory of Forms showed that if Forms were just *F* and in no way not *F*, then only Forms of substances could exist, since these Forms must constitute themselves and so could not be pure cases of accidental features. So the notion of "*F* itself" is incoherent for accidental features. But Aristotle's refutation has its own principles and dichotomies, among them the distinction between essence and accident and between substance and other categories of being. Without these dichotomies, the deconstruction will not work.

8. From the point of view of some of these dichotomies—namely, those between logical consequence and rhetorical force and between reasoning and feeling—this kind of argument commits the genetic fallacy or some other fallacy condemned from the Platonic side. Given the expanded notions of coherence and argument, if the deconstructionists are right, these fallacies are not fallacies.

9. Derrida, *Speech and Phenomena*.

10. Some followers of Wittgenstein have used this argument strategy as the basis of an "anti–ideal-language-theory" *theory*—a theory opposed to ideal-language theories—a rather delicate deformation of Wittgenstein's strategy. They start with the premise that since numerous distinctions can be made within the area covered by the dichotomy, the dichotomy must distort the phenomena. Hence there is nothing amiss in the language we already use. The language is perfectly suited for

the phenomena, if we would only pay attention to it rather than leaping ahead and idealizing. So the theory that a dichotomy would advance not only is not explanatory but even falsifies what is already clear.

This strategy, however, presupposes a theory of language built on a number of interrelated dichotomies. The typical ordinary-language argument presupposes a sharp distinction between meaning and information so that theory building in philosophy can be distinguished from theorizing and systematizing in science. Thus the distinction between the "grammatical" and the scientific is really a distinction between the merely conceptual arrangements and the material that is organized by these systems of concepts. What basically guarantees that "ordinary language" is in order is the conception, perhaps borrowed from Carnap's *Logical Syntax of Language*, that the choice of conceptual scheme is arbitrary and leaves the facts untouched. Thus this route to attacking dichotomies falls into the same difficulties as the "ideological" and philosophical attacks do.

11. Davidson, "On the Very Idea of a Conceptual Scheme."

12. Wittgenstein, *Philosophical Investigations*, pt. 1, par. 43. I replace "defined" in Anscombe's translation with "clarified" as a translation of *erclaren* in order to avoid the systematic connotations of "defined."

13. The meaning-bearing rules denied by Wittgenstein are rules that apply prior to natural language. These are the rules that apply prior to experience, the *a priori* that had become, in twentieth-century analytic philosophy, rules of language. This exclusive province of philosophy was supposed to set up conceptual schemes to provide a framework of conventions in terms of which what is the case could be stated.

14. "Theories" and the *a priori* are two parts of the same complex. On one hand, since meaning is supposed to be the basis for the *a priori*, the theory of meaning must have a deductive, analytic basis. On the other hand, the theorizing impulse sanctions the leap from the facts to a theory of facts, and a leap from the fact that the truth "Snow is white" would be false if "white" meant purple to a theory that a part of the fact that "Snow is white" is true can be isolated as the contribution of meaning.

15. Wittgenstein, *Philosophical Investigations*, pt. 1, pars. 243–449.

16. The Wittgensteinian whose work most continues this is O. K. Bouwsma, who is likewise a delight to read.

17. For a deep "metaphorics" of Platonism, see Irigaray's *Speculum of the Other Woman*.

18. Wittgenstein realized the impossibility of starting from a position outside language in the *Tractatus*, even though he overstated the point as the impossibility of metalanguages. What he should have said, rather than claiming that all metalinguistic remarks are nonsense, is that no metalinguistic remarks can be general.

CHAPTER 11

1. The choice here will make a considerable difference: Quine's notion of "theory" leads him to take mathematical logic as the model for interpretation of a natural language; Derrida takes the interpretation of texts to be the model. As applied to human language in a culture, both of these are metaphors, but metaphors that illuminate somewhat different sides of the phenomenon.

2. See especially Derrida's essay "Speech and Phenomena," an important early work in which Derrida argues that the "presence to consciousness" required of the magic language is incoherent in its most carefully worked-out presentation. This essay is also the text in which the term "deconstructive" first appears with an explanation.

3. By saying "intrinsic," I focus on traditional magic languages. Theories that posit natural historical and relational properties to give terms their reference and sense require a somewhat different discussion.

4. The theses that a natural meaning exists and that a speaker has access to that meaning are separable. Someone can deny "meaning rationalism," to use Millikan's term, and still hold, as Millikan does in *Language and Other Biological Categories*, that there is a meaning that defies interpretation. Such a theory seems to require a "given," however.

5. Quine and Davidson would often allow that the correct translation or interpretation of the terms of the distinction would be in terms of the scientifically correct distinction. Since Davidson argues against "facts" as referents of sentences, the question of "objectively right" would not arise, only truth.

6. See especially Davidson, "Truth and Meaning."

7. One discussion's "driving" us to the next is a good example of the kind of connection that has to be accommodated and criticized in a deconstruction that renounces a magic language.

8. To some extent, Derrida's discussions involve a circle since the criteria for a critique's success depend on the critique's success. This is why Derrida's discussion of Husserl in *Speech and Phenomena* and of Husserl's relation to speech-act theory and Austin in "Signature, Event, Context" and "Limited Inc." are so important. Those discussions argue for Derridean premises rather than assuming them.

9. One important point here is that the metaphors by which Derrida and Quine conceive of inconsistency are different: Derrida often uses "undecidable" to indicate how an interpretation of a single term or passage can switch the interpretation of an entire text. Thus, when a crucial word can be taken in one of two ways, and when each of those ways organizes the rest of the text in distinct ways, we have one kind of failure of unique coherence. The text, we might say, is too coherent. For his part, Quine uses "analytical hypothesis" to organize the data in a distinctive way, to which there are alternatives. For both authors, system is extremely important. No hypothesis does any interpretive job except in the context of a system.

10. A withdrawal to the purely syntactic has all the difficulties about the semantics of the metalanguage that would arise for any natural language. This is to say not that we cannot do logic or that we cannot prove things in mathematics but that such projects, to the extent that they are connected to natural languages, are subject to the same phenomena. Just think about "stipulation": Clearly we can stipulate, relative to a background language. Without the magic language, though, there is no "pure" stipulation.

11. Quine's famous discussion in chapter 2 of *Word and Object* is my main resource here. Notice the point that if the inconsistency were pervasive, in the sense that its real consequences were believed, the language users would "regard every sentence as true," which result abandons the idea that the set of marks is a language.

12. What is wrong with an inconsistent discourse? If our discourse has the proof procedure of reductio ad absurdum, then an inconsistency will allow all statements to be theorems. But this is a concern only if we think that such proof procedures are among the practices of regular discussions. We have ways, within natural languages, of defining "proof procedure" and "validity" for the restricted domains of mathematics and formal theories. I think few theorists would seriously hold that these domains can establish themselves "by stipulation."

13. Quine and Ullian, *Web of Belief.* This book readily lends itself to the extension suggested above.

14. Notice that "incoherent" and "connection" are metaphors that express a certain way of thinking about a discourse and its "structure." Such metaphors are catachreses, as Derrida has observed in "White Mythology." That is, nothing in the nature of the case makes "coherence" the correct description of a crystal structure and a logical system and a symphony. "Connection" among parts is likewise a metaphor for something that is not literally nameable, that is, not nameable in other terms.

15. Plato's view of what it is about the relationship that makes the physical world less comprehensible than mathematics seems to me to change over the course of his writings. However, his notion that the soul's categories are the structures by which reality works is constant.

16. This is a point forcefully made by Davidson in "On the Very Idea of a Conceptual Scheme."

17. I do not know how mathematical theories fit with the theses of deconstruction. Some central metamathematical results lend negative support to Derrida's self-referential discussions, but it is extremely difficult to argue from formal languages in which the mathematical results are formulated to conclusions about the discourses that Derrida discusses. One difficulty is that the notion of "proof" in a natural discourse is not formal, so the actual working out of the metatheorems, which is perforce formal, can only be analogous. The clearest ally here is Tarski, who states explicitly that he very much doubts that "true sentence" can be used consistently in a natural language. Tarski, "Concept of Truth," p. 165.

18. Derrida, "Limited Inc.," p. 123.

19. Much of the debate about the canon seems to me to be corrupted by the illusion, held on both sides, that no distinction is possible unless there is such a thing as pure aesthetic value detachable from particular circumstances. Jonathan Culler is said, perhaps apocryphally, to have claimed that comic books are equivalent to Milton, for humorous example. Nothing like that follows from the impossibility of defining the timeless aesthetic.

CHAPTER 12

1. For the primary instance of a Derridean text that parallels Plato, see Derrida, "Differance."

2. An examination of the secondary literature that agrees or disagrees with the theses advanced in this chapter about "what Plato thought" would turn the chapter into a large book of footnotes. My view is that Plato wrote dialogues instead of treatises because he was usually examining arguments rather than advancing their conclusions as theses.

3. For instance, the configurations by which Wittgenstein hoped to avoid things other than nameable objects either are or are not. If they are not, then they can do little to tie objects together in facts. If they are, then they are beings and thus are nameable.

4. If there is a God of Being that explains all beings, then that God is the sole entity that requires no explanation but exists in virtue of its own nature.

5. Plato, *Parmenides* 132a1–b3. I omit all discussion of this vast literature. I am willing to defend the interpretation that follows by demonstrating that it solves the immediate difficulty of the Third Man and that it makes sense of subsequent parts of the *Parmenides*.

6. Note that the solution to the famous Third Man regress in the first section of the *Parmenides* requires that Forms just be the characters they explain rather than being attached characters. The attached-characters picture of Form and the feature it explains lead to the thing possessed in common by the instances and the Form. However, the supposition that Justice Itself be just the character and not something besides the character requires that Justice not have other things about it, such as being a being and being different from triangularity. If it had such characters, the question of what the character itself is, apart from such additional entities, would once again arise.

7. Aristotle, *Metaphysics* A, 998a.

8. See Derrida, "Differance," p. 3.

9. For example, Derrida states: "Differance is not, does not exist, is not a present being (on) in any Form" ("Differance," p. 6). Another example: "Differance is neither a word nor a concept" (ibid., p. 7).

10. Derrida is making a point related to Sellars's in "The Myth of the Given" and "Empiricism and the Philosophy of Mind."

11. This lack of distance, Derrida argues in the first chapters of *Speech and Phenomena*, is necessary because in order to have a genuine distinction between indication and expression, a pure case of expression must be possible. The "point" character of the now in which the self talks to the self allows no "real" signs to occur when a person has an interior monologue. So the "now" must be a self-presenting point at its core, even though Husserl has himself proved that "now"-ness is a compound of protentions and retentions.

12. The pros and cons and precise definitions of haecceities would take us very far afield. Both Plato and Derrida take it to be obvious that there can be no haecceities, idealities that by their very nature can be true of only a given particular. They accept without question Aristotle's argument/observation that a particular cannot be defined. Plato does hold that some natures can have only one instance, such as the One Itself; but a question such as "Might some other particular have been the One Itself?" makes as little sense as the question to David Lewis whether there might have been other possible worlds. Since both Lewis and Plato reduce necessity to brute fact and mereology, the answer is in some sense "no."

13. Some such consideration is at work in Husserl's insistence that meanings are idealities, irreal. They can be the same in many locations.

14. Derrida, *Positions*, p. 80.

15. As soon as we imagine a field to be divided up, we have posited objects with identity conditions. Roughly, to be formed into objects, a manifold must already be an entity and, thus, already be formed.

16. The core idea of Davidson's position on the given could be put as follows: Of course there is sameness in nature. Pigs are all the same in being pigs. However, if we ask, "What is it in virtue of which pigs are the same?" we have two kinds of replies: We can cite the various biological facts and theories in virtue of which pigs are the kind of animals they are. Or we can assert the triviality that pigs are the same in being pigs. What Davidson denies is that there is something deeper than the triviality but distinct from the scientific. "Metaphysical realism" is precisely the belief in this deeper explanation of an objective sameness, an explanation that helpfully supplements "is a pig" being true of all pigs.

17. Although this would take us far afield, I would argue that Plato takes mereology to be the one kind of necessity that needs no more fundamental explanation since it is completely transparent. In this he agrees with such modal metaphysicians as D. M. Armstrong (in numerous works, most recently *A World of States of Affairs*) and David Lewis (for instance, in his *On the Plurality of Worlds*). That is, the necessities of the part/whole relation are taken as utterly obvious, not subject to deeper explanation, and as an appropriate foundation for the rest of the metaphysics of modality.

18. Sellars's demonstration that sense data cannot be both given and meaningful is in "Empiricism and the Philosophy of Mind."

19. Wheeler, "Plato's Enlightenment."

20. See Lee's "Plato on Negation and Not-Being."

21. Derrida's deconstructions are not demonstrations of the unusability of concepts but are rather akin to Wittgenstein's work in their practical import. Only on the foundationalist presuppositions that he rejects would a failure of foundationalism show the unusability of a concept that has been deconstructed. See my "Wittgenstein as Conservative Deconstructor," in the present volume. In the case at hand, the fact that something like differance would be required for an account of the origins of concepts only argues for the reality of differance if we are committed to the foundational project.

22. I belabor this point above in Chapter 6.

Works Cited

Aristotle. *The Complete Works of Aristotle.* Edited by Jonathan Barnes. 2 vols. Princeton, N.J.: Princeton University Press, 1984.

Armstrong, D. M. *A World of States of Affairs.* Cambridge, Eng.: Cambridge University Press, 1997.

Babylonian Talmud. Translated by Rabbi Dr. I. Epstein. 17 vols. London: Soncino, 1938.

Benacerraf, Paul. "What Numbers Could Not Be." In *Philosophy of Mathematics: Selected Readings,* 2d ed., edited by Paul Benacerraf and Hilary Putnam, pp. 272–94. Cambridge, Eng.: Cambridge University Press, 1983.

Beth, Evert. *The Foundations of Mathematics.* New York: Harper and Row, 1966.

Bilgrami, Akheel. "Norms and Meaning." In *Reflecting Davidson,* edited by Ralf Stoecker, pp. 121–44. New York: De Gruyter, 1993.

Bouwsma, O. K. *Philosophical Essays.* Lincoln: University of Nebraska Press, 1965.

Boyarin, Daniel. *Intertextuality and the Reading of Midrash.* Bloomington: Indiana University Press, 1990.

Brooks, Cleanth. *The Well Wrought Urn.* New York: Harcourt Brace, 1947.

Calvino, Italo. *If On a Winter's Night a Traveller.* New York: Harcourt Brace Jovanovich, 1981.

Carnap, Rudolf. *The Logical Syntax of Language.* New York: Harcourt Brace, 1937.

———. *Meaning and Necessity.* Chicago: University of Chicago Press, 1947.

Chisholm, Roderick. *The First Person.* Minneapolis: University of Minnesota Press, 1981.

———. *Person and Object.* London: Allen and Unwin, 1976.

Culler, Jonathan. *On Deconstruction.* Ithaca, N.Y.: Cornell University Press, 1982.

Davidson, Donald. "Belief and the Basis of Meaning." In Davidson, *Inquiries,* pp. 141–54.

———. "Communication and Convention." In Davidson, *Inquiries,* pp. 265–80.

———. *Inquiries into Truth and Interpretation.* London: Oxford University Press, 1984.

———. "Mental Events." In Donald Davidson, *Essays on Actions and Events,* pp. 207–24. London: Oxford University Press, 1980.

————. "Moods and Performances." In Davidson, *Inquiries*, pp. 109–21.

————. "The Myth of the Subjective." In *Relativism: Interpretation and Confrontation*, edited by Michael Krausz, pp. 159–72. Notre Dame, Ind.: Notre Dame University Press, 1989.

————. "A Nice Derangement of Epitaphs." In *Truth and Interpretation: Perspectives on the Philosophy of Donald Davidson*, edited by Ernest Le Pore, pp. 433–46. Oxford: Basil Blackwell, 1986.

————. "On the Very Idea of a Conceptual Scheme." In Davidson, *Inquiries*, pp. 183–98.

————. "Radical Interpretation." In Davidson, *Inquiries*, pp. 125–40.

————. "The Structure and Content of Truth." *Journal of Philosophy*, 87, no. 6 (June 1990): 279–328.

————. "Theories of Meaning and Learnable Languages." In Davidson, *Inquiries*, pp. 3–16.

————. "True to the Facts." In Davidson, *Inquiries*, pp. 37–54.

————. "Truth and Meaning." In Davidson, *Inquiries*, pp. 17–36.

————. "What Metaphors Mean." In Davidson, *Inquiries*, pp. 245–64.

De Man, Paul. *Allegories of Reading*. New Haven, Conn.: Yale University Press, 1979.

————. "The Epistemology of Metaphor." *Critical Inquiry*, 5, no. 1 (Autumn 1978): 13–30.

————. "Shelley Disfigured." In *Deconstruction and Criticism*, edited by Harold Bloom et al., pp. 39–73. New York: Continuum, 1979.

De Quincey, Thomas. Fourth essay on style [1841]. In his *Collected Writings*, edited by David Masson, 10: 228–36. Edinburgh: n.p., 1889–90.

Derrida, Jacques. "Differance." In his *Margins of Philosophy*, pp. 1–27.

————. *Dissemination*. Translated by Barbara Johnson. Chicago: University of Chicago Press, 1981.

————. *Edmund Husserl's "Origin of Geometry": An Introduction*. Translated by John P. Leavey, Jr. Stony Brook, N.Y.: Nicholas Hays, 1978.

————. *Limited Inc*. Translated by Jeffrey Mehlman and Samuel Weber. Evanston, Ill.: Northwestern University Press, 1988.

————. "Limited Inc. a b c . . . " Translated by Samuel Weber. In *Glyph 2*, pp. 162–254. Baltimore: The Johns Hopkins University Press, 1977.

————. *Margins of Philosophy*. Translated by Alan Bass. Chicago: University of Chicago Press, 1982.

————. *Of Grammatology*. Translated by Gayatri Spivak. Baltimore: The Johns Hopkins University Press, 1974.

————. *Positions*. Translated by Alan Bass. Chicago: University of Chicago Press, 1981.

————. "Signature, Event, Context." In his *Margins of Philosophy*, pp. 307–30.

————. *"Speech and Phenomena" and Other Essays on Husserl's Phenomenology*.

Translated by David Allison. Evanston, Ill.: Northwestern University Press, 1973.

―――. "White Mythology." In Derrida, *Margins of Philosophy*, pp. 207–71.

―――. *Writing and Difference*. Translated by Alan Bass. Chicago: University of Chicago Press, 1978.

Elder, Crawford. "Realism, Naturalism, and Culturally Generated Kinds." *Philosophical Quarterly*, 39, no. 157 (1989): 425–44.

Fish, Stanley. "With the Compliments of the Author: Reflections on Austin and Derrida." *Critical Inquiry*, 8, no. 4 (Summer 1982): 693–722.

Fishbane, Michael. *Biblical Interpretation in Ancient Israel*. London: Oxford University Press, 1985.

Frege, Gottlob. "On Sense and Reference." In Gottlob Frege, *Philosophical Writings*, edited by Peter Geach and Max Black, pp. 56–78. Oxford: Basil Blackwell, 1952.

Gödel, Kurt. *On Formally Undecidable Propositions of "Principia Mathematica" and Related Systems*. Translated by B. Meltzer. New York: Basic Books, 1962.

Goodman, Nelson. *Fact, Fiction and Forecast*. New York: Bobbs-Merrill, 1965.

―――. *Problems and Projects*. New York: Bobbs-Merrill, 1972.

―――. *The Structure of Appearance*. New York: Bobbs-Merrill, 1966.

―――. *Ways of Worldmaking*. Indianapolis: Hackett, 1978.

Grice, Paul. *Studies in the Way of Words*. Cambridge, Mass.: Harvard University Press, 1989.

Harman, Gilbert. "Quine on Meaning and Existence, I." Review of Metaphysics, 21, no. 1 (Sept. 1967): 124–51.

Hartman, Geoffrey. *Criticism in the Wilderness*. New Haven, Conn.: Yale University Press, 1980.

Hollander, John. *Rhyme's Reason*. New Haven, Conn.: Yale University Press, 1981.

Husserl, Edmund. *Logical Investigations, Volume 1*. Translated by J. N. Findlay. London: Routledge and Kegan Paul, 1970.

Irigaray, Luce. *Speculum of the Other Woman*. Translated by Gillian C. Gill. Ithaca, N.Y.: Cornell University Press, 1985.

Jeffrey, Richard, and George Boolos. *Computability and Logic*. Cambridge, Eng.: Cambridge University Press, 1980.

Kitto, H. D. F. *The Greeks*. Baltimore: Penguin, 1963.

Knapp, Stephen, and Walter Benn Michaels. "Against Theory II." *Critical Inquiry*, 14, no. 1 (Autumn 1987): 49–68.

Kneale, William, and Martha Kneale. *The Development of Logic*. London: Oxford University Press, 1962.

Kripke, Saul. *Naming and Necessity*. Cambridge, Mass.: Harvard University Press, 1980.

―――. "Outline of a Theory of Truth." *Journal of Philosophy*, 72, no. 10 (1975): 690–716.

Kuhn, Thomas. *The Structure of Scientific Revolutions*. 2d ed. Chicago: University of Chicago Press, 1970.

Lee, E. N. "Plato on Negation and Not-Being in the *Sophist*." *Philosophical Review*, 81 (1972): 267–304.

Lewis, David. *On the Plurality of Worlds*. London: Oxford University Press, 1986.

Maimonides. *The Code of Maimonides, Book X, The Book of Cleanness*. Translated by Herbert Danby. New Haven, Conn.: Yale University Press, 1954.

———. *Guide of the Perplexed*. Translated by Schlomo Pines. Chicago: Chicago University Press, 1963.

Mates, Benson. "Synonymy." In *Semantics and the Philosophy of Language*, edited by Leonard Linsky, pp. 111–36. Urbana: University of Illinois Press, 1952.

Midrash Rabbah. Translated by Rabbi Dr. H. Freedman. 10 vols. New York: Soncino, 1983.

Miller, J. Hillis. "The Critic as Host." In *Deconstruction and Criticism*, edited by Harold Bloom et al., pp. 217–53. New York: Continuum, 1979.

Millikan, Ruth. *Language and Other Biological Categories*. Cambridge, Mass.: MIT Press, 1984.

Nietzsche, Friedrich. "On Truth and Lies in the Extra-Moral Sense." In *The Portable Nietzsche*, edited by Walter Kaufman, pp. 42–47. New York: Viking, 1954.

Nozick, Robert. *Anarchy, State, and Utopia*. New York: Basic Books, 1974.

Plato. *The Collected Dialogues*. Edited by Edith Hamilton and Huntington Cairns. New York: Pantheon Books, 1961.

Putnam, Hilary. "Models and Reality." In *Philosophy of Mathematics: Selected Readings*, 2d ed., edited by Paul Benacerraf and Hilary Putnam, pp. 403–20. Cambridge, Eng.: Cambridge University Press, 1983.

———. "Realism and Reason." In his *Meaning and the Moral Sciences*, pp. 127–38. London: Routledge and Kegan Paul, 1978.

Quine, W. V. O. "Epistemology Naturalized." In his *"Ontological Relativity" and Other Essays*, pp. 69–90. New York: Columbia University Press, 1969.

———. "Necessary Truth." In W. V. O. Quine, *"Ways of Paradox" and Other Essays*, pp. 48–56. New York: Random House, 1966.

———. "Ontological Relativity." In W. V. O. Quine, *"Ontological Relativity" and Other Essays*, pp. 26–68. New York: Columbia University Press, 1969.

———. "Truth by Convention." In W. V. O. Quine, *"Ways of Paradox" and Other Essays*, pp. 70–99. New York: Random House, 1966.

———. "Two Dogmas of Empiricism." In W. V. O. Quine, *From a Logical Point of View*, pp. 20–46. New York: Harper and Row, 1963.

———. *Word and Object*. Cambridge, Eng.: MIT Press, 1960.

Quine, W. V. O., and Joseph S. Ullian. *The Web of Belief*. New York: Random House, 1970.

Rorty, Richard. *Consequences of Pragmatism*. Minneapolis: University of Minnesota Press, 1982.

―――. "The Contingency of Language." *London Review of Books*, 8, no. 7 (April 17, 1986): 3–6.

―――. *Philosophy and the Mirror of Nature*. Princeton, N.J.: Princeton University Press, 1979.

―――. "Unfamiliar Noises: Hesse and Davidson on Metaphor." *Proceedings of the Aristotelian Society*, supp. vol. 61 (1987): 283–96.

Rousseau, Jean-Jacques. *'Discourse' and 'Essay on the Origin of Languages'*. Translated by Victor Gourevitch. New York: Harper and Row, 1986.

Saussure, Ferdinand de. *Course in General Linguistics*. Translated by Wade Baskin. New York: McGraw-Hill, 1966.

Searle, John R. "Reiterating the Differences: A Reply to Derrida." In *Glyph 1*, pp. 198–208. Baltimore: The Johns Hopkins University Press, 1977.

Sellars, Wilfrid. "Empiricism and the Philosophy of Mind." In Wilfrid Sellars, *Science, Perception and Reality*, pp. 127–96. London: Routledge and Kegan Paul, 1963.

Sorensen, Roy. "The Ambiguity of Vagueness and Precision." *Pacific Philosophical Quarterly* 70 (1989): 174–83.

―――. "Vagueness Within the Language of Thought." *Philosophical Quarterly*, 41, no. 165 (Oct. 1991): 389–413.

Staten, Henry. *Wittgenstein and Derrida*. Lincoln: University of Nebraska Press, 1985.

Tarski, Alfred. "The Concept of Truth in Formalized Languages." In Alfred Tarski, *Logic, Semantics, Metamathematics*, pp. 152–278. London: Oxford University Press, 1956.

Troyer, John, and Samuel C. Wheeler. "Truth and Training." Unpublished manuscript, 1973.

Wheeler, Samuel C. III. "Aristotle of the Snub." Unpublished essay.

―――. "Attributives and Their Modifiers." *Nous*, 6, no. 4 (Nov. 1972): 310–34.

―――. "The Conclusion of the *Theaetetus*." *History of Philosophy Quarterly*, 1 (1984): 355–67.

―――. "How Paintings Can Be Joyful." In *Philosophic Essays in Honor of Martin Eshleman*, edited by Geoffrey A. Peterson, pp. 83–95. Northfield, Minn.: Carleton College, 1971.

―――. "Indeterminacy of Radical Interpretation and the Causal Theory of Reference." In *Meaning and Translation*, edited by F. Guenthner and M. Guenthner-Reutter, pp. 83–94. London: Duckworth, 1978.

―――. "Natural Property Rights as Body Rights." *Nous*, 14, no. 2 (May 1980): 171–94.

―――. "On That Which Is Not." *Synthese*, 41 (1979): 155–73.

―――. "Persons and Their Micro-Particles." *Nous*, 20, no. 3 (Sept. 1986): 333–49.

―――. "Plato's Enlightenment." *History of Philosophy Quarterly*, 19, no. 2 (April 1997): 177–88.

―――. "Reference and Vagueness." *Synthese,* 30 (1975): 367–79.

―――. "True Figures." In *The Interpretive Turn,* edited by David R. Hiley, James F. Bohman, and Richard Shusterman, pp. 197–217. Ithaca, N.Y.: Cornell University Press, 1991.

Wilson, N. L. "Substances Without Substrata." *Review of Metaphysics,* 12 (1959): 521–39.

Wittgenstein, Ludwig. *Philosophical Investigations.* 3d ed. Translated by G. E. M. Anscombe. New York: Macmillan, 1958.

―――. *Remarks on the Foundations of Mathematics.* Translated by G. E. M. Anscombe. Oxford: Basil Blackwell, 1956.

―――. *Tractatus Logico-Philosophicus.* Translated by David Pears and Brian McGuinness. London: Routledge and Kegan Paul, 1961.

Wordsworth, William. "Essays upon Epitaphs III." In *The Prose Works of William Wordsworth,* edited by W. J. B. Owen and J. W. Smyser, 2: 80–119. Oxford: Oxford University Press, 1974.

Index

In this index an "f" after a number indicates a separate reference on the next page, and an "ff" indicates separate references on the next two pages. A continuous discussion over two or more pages is indicated by a span of page numbers, e.g., "57–59." *Passim* is used for a cluster of references in close but not consecutive sequence.

Cultural Memory | in the Present

Library of Congress Cataloging-in-Publication Data

Wheeler, Samuel C.
  Deconstruction as analytic philosophy / Samuel C. Wheeler III.
    p.   cm. — (Cultural memory in the present)
  Includes bibliographical references and index.
  ISBN 0-8047-3752-5 (hardcover : alk. paper) — ISBN 0-8047-3753-3 (pbk. : alk. paper)
    1. Derrida, Jacques   2. Deconstruction.   3. Davidson, Donald, 1917–
I. Title.   II. Series.
B2430.D484 W475   2000
149—dc21   99-086425

♾   This book is printed on acid-free, archival quality paper.

Original printing 2000

Last figure below indicates the year of this printing:
09   08   07   06   05   04   03   02   01   00

Typeset by James P. Brommer in 11/13.5 Garamond